The Protection
of a Kind Providence

WASHINGTON
AND AMERICA'S EXODUS

The Protection of a Kind Providence Washington and America's Exodus

By
Captain Thomas A. Russell
(U.S. Navy Retired)
Tobacco Flower Publishing
Bolivia, North Carolina 28422

Although the author and publisher have made every effort to ensure the accuracy and completeness of information contained in this book, we assume no responsibility for errors, inaccuracies, omissions, or any inconsistency herein. Any slights of people, places, or organizations are unintentional.

ISBN-13: 978-1-7334099-0-2
LCCN: 2019948654

www.maryshawnrussell.com
Published by Tobacco Flower Publishing
Printed in the United States of America

The Protection
of a Kind Providence

WASHINGTON
AND AMERICA'S EXODUS

Thomas A. Russell

Acknowledgements

The Protection of a Kind Providence—Washington and America's Exodus would not have been possible without dedicated support from my wife, Mary Shawn Russell. It was her book, *Washington's Bloodline: The Long Lost Branch of the Washington Family Tree,* that stimulated my thoughts about this book's theme. She sustained me though this long journey of research and writing. She provided the photography of the many historical places that were so instrumental in the life of George Washington. Being a librarian in her early days, she masterfully navigated through the stacks to find those pieces of reference information that were critical to this work. As she is a Washington family descendant, I dedicate this book to her and her many Washington "cousins" who are devoted to preserving this great American name.

This work would not have been as complete without the help of the Mount Vernon Ladies' Association, specifically, Dawn Bonner and Samantha Snyder of the Fred W. Smith National Library for the Study of George Washington at Mount Vernon. Their assistance was immeasurable.

A special thanks goes to John and Kate Meyer of Cape Fear Publishers. An excellent editor, John cut, shaped, and molded this work and added clarity and readability. Regardless of your opinion of this book, you can be assured it was improved remarkably by the work of John Meyer. Kate Meyer designed the cover and her talent speaks for itself; she is a pro.

Trophies of War—Yorktown Battlefield

Table of Contents

Table of Illustrations

Table of Illustrations

Table of Illustrations

Preface

The Evolution of a Book

While helping my wife conduct research for her book, *Washington's Bloodline: The Long Lost Branch of the Washington Family Tree,* I became intrigued by little-known events in the Washington family's history. These events led me to believe that George Washington was destined to lead America's founding. Those events started with George Washington's great-grandfather and grandfather. John Washington was the first Washington to migrate to America. What caused George's great-grandfather, John Washington, to travel to America instead of establishing an occupation in England? Once in America, the grounding of his ship at Mattox Creek on what was to have been his return voyage to England kept him in America instead of returning as planned.

Then there was the lawsuit for custody of George Washington's father, Augustine Washington. Had the suit been settled under different circumstances, Washington's father could easily have remained in England, never to return to America to raise a family—a family that fathered the first president of the United States. Had those events, and many more, occurred differently, there would not have been a George Washington to lead America's founding.

Researching events in the personal life of George Washington revealed that time and time again a miracle would manifest itself at the appropriate moment to save his career, his army, or in some cases his life. So frequently have these miracles been chronicled that I argue some power greater than the performers themselves influenced the events. Everything was just too well-coordinated and too filled with cohesive systems of cause and effect to be held together by just luck or fate. A plan had to exist somewhere, but where?

Many of our founding fathers expressed the opinion that Divine Providence guided them and provided protection over them during our country's founding. In a letter to his brother John Augustine Washington, dated July 18, 1755, George Washington writes:

> "By the all-powerful dispensations of Providence, I have been protected
> beyond all human probability and expectation; for I had four bullets
> through my coat, and two horses shot under me, yet escaped unhurt, altho'

death was leveling my companions on every side."[1]

Letters from John Adams, Benjamin Franklin, and Thomas Jefferson all routinely gave thanks to "Providence."

According to Tony Evans in *Detours: The Unpredictable Path to Our Destiny*, Providence is God either causing or allowing things to happen for his purpose.[2] That being said, God clearly had a purpose and a destiny for George Washington.

I initially thought a book detailing George Washington's destiny and the miracles of Divine Providence that supported that argument about his destiny would be a great adventure. Although George Washington is its central character, I discovered that the story was bigger than just him. I started my research looking at the Church of England and the religious dissent that drove the Pilgrims and other Separatists to America. That same religious dissent and revolution in England was the reason for the venture to America of George Washington's great-grandfather, John Washington.

Washington as America's Moses

This book's research also revealed a striking similarity to the Biblical story of Moses and the Exodus. The Bible's Book of Exodus describes Moses leading the enslaved Israelites out of Egypt to God's "promised land." The similarities between the enslaved people of Israel in Egypt and the American colonies under British rule; resemblances between the Egyptian pharaoh and King George III; and parallels between Moses and George Washington are striking.

These comparisons are not new revelations. Early in the Revolutionary War, American Patriots began to see that struggle as their escape "from the worse than Egyptian bondage of Great Britain." "Deliverer of America" was one of Washington's many popular post-war titles. Before Washington's death, it had become fairly commonplace for Americans to refer to the Revolution as "our miraculous deliverance from a second Egypt—another house of bondage." Early Americans likened the Fourth of July to the day the Hebrews "came up out of Egypt," and insisted that "God (had) raised up a Washington" just as he had earlier "qualified and raised up Moses."[3] The American Patriots saw themselves as the new Israelites and King George III as the modern-day pharaoh. When Pharaoh pursued the Israelites, God destroyed the Egyptian army at the Red Sea. Similarly, in the American Revolution, God allowed for the defeat of the greatest armed force on earth by a rag-tag, ill-equipped force consisting of farmers and merchants with limited military expertise.

---

1   W.W. Abbot, ed., *The Papers of George Washington,* Colonial Series, vol 1, *7 July 1748 – 14 August 1755* (Charlottesville: University Press of Virginia, 1983), 343.

2   Tony Evans, *Detours The Unpredictable Path to Your Destiny* (Nashville, Tennessee: B&H Publishing Group, 2017), 138.

3   Robert P. Hay, "George Washington: American Moses," *American Quarterly* Volume 1 No 4, 781-782.

George Washington 1795 by Charles Willson Peale

This book makes the argument that America's founding was much like that of Israel. Like Moses, George Washington led the American Patriots to our "promised land" through the acts of personal sacrifice, bravery, and the help of a Divine Providence.

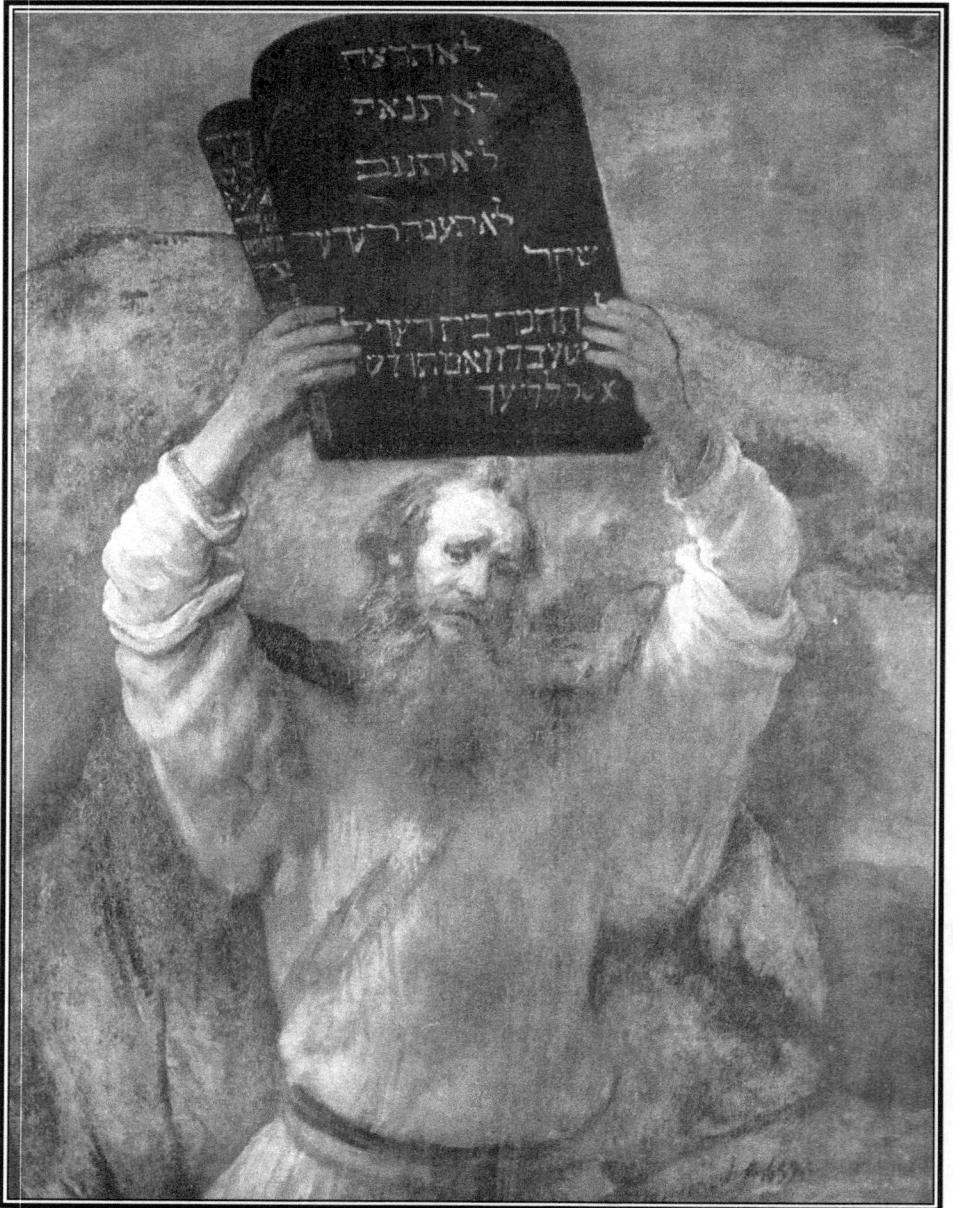

Moses by Rembrandt

Introduction

The Bible's Book of Exodus conveys that four hundred years had passed since Joseph moved his Hebrew family to Egypt. These descendants of Abraham had grown to over two million. To Egypt's new ruler, these immigrants were foreigners, and their numbers were frightening. Pharaoh decided to make them slaves so they wouldn't upset his balance of power. To control the expanding Hebrew population, Pharaoh decreed that all newborn Hebrew boys were to be killed. As it turned out, that was his biggest mistake. God intervened and came to the rescue of the Hebrew people.[4]

Through a series of strange events that could be described as acts of Divine Providence, a Hebrew boy named Moses, born at the time of that murderous decree, survived to become a prince in Pharaoh's palace. After defending a Hebrew slave by killing the slave's taskmaster, Moses departed Egypt to become an outcast in the wilderness. God visited Moses in the mysterious flames of a burning bush. Afterwards, Moses agreed to return to Egypt to lead God's people out of slavery.

Moses confronted Pharaoh. Through a cycle of ten plagues God perpetrated on the people of Egypt, Israel was torn from Pharaoh's grasp, given its freedom, and allowed to depart Egypt on a journey Moses led to God's "promised land." [5]

Like Moses, George Washington's destiny was aided by decisions made by his great-grandfather, John Washington; his grandfather, Lawrence Washington; his grandfather's cousin, John Washington of Chotank Creek; and his father, Augustine Washington. There are many similarities in the circumstances surrounding the births of Moses and Washington. Moses had been born in fertile Goshen, "one of the best" provinces of Egypt. He was "from an honorable lineage." His "ancestors in a particular covenant with the Most High, [had] moved thither by invitation and divine confirmation, to secure themselves against the devastation of famine." Similarly, Washington had been born in Virginia, a British colony "well known of its profusion and wealth." He was "from a respectable parentage." His ancestors had emigrated from Britain "for views to enjoy on this side of the Atlantic, greater advantages both civil and religious." By luring the forebears of Moses and Washington to new lands, Providence had made preparation for the time when their offspring would be needed.[6]

---

4   *The Bible Life Application Study*, King James Version (Wheaton, Illinois: Tyndale House Publishing 1996), 115.

5   Ibid.

6   Hay, 783.

George Washington, too, was raised within his future enemy's established society. He was the protégé of William Fairfax, the proprietor of the Northern Neck in England's Virginia colony. George became the primary instrument of Governor Robert Dinwiddie, the English royal governor of the Virginia colony during the conflict that became known as the French and Indian War. Like Moses, Washington broke from the established government—England—in order to deliver the American people to their "promised land"

Moses led the Hebrews out of Egypt to the Red Sea, where they were trapped and about to be slaughtered by Pharaoh's army. God saved the Hebrews by parting the Red Sea and providing for their escape. When the Egyptians pursued them across the Red Sea, God returned the sea to its normal state and the army was destroyed.[7]

On several occasions during the Revolutionary War, General Washington found himself trapped against his own "Red Sea," but through a miracle, he managed to escape with his army intact. Like the Egyptians in their time, the greatest military force on the earth was inexplicably defeated.

God provided the direction of travel into the wilderness for Moses and the Hebrew nation through pillars of cloud and fire. God continued to perform miracles by providing protection, food and water to the Hebrew people. Despite continual evidence of God's love and power, the people complained and began to yearn for their days in Egypt. Moses eventually led the Israelites to Mount Sinai where God provided Moses his laws for living, the Ten Commandments. God was forging a holy nation, prepared to live for and serve him alone.[8]

The same can be said of General Washington as he struggled to hold his army together despite shortages of food, shelter, clothing and ammunition. Somehow, he found a way to provide for his men during the severe winters at Valley Forge and Morristown. During Washington's 1776 retreat across New Jersey and into Pennsylvania, many New Jersey colonists lost faith in the Revolution. They "yearned for their days in Egypt" by signing British loyalty oaths.

On the banks of the Jordan River, Moses assembled the tribes of Israel. He delivered God's laws by which they must live in their new land. He passed his authority to Joshua, under whom they would possess the land. Moses then went up Mount Nebo, to the top of Pisgah, looked over the promised land of Israel spread out before him. He died at the age of one hundred and twenty, never to enter the promised land.

George Washington too, delivered the laws for this nation when he presided over the Constitutional Convention of 1787. This Constitution, which today is both the shortest and the oldest still in existence, was flawed in many ways but was an accepted compromise that achieved ratification throughout all the colonies, both north and south. Shortly after spending two terms as the first president of the United

7   Ibid.
8   Ibid, 115-116.

Pilgrims Land at Plymouth Rock by Peter Frederick Rothermel

States, Washington died at Mount Vernon. He was within sight of but outside his promised land, our nation's new capital, Washington, D.C.

The American Exodus Story

A large number of American colonists, particularly in New England, thought of their suppression under British rule as equal to what the ancient children of Israel suffered during their enslavement in Egypt. The Pilgrims set sail on the *Mayflower* in September 1620, searching for a haven where they could practice their religion free from persecution. For these devout Puritans, their "American Exodus" to the New World essentially brought with it a "deliverance" that equaled that of Moses.

As Bruce Feiler, the author of *America's Prophet: How the Story of Moses Shaped America*, has noted, the Pilgrims viewed themselves as reliving the Exodus saga. Feiler writes, ". . . they described themselves as the chosen people fleeing their pharaoh, King James." While still on the Atlantic, the Pilgrims' leader, William Bradford, proclaimed their journey to be as vital as "Moses and the Israelites when they went out of Egypt." And when they arrived in Cape Cod, "they thanked God for letting

3

King George III by Benjamin West

them pass through their fiery Red Sea."[9]

A decade later, in 1630, a second wave of Puritans made their way across the Atlantic on board the ship *Arbella*. While sailing to what would become the Massachusetts Bay Colony, John Winthrop delivered a sermon to the passengers entitled "A Model of Christian Charity," in which he too invoked comparisons with the "Children of Israel."[10] Winthrop's proclamation of their settlement as a "shining

---

9   Michael Freund, "How the Exodus Story Created America," Pundicity Informed Opinion and Review, March 29, 2013, www.michaelfreund.org/13124/exodus-america. (January 18, 2017).
10   Ibid.

city on a hill" was certainly reminiscent of America as a second Jerusalem of sorts.

When more than a century and a half after the Pilgrims' arrival, the American colonies went to war against their British masters, the revolutionaries were also very much stirred by the story of the Israelites. With the arrival of the American Revolution, this theory was taken to the next level. One could argue that the Puritans had William Bradford as their Moses, leading them to their promised land. I argue that the chronology of events and particularly the miracles associated with the life of George Washington and the American Revolution have not been exceeded at any point in our nation's history.

When looking at the complete picture of American history, a more compelling argument would be that the Pilgrims' arrival in the New World was the start of the American Exodus story. That would equate to the Biblical story of Joseph's family moving to Egypt. I argue that the Puritans had a significant role to play in the American Exodus story, not only because of their arrival in Massachusetts, but for their rationale for coming to America. That was to achieve religious freedom and to establish a governmental ideology that still resides in America. Certainly the Hebrews had their pharaoh, who worshiped idols; the colonies had King George III, who was the head of the Anglican Church. Both had "hardened hearts," which contributed to their downfall.

The end result was a new nation based on a new order of freedom unseen before in the world. The odds against this outcome were immense. Each Revolutionary War battle was critical, and each reveals more about the precarious nature of America's march to freedom and the presence of God's providential hand at each critical moment.[11]

My purpose in writing this book is to tell the remarkable story of America's founding and to illuminate the source of America's greatness. I stand in company with most of the founding fathers themselves in believing that Divine Providence was at the center of this pivotal historical event. My primary focus is on actual historical information. I do draw conclusions, but you are encouraged to formulate your own.

The skeptic may disbelieve my interpretation of events I describe here. The miracles mentioned can be viewed as natural phenomena. Taken as a whole, however, there is a resounding case that something other than luck orchestrated the astonishing sequence of events that led to the life of George Washington, and the incredible sequence of military engagements that led to victory for America. I do not assume that you will share my beliefs but challenge you to explore your own. I do promise that no matter what you conclude, you will be uplifted by this incredible story.

---

11   Larkin Spivey, *Miracles of the American Revolution Divine Intervention and the Birth of the Republic* (Chattanooga, Tennessee: God and County Press, 2010), 13.

Part I

Moses and Washington
Their Destiny—Luck or Divine Providence

The reflection upon my Situation, & that of this Army, produces many an uneasy hour when all around me are wrapped in Sleep. Few People know the Predicament we are In . . . If I shall be able to rise superior to these, and many other difficulties, which might be innumerated [sic], I shall most religiously believe that the finger of Providence is in it.

George Washington to Joseph Reed
January 14, 1776

George Washington remains one of the most significant stories in the history of the United States. Some men are symbols for an age. Washington was far more: he was a mirror reflecting the beliefs of generation after generation of Americans. Indeed, in their remembrances of the Father of his Country are registered in large measure the entire ideological development of the American people.[12]

Part One compares the parallels and similarities between the life of Moses and that of George Washington. The purpose of this part is to explore what the greater story of Washington symbolizes: the widely held idea that "As the deliverer and political savior of our nation, he has been to us, as Moses was to the children of Israel." Through historical facts, I make the argument that Washington's ascent from birth to first president of the United States was more than "being at the right place at the right time." Instead, it was a customized life's calling, for which God equipped and ordained him. It was his destiny.

---

12   Hay, 781.

Chapter 1

Moses and Washington—Their Destiny

He whom the Almighty has chosen to be an Instrument, in his hands, to do much good, may well be hail'd. O thou highly favored of the Lord, who has received skill and understanding, fear not, peace unto Thee, be strong, yea be strong, for He will give his Angels charge over Thee, to keep Thee in all thy ways.[13]

Arthur Campbell to John Adams
December 1799

Was George Washington preordained by a divine power to lead a fragmented people to independence and nationhood? Certainly, circumstances could lead one into this belief. Many unusual events occurred to ensure that both Washington and Moses were available to lead their nations to their "promised land."

Were these events luck or something more? We talk about being lucky. We call someone a lucky dog. We wish people luck. We talk about lady luck, tough luck, good luck, bad luck, blind luck, rotten luck, lucky stars, and lucky charms. Luck is the concept of seeing events as random things that happen to affect one's life, fortune, future, or lot in life. It is that inanimate force that just sort of shows up unexpected, unanticipated—for either our benefit or our harm. Far too many of us embrace this mentality as a primary way of thinking.[14]

Robert Ohotto defines destiny in *Transforming Fate to Destiny* as a dynamic, active, and progressive process that continues to unfold throughout your life. It's activated from the very first breath you take on this planet and doesn't finish until your very last. It requires you to deliver a unique contribution to this world.[15] Tony Evans,

---

13   "To John Adams from Arthur Campbell, 21 December 1799," *Founders Online*, National Archives, version of January 18, 2019, https://founders.archives.gov/documents/Adams.99-02-02-4098. (March 22, 2019).
14   Evans, 126.
15   Robert Ohotto, *Transforming Fate into Destiny A New Dialogue with Your Soul.* (Carlsbad, California: Hay House Inc, 2008), 169.

in *Detours The Unpredictable Path to Your Destiny,* says each person has been custom-designed by God's loving, sovereign hand.[16]

Providence is how God uses his sovereignty to integrate, connect, attach, detach, arrange, and hook things up to facilitate his purposes.[17] As Evans puts it, what you, we, and others may look at as random events, chance encounters, or arbitrary connections are actually orchestrated events in both the purpose and plan of God. Evans says, "Let me put it another way—this mysterious thing called Providence means that God is sitting behind the steering wheel of history."[18] Providence is God either causing or allowing things to happen for his purpose.[19]

Whether the stories of Moses and George Washington were associated acts of luck or Divine Providence, you can decide. The historical facts speak for themselves. Letters from Washington reveal that he believed in destiny and Divine Providence. In a letter to Mrs. George William Fairfax, written on September 12, 1758, he said:

> "There is a Destiny which has the control of our actions, not to be resisted by the strongest efforts of Human Nature."[20]

Early in the lives of both Moses and Washington, they had been providentially rescued from lesser fates. Through the actions of loving mothers, heaven had saved them from ends that it had not intended.[21] The life of Moses should have been terminated shortly after his birth. But unusual events saved his life and elevated him, despite his Hebrew heritage, to the highest positions in the Egyptian government. Washington too, was the product of events that ensured he was born American, remained in America, and lived to lead our nation's founding. One telling example: Washington's mother refused to allow George to make a career in the British navy.

Moses Survives Pharaoh's Decree

When the Book of Exodus begins, the Hebrews were living in Egypt. After a time they grew in number and the new ruler put them into slavery to control his nation's population. The Hebrew slaves had reproduced so fast that Pharaoh felt threatened, fearing a potential revolt against his authority. He gave orders that no more newly born Hebrew boys should be allowed to live. To save the infant Moses from Pharaoh's decree, his mother made a little vessel of papyrus. She waterproofed it with asphalt and pitch. She placed Moses in the vessel and floated it among the reeds on the bank of the Nile River.

By God's providence, Moses, the child of a Hebrew slave, was found and

---

16   Evans, 6.
17   Ibid, 129.
18   Ibid, 131.
19   Ibid, 138.
20   W.W. Abbot, ed., *The Papers of George Washington,* Colonial Series, vol 6, 4 September 1758 – 26 December 1760 (Charlottesville: University Press of Virginia, 1988) 10-13.
21   Hay, 784.

adopted by an Egyptian princess, the daughter of Pharaoh himself. Moses was reared in the royal court as a prince of the Egyptians and saved from a certain early death.[22]

Establishment of the Washington Family in America

In 1732 George Washington was born into the gentry, in a prominent Virginia family that, like all their peers at the time, was loyal to the British government. However, were it not for world events and decisions made by the boy's great-grandfather, grandfather, and other relatives, there may never have been a George Washington to lead America's founding.

John Washington—Great-Grandfather of George Washington

George Washington's great-grandfather, John Washington, was the first of his family to immigrate to America. He was a well-educated son of an English clergyman named Lawrence Washington.

Lawrence spent the better part of his childhood at Sulgrave Manor in Oxfordshire. He earned two degrees at Oxford's Brasenose College .[23] He was a casualty of an early rebellion against royal authority and for religious liberty. During the English Civil War, Lawrence was persecuted by the Puritans as a "scandalous, malignant priest." In 1643, he was removed from his parish in the Puritan cleansing of the Church of England under Oliver Cromwell.[24] He was accused, probably falsely, of being "a common frequenter of ale houses" and "oft drunk."[25] After 120 years of ownership, the Washington ancestral home at Sulgrave Manor was seized.[26] The Washingtons were forced from their home.

Most historians argue that Lawrence's problems with the crown caused his son, John, to seek his fortune in the tobacco trade in North America.[27] It's noteworthy that religious dissent in England, specifically by the Puritans, that caused John Washington to go to America was also the cause for the Pilgrim's move to America. It is interesting that the descendants of the Pilgrims and other Puritans, who were guided by a dissident Protestant tradition that established a de facto independent and self-governing commonwealth in New England, were the first to revolt against the British government during America's Revolution.

So both the Washington family establishment in America and the leaders who

---

22   *The Bible*, Life Application Study, King James Version (Wheaton, Illinois: Tyndale House Publishing, 1996), Exodus 2:1-10.

23   Ron Chernow, *Washington a Life* (New York: Penguin Books 2010), 3.

24   Ibid.

25   Douglas Southall Freeman, *George Washington* Volume 1 *Young Washington* (New York: Scribner's and Sons 1948), 15.

26   "Col. John (G-Grandfather to George) Washington & Descendants," http://oursouthern-cousins.com/Descendants, August 3, 2007, (February 23, 2017), 2.

27   Ibid, 3.

first revolted against the English government during the Revolution can be traced back to religious dissent against the Church of England.

Running Aground in America

George Washington's great-grandfather, John Washington, at age twenty-five served as mate and partner on the ketch *Sea Horse of London,* which arrived in Tidewater Virginia in 1657.[28] But just as the ship sailed to return to England, loaded with a cargo of tobacco, a winter storm drove it aground on a shoal near the mouth of Mattox Creek in the Potomac River. The ketch sank. The tobacco was ruined. While attempting to raise the sunken vessel, John Washington met Nathaniel Pope, a rather rich Marylander, who had a marriageable daughter, Anne.[29] John became infatuated with Anne and determined to stay in America instead of returning to England.

The religious dissent in England; John Washington's decision to make his living in the American tobacco trade; his ship's grounding; his friendship with Nathaniel Pope; and his marriage to Pope's daughter were the chain of events that established the Washington family in America. Were these events all acts of "luck" or was something else in play? Was it Divine Providence? You decide.

Marriage to Anne Pope

The *Sea Horse of London's* master, Edward Prescott, held that Washington was partly responsible for the damage to his vessel. He pressed charges. Nathaniel Pope came to Washington's defense by paying his bond in beaver skins.[30] John Washington and Anne Pope were married in late 1658, receiving seven hundred acres of land and a loan for £80 from Nathaniel Pope.[31] They settled in a riverfront part of Westmoreland County, Virginia called Bridges Creek. They soon expanded their lands to include nearby Mattox Creek.

Ron Chernow gives this depiction of the great-grandfather of George Washington in *Washington a Life:*

"a bottomless appetite for land, and avidity for public office, and a zest for frontier combat—that foreshadowed his great-grandfather's rapid ascent in the world . . . John also set a precedent of social mobility through military laurels after he was recruited to fight Indians in Maryland and was rewarded with a colonel's rank. In this rough-and-tumble world, he was accused of slaughtering five Indian emissaries and cheating tribes of land,

28 Mary Shawn Russell, *Washington's Bloodline, The Long-Lost Branch of the Washington Family Tree* (Bolivia, NC: Tobacco Flower Publishing, 2018), 2.
29 Freeman, 15-16.
30 Justin Glenn, *The Washingtons a Family History* Volume One *Seven Generations of the Presidential Branch* (California: Sava Beatie, 2015), 1.
31 Freeman, Vol 1, 16.

activities that won him the baleful Indian nickname of Conotocarious, which meant 'Destroyer of Villages' or 'Town Devourer.' John piled up an impressive roster of the sort of local offices—justice of the peace, burgess in the Virginia assembly, lieutenant colonel in the county militia—that signified social standing in colonial Virginia. Most conspicuous was his omnivorous craving for land. By importing sixty-three indentured servants from England, he capitalized upon a British law that granted fifty acres [for each servant imported], with the single largest property bordering the Potomac River at Little Hunting Creek the future site of Mount Vernon."[32]

Starting the Washington Family

In 1659 John Washington and Anne Pope had a son. They named him Lawrence. The boy would become the grandfather of George Washington. For clarity he will be referred to as Lawrence Washington II to distinguish him from John Washington's father, Lawrence Washington I. One of the many points of confusion that comes to light when someone from the twenty-first century attempts to research history back to the eighteenth century is the matter of names. How many Lawrence Washingtons or John Washingtons were there, and which one are we referring to? The problem stems from the fact that throughout the eighteen and nineteenth centuries, English-speaking families often followed a basic naming convention. Many children's given names originated from their ancestors. For example, while there were exceptions, the first son was usually named after the father's father. The chart to the right shows the commonly accepted pattern:[33]

First son	Father's father
Second son	Mother's father
Third son	Father's eldest brother
Fourth son	Mother's eldest brother
First daughter	Mother's mother
Second daughter	Father's mother
Third daughter	Mother
Fourth daughter	Mother's eldest sister

Common English Naming Pattern

So John and Anne Pope Washington named their first-born son after John's father, Lawrence I. By 1668, Anne had borne John four more children: John Junior, Anne, and two children who died young.

Death of John Washington and Anne Pope

Anne Pope died in 1668 and John Washington died in the fall of 1677. His will was admitted to probate on September 26, 1677. His estate consisted of more

---

32   Chernow, 3.
33   Russell, xvi.

Washington Family Cemetery at Bridges Creek, Virginia. John Washington and Anne Pope are in center crypt.

than eighty-five hundred acres of land.[34] The will divided his lands among his three living children, Lawrence, John and Anne. In accordance with primogeniture, customary in Virginia, Lawrence as the oldest inherited the largest share.[35] Both Anne Pope and John Washington are buried in the Washington Family Cemetery at Bridges Creek, Virginia.

The chain of events leading to the birth of George Washington continue through the life of George's grandfather, Lawrence II, and one of his distant cousins.

Lawrence Washington II

Lawrence Washington II, John's oldest son, was born at Mattox Creek, Virginia.[36] Lawrence was sent to England for his education and was still there when his father died.[37] Lawrence's education focused on law. By 1679 he had returned to Virginia where he took up some of the same public duties his father had discharged.

Lawrence became justice of the peace and sheriff, positions that complimented his work as an attorney.[38] As sheriff, in 1692 he hired two deputies, one being his cousin John Washington, the son of his father's brother.[39] Cousin John Washington did not serve out his term as deputy sheriff but chose to move northwestward to Stafford County, where he settled in an area called Chotank.[40] Chotank Creek is up the Potomac River some twenty miles from Mattox and Bridges Creeks, near present-day Dahlgren, Virginia. For clarity, we will identify him as John Washington of Chotank, not be confused with his grandfather, John Washington the father of Lawrence Washington II. After the death of Lawrence II, cousin John of Chotank Creek would play a pivotal role in American history that has gone mostly unrecognized by historians.

---

34   Glenn, Vol 1, 2.
Freeman, Vol 1, 29-30.
35   Ibid.
36   Ibid, 30.
37   Glenn, Vol 1, 4.
38   Chernow, 4.
39   Charles Hatch, Jr, *Chapters in the History of Popes Creek*, (Washington DC: US Department of Interior December 1, 1968), 20.
40   Ibid.

Selected to the House of Burgesses

By age twenty-five, Lawrence II was elected to represent Westmoreland County. in Virginia's colonial legislature, the House of Burgesses. It was presided over by a royal governor appointed by the king. Lawrence never showed interest in farming or increasing his land holdings, perhaps being satisfied with his compensation from public office.[41] His acquisitions were modest by the standards of his time; he increased his holdings by only some 440 acres. He made few improvements to his estate at Bridges Creek.[42]

Augustine Warner
Courtesy of Biography.com

Warner Hall—Home of Augustine Warner

Marriage to Mildred Warner

As John, the first Washington to immigrate to America, had added the family name to Virginia's gentry class, it was Lawrence II who added social distinction to the Washington name by marrying Mildred Warner. That occurred around 1691.[43] Mildred Warner was of "established position," as her father was Augustine Warner of Gloucester County, speaker of the House of Burgesses and a member of the King's Council.[44]

Some of the most recognized names in American history are direct descendants of Augustine Warner: Robert E. Lee, the famous Civil War general, and Captain Meriwether Lewis, the renowned explorer of the Lewis and Clark expedition.[45] Queen Elizabeth II, the current monarch of England, is a direct descendant of

---

41   Freeman, Vol 1, 30.
42   Ibid.
43   Chernow, 4.
44   Freeman, Vol 1, 30.
45   Theresa F. Stavens, "History," *The Inn at Warner Hall*, http://warnerhall.com/historic-virgin-ia-bed-and-breakfast/. (February 6, 2017).

Augustine Warner through the Bowes-Lyon family and the Earl of Strathmore.[46] Augustine Warner's wife was Mildred Reade. Her lineage can be traced back to the ancient rulers of England.

Family of Lawrence Washington II and Mildred Warner

As Douglas Southall Freeman writes in *George Washington Volume 1, Young Washington,* Lawrence II began at a higher level economically and socially than his father, and went farther.[47] Lawrence and Mildred produced three children: John, Augustine, and Mildred. It was the second child, Augustine, who would become the father of George.

Death and Will of Lawrence Washington

Sometime after March 11, 1698, in his thirty-eighth year, Lawrence died.[48] All the children were still young. In Lawrence's will, he gave John, his oldest child, the home tract and other lands. Augustine was given

Crypt of Lawrence Washington

approximately eleven hundred acres.[49] Mildred received twenty-five hundred acres included patents at the "freshes" of the Potomac River.[50] Those "freshes" of the Potomac included Little Hunting Creek, which Mildred would later sell to her brother Augustine. Little Hunting Creek would become Mount Vernon, the home of George Washington. It is important to note that Lawrence's will is the document that allows for the unbroken chain of events leading to George's birth. Lawrence stipulated in his will that while his children were minors, or until their marriage if that was before they became of age, John, Augustine, and Mildred were to "remain under the care and tuition of their mother," who was to have "the profits of their estates" to pay for their support and schooling."[51] This specific language would later become an issue after the early death of his widow Mildred. Lawrence Washington's will is historically significant for America's future.

---

46   Ibid.
47   Freeman, Vol 1, 30.
48   Ibid.
49   Freeman, Vol 1, 31.
50   Ibid.
51   Ibid.

Mildred Warner Washington Remarries

Within two years after the death of Lawrence II, Mildred Warner Washington remarried. This was in 1700, to George Gale of Whitehaven, England.[52] Gale took Mildred and the three young children of Lawrence Washington II with him to Whitehaven, where Mildred died on January 30, 1701.[53] Mildred Warner Washington Gale was buried in Saint Nicholas Church in Whitehaven. That left the three children, including Augustine, the future father of George, living in England. Both their natural parents were dead. They were under the care of their stepfather, George Gale, and all owned sizeable estates from their inheritance in America. They were too young to take possession or manage their claims.

Litigation for the Children of Lawrence and Mildred Washington

George Gale accepted his responsibility as parent to the Washington children. Almost immediately, he placed Augustine and his brother in the Appleby School, about fifty miles from Whitehaven. Gale also continued the care and nurturing of little Mildred, still of pre-school age.[54]

When the word of Mildred Warner Washington Gale's death reached Virginia, and the terms of her will became known, John Washington of Chotank, cousin to and executor of Lawrence II's will, disputed the validity of Mildred Gale's actions

Lawrence left his three children sizable estates in which Gale had no legal interest. According to the will of Lawrence Washington, the children's inheritance had been assigned to their mother during her lifetime and could not be passed on to Gale while he was their guardian. According to the court, Lawrence's cousin John Washington, the executor of his will, was correct. The court's opinion was that Mildred's interest in her children's estates ended with her death. She could not transfer the property, income, or custody of the children to her husband. Based on this opinion, the court ordered Gale to return the orphans and their property to Virginia and into the custody of John Washington of Chotank. [55]

As ordered by the court in the year 1704, George Gale returned to Westmoreland County. He brought the children of Lawrence II, John, Augustine and Mildred, and delivered them and their estates to John Washington of Chotank, as executor of their late father's will.[56] John of Chotank then raised his cousin's children. Lawrence's foresight in articulating his children's specific legal rights and John of Chotank's courage in attesting that will would have lasting implications for America. Had the

---

52 Glenn, Vol 1, 4.

53 Hatch, 26.

54 Freeman, Vol 1, 32.

55 Ibid.

56 Clayton Torrence, "A Virginia Lady of Quality and Her Possessions: Mrs. Mildred Willis of Fredericksburg," *The Virginia Magazine of History and Biography* Volume 56, No. 1, January 1948, 44.

children not returned to America, Augustine Washington would not have married Mary Ball. Without that marriage, George Washington would not have existed and the future of America might have taken a different course.

Was the chain of events leading to the George Washington's birth just plain luck or was Divine Providence at work? You can decide for yourself, but these are the facts. Like the vulnerable Moses in the basket floating in the Nile, for Washington to have been born in America depended on the decisions of many of his ancestors. Any one of the players could have made decisions that would have broken the chain of events that led to George's birth. I argue that it was through Divine Providence that this chain was not shattered.

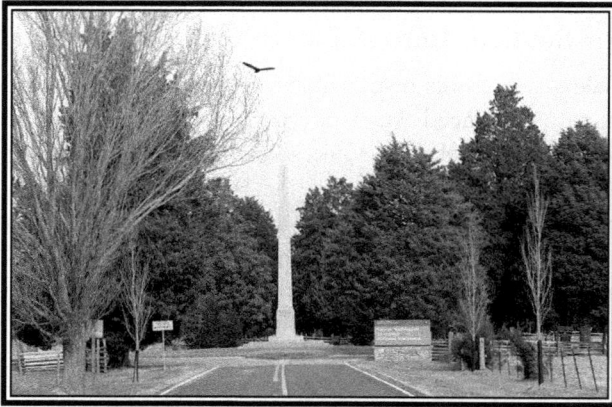

George Washington Birthplace National Monument

Chapter 2

Washington's GPS

We are not in a world ungoverned by the laws and power of a superior agent. Our efforts are in his hand and directed by it; and he will give them their effect in his own time. [57]

Thomas Jefferson to David Barrow
April 30, 1789

O n Friday, June 16, 1775, John Hancock, president of the Second Continental Congress, announced that George Washington had been chosen general and commander in chief of the army of the United Colonies of America, which was in revolt against England. Washington stood modestly at his seat in Philadelphia's red-brick State House and replied:

> "Mr. President, tho I am truly sensible of the high honor done me in this appointment, yet I feel great distress from a consciousness that my abilities and military experience may not be equal to the extensive and important trust. However, as the congress desire it, I will enter upon the momentous duty and exert every power I possess in their service and for the support of the glorious cause."[58]

How had someone born into the planter class of Virginia, without formal education, risen to the most important position in America? Similar to how Moses, who was born into a Hebrew slave family, rose to one of the highest positions in Egypt, Washington's life's destination relied on those who guided him as precisely as if he were taking directions from a Global Positioning System (GPS). Washington took directions from his "GPS" and adroitly took advantage of the opportunities that presented themselves during his journey.

Preserving both Moses and Washington from meaner fates was only one way that God manifested his very specific care. Throughout his youth, the facts of the George Washington story appear to reveal that he was being tailored "exactly" for

---

57 Carol Kelly Gangi, *The Essential Wisdom of the Founding Fathers* (New York: Fall River Press 2018), 65.
58 Philander D. Chase, ed., *The Papers of George Washington*, Revolutionary War Series, vol 1, 16 June 1775 – 15 September 1775, (Charlottesville: University Press of Virginia, 1985), 1-3.

the preordained American Exodus, just as Moses had been before him.[59] Several individuals can be credited with setting the destination into George Washington's "GPS". The most influential are discussed in this chapter. They made a significant impact on the direction that George took in his life. As you read, ask yourself if these people and events were just "luck" or was it the work of Divine Providence?

Augustine Washington—Father of George Washington

George Washington's father, Augustine, did not have a major role to play in raising his son. Augustine died before George reached his teenage years. The truth is, we know little about Washington's relationship with his father. In all his voluminous correspondence, he mentioned his father on only three occasions and then only cryptically. As for his mother, Mary Ball Washington, we know she was a tall and physically strong woman who lived long enough to see her son elected president but never extolled or even acknowledged his public triumphs.[60] It was actually father Augustine's early death that steered George's life direction from what was expected to what he actually became.

Augustine inherited eleven hundred acres through his father's will and acquired another 1,750 acres from the dowry of his first wife, Jane Butler.[61] Augustine or Gus, as he was known, is described as a remorseless, hard-driving businessman who specialized in tobacco farming until he began buying properties on the Rappahannock River that were rich in iron.[62] Like his father and grandfather, he soon became a justice of the peace and took his seat on the bench of the Westmoreland County Court.[63] His marriage to Jane Butler produced three children, Lawrence III (named after the father's father), Augustine Junior (referred to as Austin), and Jane. About 1717 Gus purchased lands that adjoin the Washington family estate at Bridges Creek[64]

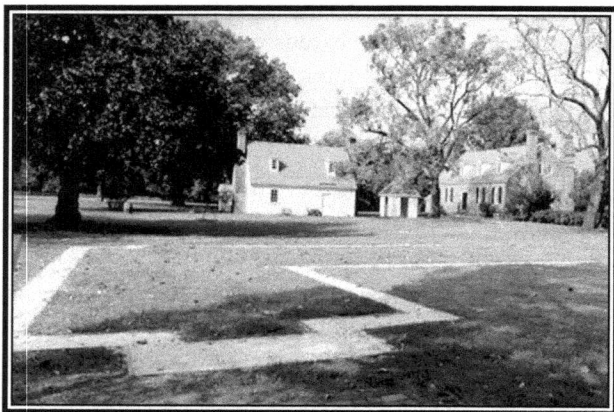

Wakefield at Pope's Creek, Virginia

59   Hay, 784.
60   Joseph J. Ellis, *His Excellency George Washington* (Vintage Books: New York) 2005, 8.
61   Chernow, 5.
62   Ibid.
63   Freeman, Vol 1, 34.
64   U.S. Department of Interior, National Park Service, *George Washington Birthplace National Monument,* 1941,Washington, D.C.: National Park Service 1941, 5.

This adjoining property, acquired from one Joseph Abbington, was called Pope's Creek. Approximately ten years later, Gus completed a home on Pope's Creek, about three-quarters of a mile from where it empties into the Potomac River. The site was approximately a mile and an eighth northwest of the Washington family burying ground. The structure was not given a name but was known many years later as Wakefield.[65]

Iron Furnace

Gus bought more agricultural land to cultivate or to resell in the Chotank region along the Potomac and began to share in the development of ore-bearing land and iron furnaces.[66] Whether it was his own search or that of his iron furnace manager, John England, someone discovered rich iron deposits on a tract along Accokeek Creek. This lies between the Potomac and Aquia Creek and near Marlborough Point, about eight miles from Fredericksburg. Gus received patents on this land and by January 1725 signed an agreement with the Principio Iron Works and John England for mining iron. [67] Augustine and Jane were not rich, but they were prospering, allowing Gus to discharge the duties and holdings of the offices that usually fell to a gentleman of the county.[68] In 1728, while Gus was away in England settling a deal involving the iron ore business, his wife Jane Butler died. Saddled with the care of three young children, Gus now had an urgent quest to find a new bride.[69]

On March 31, 1731 (New Style Calendar) [70], the thirty-seven year old Gus married twenty-three year old Mary Johnson Ball.[71] They resided in the home Gus had built at the Pope's Creek farm.[72] George Washington was the first child of the marriage of Gus and Mary Ball. He was born at Pope's Creek around 10 a.m. on February 11, 1732.[73]

George was raised amid the rich, open farmland of Virginia's Tidewater section, where four rivers dominated the region: the James, York, Rappahannock, and Potomac. [74] Large tobacco fields thrived in the coastal plain, broken only by a

---

65   Freeman, Vol 1, 35.
66   Ibid, 37.
67   Ibid, 38.
68   Ibid, 41.
69   U.S. Department of Interior, 6.
70   Old style vs. new style calendar dates. Great Britain and its colonies did not convert from the old Julian Calendar to the new Gregorian Calendar until September 1752. By then, the old style calendar lagged eleven days behind the new. To compensate, the British Empire directed that the day after September 2, 1752, be designated September 14, 1752. This reform also dictated that the new style calendar began each year on January 1, where the old style calendar had begun the year on March 25.
71   Chernow, 5
72   U.S. Department of Interior, 5.
73   Chernow, 6.
74   Ibid.

View of Potomac River from Little Hunting Creek

sprinkling of tiny, isolated towns.[75]

In addition to his older siblings from the marriage of Jane Butler, Gus and Mary delivered to George five additional brothers and sisters: Betty, Samuel, John Augustine, Charles, and Mildred. [76] George straddled two families, which perhaps forced him at an early age to hone the diplomatic skills he would demonstrate later.[77] While the two older half-brothers were away in England being educated, George probably helped his mother care for his younger siblings.

Move to Little Hunting Creek (Mount Vernon)

In 1735 Gus moved the entire family sixty miles up the Potomac to a location that he bought from his sister, Mildred Washington Lewis Gregory. This land was known as Little Hunting Creek. Mildred had inherited it from her and Gus's father, Lawrence II. Mildred sold this twenty-five-hundred-acre tract to Gus, who decided to make it his home. Little Hunting Creek provided a more convenient access by road to his iron furnace. on Accokeek Creek near Fredericksburg.[78]

At Little Hunting Creek, Augustine owned a dwelling that may have been built by his father. It was not large, but neither was his household. Only five in the family lived there, the parents and children: George, Betty, and Samuel. The two older brothers, Lawrence III and Augustine Junior were still in England; the youngest children had not yet been born. Cabins for the servants were erected and a mill was built on Dogue Run Creek. This completed the task of making the plantation self-sustaining.[79]

Accokeek was thirty miles from Little Hunting Creek with several streams and marshes in between. The distance and difficult topography were enough to discourage

---

75   Ibid.
76   Ibid, 7.
77   Ibid.
78   Paula S. Felder, *George Washington's Fredericksburg*, (Virginia Beach, Virginia: The Donning Company Publishers, 2011), 16.
79   Freeman, Vol 1, 53.

Ferry Farm—Washington's Childhood Home

frequent journeys but not so great, perhaps, as to deter Gus from attempting to keep in touch with his iron enterprise.

The death of John England, who had managed the iron furnace, probably forced Augustine to take a larger part in running the business. This proved to be as hard to execute from nearby Little Hunting Creek as it had been when Augustine lived at the more distant Pope's Creek.[80]

Young George's initial stay at Little Hunting Creek was short-lived. His father would negotiate a better business deal with the investors in his Principio iron furnace. At the same time, a more convenient residence was up for auction near Fredericksburg. In 1738, Gus bought the working farm of William Strother, on the bluff just below and opposite Fredericksburg. This was a convenient eight miles from the iron works on Accokeek Creek.[81]

Move to Ferry Farm – Fredericksburg, Virginia

After living three years at Little Hunting Creek, at age six George moved again. This time, his new home was a six-hundred-acre farm poised on the brow of a hill, slightly recessed from the Rappahannock River, with plenty of woods and broad fields for growing tobacco, wheat, and corn. The property had pure streams for drinking water and it overlooked the town of Fredericksburg The Washington

---

80   Ibid, 58.
81   Russell, 46.

family called this place Ferry Farm, since the ferry to Fredericksburg landed on the property.[82] George would reach adulthood while living on Ferry Farm.

Douglas Southall Freeman describes the place as a livable residence of eight rooms with nearby storehouses and an adequate number of outbuildings. The gardens were on the north. Eastward from the main structure was a strip of woodland; to the south were open fields, less elevated; on the west was another modest stretch that fell away toward the river. The site was high and fine, but had an unhappy difference from Little Hunting Creek: the size of the river. Compared with the width of the gracious tidal Potomac, the Rappahannock at Fredericksburg was a mere creek.[83]

At Ferry Farm, George witnessed something he had never before experienced. His new home was directly across the river from a sizeable town, something he had not seen before age seven.

After the move to Ferry Farm, George's older half-brother, Lawrence III, returned from being educated in England. Lawrence took up residence at Little Hunting Creek to operate the farm there. It was at this time that George set eyes for the first time on his older brother, to him a quasi-mythical figure who had been polished by his years at the Appleby Grammar School, in England. "Tall and debonair," as Chernow described him, "Lawrence must have radiated a mature, well-traveled air of worldly sophistication for young George, who was fourteen years his junior."[84]

First Exposure to War

George's first exposure to war came through his older brother. In 1739 England clashed with Spain in the Caribbean in a conflict known as the War of Jenkins's Ear. Robert Jenkins was a British captain whose ear was allegedly mutilated by the Spanish. The British enlisted colonial support, raising an American Regiment for an amphibious expedition to Cartagena on the northern coast of South America. Lawrence Washington III was awarded a spot as captain of a Virginia infantry company. The expedition was a bloody disaster. Lawrence III never disembarked from his transport ship. But his return with thrilling tales of war made an impression on young George that that he would mimic years later.[85]

Lawrence III had mixed feelings about his British superiors. He did not have high regard for Brigadier General Thomas Wentworth, who sneered at colonial troops and kept them cooped up aboard the ship. But he "retained clear affection for Admiral Edward Vernon and in a burst of Anglophilia, would rename the Little Hunting Creek estate Mount Vernon, hanging the admiral's portrait in an honored place there."[86]

82   Chernow, 8.
83   Freeman, *Vol 1*, 59
84   Chernow, 8.
85   Ibid, 9.
86   Ibid.

Death of Augustine Washington

In 1742, George's other half-brother, Augustine Junior, returned from his stint at the Appleby School . It was expected that shortly George himself would be enrolled in the English boarding school. That dream was crushed later that year when his father fell ill and on April 12, 1743, died at age forty-nine.

With the coming of spring and the approach of Easter, George had been permitted to go to the Chotank region to visit his cousins. He was there when calamity came across the fields. A messenger rode up with instructions for George to return home at once. His father was dangerously sick. When George reached home he found his family despairing and Augustine's great form spread out on a bed. The stricken man had made his will and now faced death with his soul content.[87] His death was eerily similar to George's own some fifty-six years later. Gus had ridden out in a storm and gotten sick. His father's premature death highlighted a central theme in George's life: that "although he was a superb physical specimen, with a magnificent physique, his family's medical history was blighted by truncated lives."[88] Augustine Washington was buried in the family graveyard on Bridges Creek.[89] Because of Augustine's early death, George was not able to pursue the formal education in England his older brothers had received.

Augustine's will left sizeable estates to each of his male children. Lawrence III inherited Mount Vernon and the iron mine. Augustine Junior inherited the farm at Pope's Creek. George received Ferry Farm, a half share in a tract upriver called Deep Run and assorted lots in Fredericksburg.[90] George also found himself, at age eleven, the owner of ten human beings.[91]

Education

George probably learned his ABCs from John Hobby, who lived a few miles south of Ferry Farm. At age twelve, his mother learned of an opportunity for her children to be taught across the river in Fredericksburg. The Reverend James Marye had been minister for Saint George's Parish since 1735. Marye was educated in France by Jesuit priests, but as a Huguenot, had become a victim of religious upheaval. He moved to England, was accepted into the Anglican Church and was sent to Virginia[92]

Marye taught both boys and girls. George Washington attended his school for several terms between 1743 and 1746.[93] Cousin Lewis Willis, the son of George's aunt and godmother, Mildred Washington Lewis Gregory Willis, attested to George's

---

87   Freeman, Vol 1, 72.
88   Chernow, 9-10.
89   Freeman, Vol 1, 73.
90   Chernow, 9-10.
91   Ibid.
92   Ibid.
93   Ibid.

serious demeanor and withdrawn behavior. According to Lewis, "George applied himself in math while the others played at field hockey."[94] A single incident, George's spontaneous romp with one of the largest girls in the class, so astonished everyone that Lewis remembered it in his old age.[95]

Lewis Willis was the source of many a boyhood anecdote that has been elevated to a myth over the course of history. Willis recalled that cousin George once threw a rock across the Rappahannock River at the ferry landing. This recollection has been elevated by time to unhuman feats of strength, featuring silver dollars thrown across the much wider Potomac.[96]

The death of his father not only robbed George of a formal education but threw the boy back upon his own resources, stealing any chance of a playful youth. Because his mother never remarried, George developed the deeply rooted hardness common in youths forced to function as adults at an early age. Mary Ball Washington appears as an unbending, even shrewish, disciplinarian. One can only imagine the unspoken dread that she too, experienced at being widowed at thirty-five. This left her to perform her late husband's duties. Her tasks were to manage Ferry Farm, raise five children ranging from six to eleven, and oversee dozens of slaves. Her husband's death forced Mary to eliminate any frills of family life. Her spartan style as a businesswoman, thrifty and demanding, had a discernible impact on George.[97]

George's inability to go to England for schooling turned out to be one of the greatest detours of his young life, which turned to the benefit of America. Staying in Virginia afforded him the opportunity to be guided by his older brother Lawrence III. I argue that Lawrence III provided the single biggest impact on the destination set in George's "GPS." The timing was perfect. Lawrence had returned from schooling in England and military service. George was not sent to England to spend years being educated; he was not separated from his brother. That meant those years would be spent with Lawrence providing the guidance, direction and connections for George's future.

Lawrence Washington III—Brother to George

Lawrence III became George's surrogate father and felt responsible for managing the career options of his younger brother, who had little hope of inheriting enough land to permit easy entrance into the planter class of Chesapeake society.[98] When George was about fourteen, Lawrence urged George's mother to consider enrolling her son as a British naval cadet. Mrs. Washington did not approve of the suggestion, nor did his uncle in England, who forwarded the negative opinion that the navy would "cut him and staple him and use him like a Negro, or rather like

94   Ibid, 12.
95   Felder, 24.
96   Ibid.
97   Chernow, 10.
98   Ibid.

a dog.'"[99] Posterity has certainly benefited from Mrs. Washington's wisdom.[100] Had the impressionable juvenile continued along this course that his natural curiosity dictated, he would have hazarded his morals, his "future usefulness," perhaps even his life. But in God's plan it was not to be. As the historian Robert P. Hay put it, "Providence snatched him from the brink of ruin, in almost as singular a manner as he did the Hebrew child, Moses."[101]

Lawrence's three other contributions to Washington's career were significant. The first two were ironic.

In 1751 Lawrence III traveled to Barbados in search of a tropical cure for his tuberculosis. He took George along as a companion. This turned out to be George's only trip abroad. During the trip George contracted a mild case of smallpox, which his own bodily defenses defeated. The case gave him an immunity against the era's most feared and fatal disease. This event probably saved Washington's life during the Revolutionary War, when smallpox coursed its way through the ranks of the Continental Army. [102]

Lawrence Washington III
**Courtesy of Mount Vernon Ladies'
Association**

The second event was when Lawrence III lost his battle with tuberculosis. His Mount Vernon estate would become his brother George's property after the deaths of Lawrence's wife and child.[103]

George had begun to spend much of his time at Mount Vernon around 1747. He lived with his brother and Lawrence's new wife, Ann Fairfax. Her family's estate was at nearby Belvoir. The head of the Fairfax dynasty was Lord Thomas Fairfax, an eccentric member of the English peerage. Thomas Fairfax's disdain for women and love for horses and hounds soon carried him across the Blue Ridge Mountains to pursue his passion for fox hunting, uninterrupted by the burdensome duties of managing his estates. He controlled more than five million acres in the Northern Neck of Virginia.

Lord Thomas's cousin William was Anne's father. William served as his cousin's proprietor and assumed the responsibility of selling and leasing his vast land holdings between the Potomac and Rappahannock Rivers. That made William Fairfax the most influential man in the region. The Fairfaxes were a living residue of European feudalism and English-style aristocracy, firmly entrenched among Virginia's more provincial version of country gentlemen.

---

99   Ibid.
100   Felder, 24.
101   Hay, 784.
102   Ellis, 10.
103   Felder, 24.

Lord Thomas Fairfax, Sixth Lord Fairfax of Cameron
Courtesy of Biography.com

"Though Washington was destined to lead a revolution that eventually toppled this whole constellation of aristocratic beliefs and presumptions, he was initially a beneficiary of its powers of patronage."[104]

Doesn't that comment from the historian Paula Felder sound similar to how Moses, the beneficiary of his standing in the Egyptian high court, would only later lead a revolution against it?

On July 19, 1743, a little more than two months after Augustine's death, Ann Fairfax became the wife of Lawrence Washington III. For both Lawrence and George, it was a fortunate day. To Lawrence it meant alliance with the most powerful interests of the Northern Neck through marriage to a girl who already had valuable lands. Before many more years, she was to hold patents for a total of four thousand acres. George, in his turn, found new and desirable associations. Increasingly, after Lawrence's marriage, George visited Mount Vernon and its neighbor, Belvoir, where he came under the influence of both William and Lord Thomas Fairfax.[105]

---

104   Ibid.
105   Freeman, Vol 1, 76.

William and Thomas Fairfax—George's Mentors

Lawrence III's third contribution to George's career was his introduction to William Fairfax. With his wealthy neighbor, George found a mentor with significant influence in the American colonies.

Lord Thomas Fairfax, living at Belvoir at the time, also took an interest in young George Washington, writing his mother, Mary Washington:

"Young George has what my friend, Mr. Addison, was pleased to call the intellectual conscience. The Lord deliver him from the nets of those spiders, called women, who will cast for his ruin. I wish I could say that he governs his temper for he is subject to attacks of anger on provocation, and sometime without just cause, But time will cure him."[106]

During his visits to Mount Vernon and Belvoir, George quickly became motivated by talk of patents, of surveys, of trails, of settlements, and of the profits that might be made by organizing land enterprises beyond the western frontier west of the Blue Ridge Mountains. He wanted to be like Lord Fairfax, Colonel Fairfax and his brother Lawrence, not merely the owner of a farm of moderate size.[107]

The means for George's advancement were at hand. In the storehouse at his home were the surveyor's instruments that had belonged to his father. Across the river in Fredericksburg and elsewhere in the neighborhood lived men who knew how to use the surveyor's compass. One such man was George Hume. From 1746 to 1747 George Hume quickly taught George Washington the elements of surveying. [108]

On March 11, 1748, at age sixteen, George Washington received his first job. He accompanied George William Fairfax, the son of William Fairfax, on a surveying expedition in the Shenandoah Valley.[109] It was an important date in George's life both because it marked his farthest journey from home and because it was his first personal contact with the new frontier about which there was constant talk among the elders.[110]

Washington recorded his adventures in a diary entitled *A Journal of My Journey over the Mountains*. He relays stories of incredible adventures: fording swollen rivers, fending off hungry bears, shooting wild turkey, and sleeping rough under the stars. He met Native warriors, fresh from battle, carrying scalps. He shared their meals, watched them dance and get drunk![111] From his journal Washington writes:

---

106   Hugh Fairfax, *Fairfax of Virginia, The Forgotten Story of America's Only Peerage, 1680-1960* (London: The Fairfax Family Publisher, 2017), 39.
107   Freeman, Vol 1, 197.
108   Ibid.
109   Felder, 24.
110   Freeman, Vol 1, 203.
111   Fairfax, 39.

"Went into the Bed as they call'd it when to my Surprize I found it to be nothing but a Little Straw – Matted together without Sheets or any thing else but only one Thread Bare blanket with double its Weight of Vermin such as Lice Fleas & c."[112]

This job became possible because of the introductions Lawrence III provided to his brother: to William Fairfax and to George Hume, who taught him the skills of surveying.

In 1752, Lord Thomas Fairfax moved his headquarters for managing Virginia's Northern Neck from his cousin's home at Belvoir into the heart of the Shenandoah Valley. He built his home below the slopes of the Blue Ridge not far from present-day Winchester, Virginia. He named the house Greenway Court. It was here that the relationship between Lord Thomas and George Washington blossomed, much as that between a tutor and his pupil.[113]

The surveying expeditions that Washington undertook for Lord Thomas taught him much about living on the land, and familiarized him with this previously unsettled region. These skills he later put to good as a soldier. More important, Thomas Fairfax shared the worldly knowledge and wisdom he had gained over the course of his more than sixty years. Fairfax taught George all he knew about politics, culture and society in Georgian England.[114] It was Washington's talent in surveying and the influence of Lord Thomas and William Fairfax that opened the door to the young man's future. It all started with surveying and the Fairfaxes, and that all came through the connections of George's brother, Lawrence Washington III.

Washington's friend George William Fairfax **Courtesy of Biography.com**

George Washington Starts his Career

George William Fairfax became George's best friend, and George William's father, William, would forever use his influence to obtain George a place in Virginia's upper class. His surveying experience, coupled with an ethic of hard work, brought Washington his first income and was excellent preparation for the next chapter in his life. At seventeen, with the help of his Fairfax mentors, George received an appointment as surveyor of the new county of Culpeper. By the time he was eighteen, his thrifty habits allowed him to save enough to acquire land he had scouted in the Shenandoah Valley. The knowledge gained of terrain in this little-traveled area of Virginia would be invaluable in his later military service during the French and Indian War. That war in turn was the groundwork of his military career.[115]

---

112   Ellis, 11.
113   Fairfax, 40.
114   Ibid.
115   Felder, 25.

Death of Lawrence Washington III

The death of Lawrence Washington III in 1752 left vacant the position of adjutant in the Virginia Militia. Without any military experience or training, his brother George decided to seek appointment to succeed his deceased brother. Thanks to William Fairfax's influence with Governor Robert Dinwiddie, George was appointed to the position with the rank of major.[116]

Programming his GPS

If Washington's GPS was programmed to his final destination as first president of the United States, then certainly the waypoints along his route, as identified in this chapter, paved the way. The death of Augustine Washington caused George Washington to stay in Virginia instead of being educated in England, as was the original plan. Being raised in Virginia led George to his older brother Lawrence III, who guided him and introduced him to the Fairfaxes. Associations with brother Lawrence and William Fairfax steered George into the skill of surveying. Colonel Fairfax mentored George and gave him his first job as surveyor, then his appointment of official Surveyor of Culpeper County. William Fairfax also recommended and received approval from Virginia's governor for George to become adjutant of the Virginia Militia. Lord Thomas Fairfax had personally tutored George on worldly issues of politics, culture and society. The stage was now set. All that remained was an opportunity to excel. That opportunity presented itself in 1753 when someone was needed for a diplomatic mission into the western frontier. These lands were known by only a few British colonists. The requirements for the person were:

√ Trusted by Virginia's governor (Washington)
√ Could represent the British government (Washington)
√ Familiar with the western frontier (Washington)

George Washington met these requirements and was selected by Governor Dinwiddie. The rest is history.

Could the events described in this chapter have all been attributed to "blind luck" or an act of Divine Providence? Not convinced? Read further.

---

116   Ellis, 12.

Fort Necessity, with Swivel Gun on Earthworks
Photo by John Meyer

Chapter 3

Learning the Art of War

I am chief and ruler over my tribes. My influence extends to the waters of the great lakes and to the far blue mountains. I have traveled a long and weary path that I might see the young warrior of the great battle. It was on the day when the white man's blood mixed with the streams of our forest that I first beheld this chief (indicating Washington). I called to my young men and said, "Mark yon tall and daring warrior? He is not of the red-coat tribe— he hath an Indian's wisdom, and his warriors fight as we do—himself is alone exposed. Quick! Let your aim be certain, and he dies." Our rifles were leveled—rifles which, but for you, knew not how to miss. Twas all in vain; a power mightier far than we shielded you. Seeing you were under the special guardianship of the Great Spirit, we immediately ceased to fire at you. I am old, and soon shall be gathered to the great council fire of my fathers in the land of shades; but ere I go, there is something bids me speak in the voice of prophecy. Listen! The Great Spirit protects that man (again indicating Washington), and guides his destinies—he will become the chief of nations, and a people yet unborn will hail him as the founder of a mighty empire. I am come to pay homage to the man who is the particular favorite of Heaven and who can never die in battle.[117]

Chief White Mingo
1770, Conversation with Washington and Dr. James Craik
Describing the 1755 Battle at the Monongahela

The story above was told to both George Washington and Doctor James Craik in the year 1770 by a Native American chief named White Mingo, who participated in the Battle at the Monongahela River during the French and Indian War. True to the chief's prediction and because God sovereignly and divinely protected him, Washington not only did not die in that 1755 battle but he was not even wounded, not in that or in any of the numerous subsequent battles in which he fought.[118]

How did Washington find himself in such a position in 1755 fighting on the side of the British against the French and their Native American allies? George

117   David Barton, *The Bulletproof George Washington* (Aledo, Texas: WallBuilders, 2016), 67.
118   Ibid.

had no military experience, did not speak French or any Native dialects, and was inexperienced in the matters of diplomacy. In order to understand the ending we must go back to the beginning.

English and French Expansion in America

In the early 1740's the population of the American colonies had grown to approximately 1.5 million people. To continue to grow in population, the colonies needed to expand. The British colony of Virginia expanded westward into regions beyond the fall lines of the navigable rivers.[119] The Virginia Tidewater area that these English immigrants left behind was defined as extending along and between the banks of the rivers—Potomac, Rappahannock, Mattaponi, Pamunkey, and James—that flowed southeast into the Chesapeake Bay. Immigrants and their descendants had been ascending these rivers since the 1600s, claiming land and establishing farms and producing their crops (mostly tobacco) to ship down river and across the Atlantic to England.[120] The Tidewater region ended at the fall line, that point in each river beyond which ocean-going ships were unable to sail.[121] Early colonists seldom ventured beyond that line.[122] It was not until the eighteenth century that development began to spread farther west into the hilly region that would become known as the Piedmont.[123] This migration was caused by English desires to populate their colonies, combined with dwindling opportunities to obtain land in the Tidewater region, and soil depletion caused by decades of tobacco cultivation.

As British immigrants migrated west, another European country also had land claims in North America. France controlled the Mississippi River and lands west of the Mississippi. It also had colonies in Canada, and was actively trying to link those realms with trade routes in the Ohio Valley region. Native Americans who were being forced west by new English settlements began to stand their ground and contest this migration. As both the French and English had vital interests in the Ohio River Valley, they were set on a collision course for supremacy in North America. This Ohio Country spread west from the Appalachian Mountains all the way to the Mississippi River. Many in both England and France considered it a strategic key to controlling the continent. After all, it was a land extending thousands of miles, covered by enormous forests with plentiful supplies of timber and able to meet the growing demands of both the Old World and New. It was a country containing limitless mineral wealth, with a climate varied enough to support diverse types of agricultural production and the potential for numerous industries.[124]

119   Carolyn Jones Elstner and Katherine Porter Clark, *Dear Old Ellwood* (Washington VA: Rappahannock Historical Society 2016), 12.
120   Ibid.
121   Ibid.
122   Ibid.
123   Ibid.
124   Barton, 8.

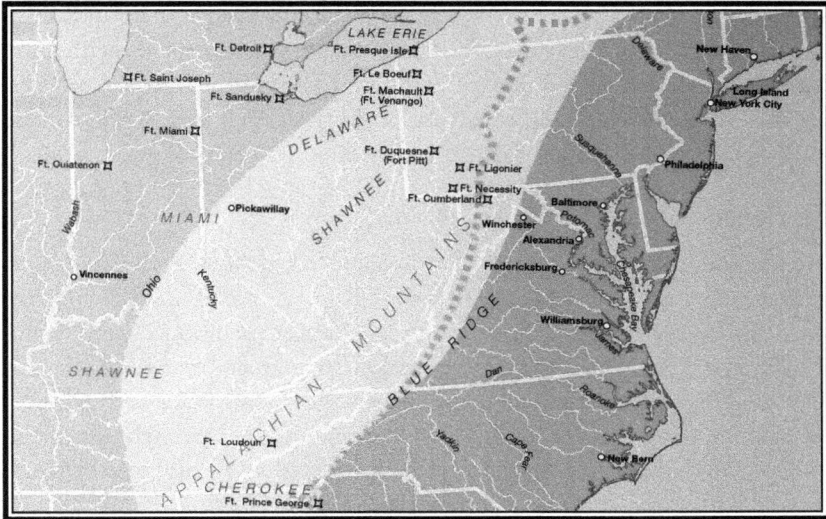

Forts in the Disputed Lands
Courtesy of the National Park Service

The two nations' rival claims to the vast territory along the Ohio River approached a climax around 1750. A group of Englishmen and Virginians, including Lawrence Washington III, obtained a large grant of two hundred thousand acres in the upper Ohio Valley. The group formed a partnership called the Ohio Company. Their goal was to realize the area's economic and financial potential. From a post at Wills Creek—now Cumberland, Maryland—the Company planned expanded settlements in the region and started to open an eighty-mile road to the Monongahela River.[125] That would provide a link between the Atlantic, via the Potomac, and the entire Ohio and Mississippi valleys.

At the same time, the French considered the Ohio River a vital link between their colonies in New France (Canada) and Louisiana. By controlling the Ohio River, the French had a natural water highway connecting their vast lands. The French governor of Canada ordered that a chain of forts be built on lands the English claimed. So the French began erecting a chain of forts from the Great Lakes to the Illinois River, to the Mississippi River, and finally to the Gulf of Mexico.[126] The purpose was to draw a French line across the American continent from north to south, thus keeping English settlements confined to the Eastern Seaboard east of the Allegheny Mountains. But by this time the English had already moved well west of the Alleghenies.

While the French moved south and the English moved west, the Native Americans were caught in the middle. All three laid claim to this land, and all thought

---

125   U.S Department of the Interior, National Park Service, *Fort Necessity,* Washington, D.C.
126   Ibid.

they were in the right. Both the French and the English sought the goodwill and aid of the Native peoples. Their concept of land ownership conflicted with European values and culture, causing their claims to the area to be ignored. In order to hold on to their lands, the tribes played French and English against each other, often siding with the force they perceived as the most powerful.

Washington's Diplomatic Mission

In late 1753 Virginia Governor Dinwiddie learned the French had built Fort Presque Isle on the shore of Lake Erie and Fort Le Boeuf in part of the Ohio Country claimed by Virginia. He sent an eight-man expedition led by twenty-one year old George Washington to deliver a diplomatic objection to the French at Fort Le Boeuf. [127] Dinwiddie's formal document set forth the nature and extent of the English claim to the Ohio Valley and sternly warned the French against further intrusion into that region. This would be the most important diplomatic mission yet undertaken in America, and its most dangerous.

On October 31, 1753, Washington departed Williamsburg. He enlisted the assistance of a French-speaking interpreter, four experienced woodsmen, and a well-known surveyor, Christopher Gist, who was knowledgeable in the customs and to some degree, the language of Native peoples in the region. Gist served as guide, translator and assistant.[128] After traveling hundreds of miles across the Allegheny Mountains in the dead of winter on poorly established trails, through rugged and treacherous wilderness, George received a polite rejection when he delivered his letter from Virginia's governor that demanded the French withdrawal from the region. The French general, Jacques de Saint Pierre, told Washington that his orders required him to eject every Englishman from the Ohio Valley and he meant to carry out those orders to the letter. Saint Pierre, stated that France claimed the area and intended to make good its claim by force of arms if necessary.[129]

Anxious to return and report the news to Governor Dinwiddie, Washington departed the French fort on December 14, despite the weather's turn to the worse with cold temperatures and blowing snow. Twice he escaped near death on the return trip. A hostile Indian's bullet came close to hitting him. Later he almost lost his life when he slipped from a raft trying to cross the ice-choked Allegheny River and was nearly swept away.[130]

Washington managed to arrive back in Williamsburg on January 16, only eleven weeks after his departure. During his journey, he kept a daily journal. Upon his return, the *Maryland Gazette* published that account, which was circulated throughout

127   Felder, 27.
128   George Washington's Mount Vernon, *Allegheny Expedition*, www.mountvernon.org/digital-encyclopedia/article/allegheny-expedition, 2018, (February 19, 2018).
129   Barton, 12.
130   Glenn, Vol 1, 19

Washington—Colonel of Virginia Militia by Charles Willson Peale

the colonies and in England. The result was widespread public praise for the young Washington.[131]

Dinwiddie responded immediately to the French rejection of his ultimatum. In January 1754, shortly after Washington's return, the governor sent a small force of Virginians to build a fort at "The Forks" where the Monongahela and Allegany Rivers meet to form the Ohio. This is modern-day Pittsburgh. The small force carried only the essentials needed to survive the trip and build the fort.

Battle of Jumonville Glen

By the spring of 1754, Dinwiddie recognized the need to resupply and fortify the fort at "The Forks." He raised a regiment of Virginia Militia with now Lieutenant Colonel George Washington as second in command. The regiment was sent west to build a permanent road to Redstone Creek on the Monongahela River and afterwards to protect the western settlers from both the French and Indians. When the force's leader, Colonel Joshua Fry, was fatally injured during their march, twenty-two-year-old George became the officer in charge of the regiment.

It was April 1754 when Fry and Washington left Alexandria, Virginia, leading 160 troops to carry out their mission. The next five years would be George's crash course in the art of war.

Soon Washington learned that a French force of more than a thousand had seized the half-built fort at "The Forks," renamed it Fort Duquesne, and was proceeding to radiate French influence over the several Native American tribes in the region.

After three weeks of marching, Washington's force reached a place in southern Pennsylvania called the Great Meadows, some sixty miles from Fort Duquesne. The meadow was mostly marsh, but the militarily inexperienced Washington believed it "a charming field for an encounter." The meadow also provided an ideal location to graze his cattle and horses in an area almost totally wooded. Faced with a vastly superior enemy force, Washington decided to build a makeshift fort in the meadow. It was near the camp of Tanacharision, also known as Half-King, a Seneca chief who had been Washington's ally on his previous western expedition. Washington hoped to rally whatever Indian allies he could find, and wait for reinforcements. He had learned, before leaving Alexandria, of plans for reinforcements from independent militia companies from North Carolina, South Carolina and New York. He named the small stockade, built in the open meadow, Fort Necessity.[132]

On May 27, Half-King reported the appearance of French troops nearby, along the Youghiogheny River only a few miles from Fort Necessity. With Half-King was a delegation of warriors to join Washington's garrison. On the morning of May 28

131 Barton, 14-15.
132 George Washington's Mount Vernon.

Site of the French Camp at Jumonville Glen

Washington found a French patrol of thirty-two soldiers camped in a forest glen at the base of a cliff. At this moment in history the French and English were not at war. But Washington knew the French had already forced the earlier English expedition to evacuate its fort at The Forks of the Ohio.

Washington's detachment of forty, plus the Seneca Indian allies under Half-King, encircled the French camp. The Americans cautiously advanced, intending to surprise and capture the French. However, the French were on the alert. Seeing the approaching Americans, they flew to their arms.[133] What happened next, at what came to be called Jumonville Glen, soon became an international controversy about who fired the first shot in the French and Indian War.

It has remained a matter of scholarly debate ever since, both because it was Washington's first combat experience and because there is good reason to believe Washington found himself overseeing a massacre. Eyewitness accounts conflict, but the most plausible version of the evidence suggests that the French troops, surprised and outgunned, threw down their weapons after the initial exchange of fire and attempted to escape. As they fled, the French ran directly into a line of Half-King's warriors.

Reasoning that a surrender to the Virginians was preferable to surrendering to Half-King, the surviving French turned around and surrendered to Washington. The French commander, Joseph Coulon de Villiers, sieur de Jumonville, had been

---

133   Barton, 16.

wounded in the exchange. He tried to explain that he had come on a peace mission on behalf of his monarch, Louis XV, claiming sovereignty over the disputed Ohio Country.[134] Documents found on the French soldiers confirmed this, but also included correspondence indicating they were spying on the British forces.

As Washington sought to understand the translation of Jumonville's diplomatic message, Half-King—who apparently spoke fluent French—decided to take matters into his own hands. The chief stepped up to where Jumonville lay, and in French declared, "Thou art not dead, my father," then sank his hatchet into Jumonville's head, splitting his skull in half. Half-King then proceeded to pull out Jumonville's brain, and washed his hands in the mixture of blood and tissue. His warriors then fell upon the wounded French soldiers, scalped them, and decapitated one and put his head on a stake. This all happened under the eyes of the shocked and hapless commanding officer, Lieutenant Colonel George Washington.[135]

Washington's forces and his allies killed ten Frenchmen and wounded twenty-one.[136] One French soldier escaped and returned to Fort Duquesne to relay the news to the French garrison there. This event was the salvo that started the seven-year-long war between the British and the French that became known as the French and Indian War.

Washington's Surrender at Great Meadows

Washington was convinced that Jumonville's claim to be on a diplomatic mission was "a pure Pretense; that they never intended to come to us but as Enemies." Some argue that Washington was rationalizing the massacre to himself. In a letter home to his brother, he glossed over the killings by focusing on his personal response to the sense of danger:

"I heard Bullets whistle and believe me there was something charming in the Sound." [137]

This self-promoting statement made it into the Virginia newspapers, prompting a flurry of stories depicting Washington as America's first war hero. The bravado remark even made the rounds in London, where King George II reportedly dismissed it as youthful bragging. Whether he was a hero, braggart, or an accomplice in murder, the skirmish at Jumonville Glen had convinced Washington that his forces could hold their own against the numerically superior French until reinforcements arrived.[138]

Returning to Fort Necessity, Washington felt pretty confident after a month had transpired and he had heard nothing from the French. After he finished building the

134 Ellis, 13-14.
135 Ellis, 14.
136 Fort Necessity.
137 Ellis, 14-15.
138 Ellis, 14-15.

stockade, it was Washington's belief that with support from local Indians, he would have no fear of an attack from as many as five hundred men.[139] Dinwiddie concurred and Washington and his forces remained at Fort Necessity, awaiting the promised reinforcements. By then a small militia detachment of about two hundred from South Carolina was on its way.

Unfortunately for the English forces, Half-King and his council of Indians from the Iroquois Confederacy were not persuaded by Washington's official position. He argued that the English had no plans to acquire Indian lands, but were there only to support their Native allies in repelling the French. More important, Washington had little food to be able to share with his Indian allies. Whether out of disenchantment with Washington, or in search of game, Half-King led all the friendly Indians into the woods, leaving Fort Necessity to its fate. Shortly thereafter, the small militia force from South Carolina arrived.[140]

Road to the Monongahela

Waiting for further reinforcements, Washington began to cut a road across the rough country in the direction of the French fort. That effort extended the road a total of twenty miles.[141] By then his force totaled around three hundred men.

In response to Jumonville's defeat and death, the French and their Indian allies collected a much larger force and strengthened their position at Fort Duquesne. Washington, deciding he could wait no longer for reinforcements, set out to dislodge the enemy. After advancing only thirteen miles, his scouts reported that French General Louis de Villiers was approaching with a massive army of more than eleven hundred French and Indians. De Villiers, as it happened, was the angry brother of the slain Jumonville.

Washington realized his military disadvantage and fell back to Fort Necessity to save his soldiers. He had no sooner secured the fort when De Villiers arrived and surrounded it. The battle did not go as Washington had planned. The French and Indians refused to engage in the open field. Instead they fired two musket volleys then stationed themselves in the woods. Many of the Indians climbed into the trees where, concealed by thick vegetation, they fired down upon the Americans in the fort.

139   Ibid.
140   Ellis, 15.
141   Barton, 17.

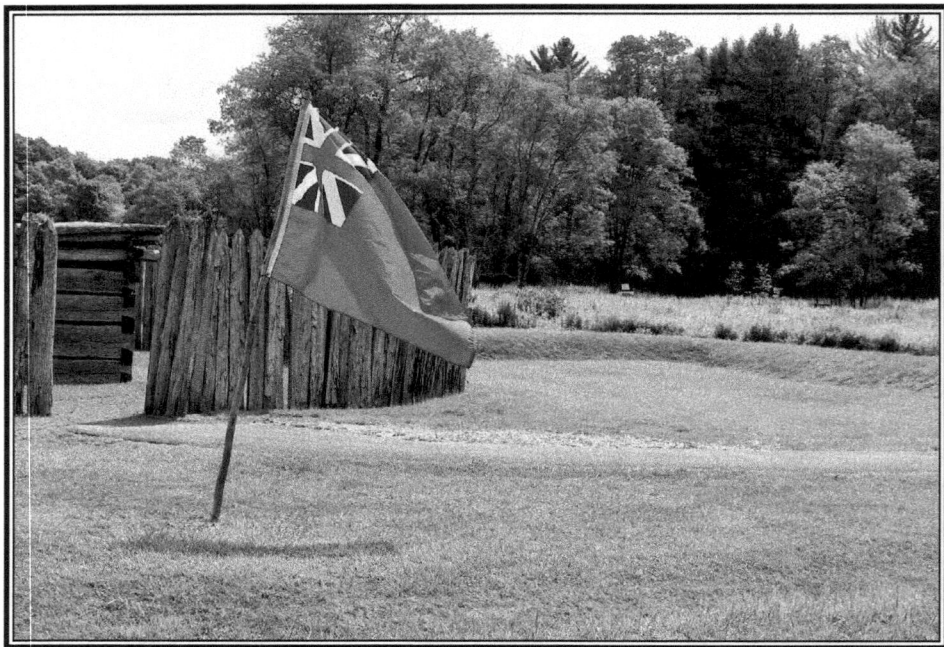

Fort Necessity: Reconstruction on Original Foundation

Washington's troops were fatally exposed as they scrambled into the fort's trenches. Here Washington's inexperience again worked against him. Instead of building the fort in the center of the meadow, allowing for an extended field of fire on all sides, he had placed it too close to the woods. That allowed the French to conceal themselves from Washington's troops. For nine long hours, a continuous shower of musket balls was poured in upon the Americans.[142] The Americans returned the French fire with vigor, but Washington's men were increasingly being killed by gunfire from elevated and concealed positions. Greatly outnumbered, unreinforced, and without sufficient food and supplies, Washington knew it would be impossible to hold out much longer.[143] It was only after moisture from a torrential rain had rendered his troops' musket cartridges and firelocks unusable that he was forced to surrender. Signing the French surrender document, Washington admitted responsibility for the murder of the French commander he had recently ambushed.

In the Articles of Capitulation, the French referred to "the Assassination of M. de Jumonville," meaning Washington's signature endorsed the conclusion that the British in general and he in particular were responsible for murdering a diplomatic emissary of the French crown. The French interpreted this to mean the British were responsible for the hostile action that launched the French and Indian War.

142   Ibid.
143   Ibid.

Washington went to his grave claiming he never realized that the word "assassination" was included in the Articles of Capitulation. Washington later explained that he was relying on his interpreter, who had translated the word as "loss" or "death" from the rain-soaked document.[144]

On July 4, 1754, his force, which was allowed to keep its remaining equipment and provisions, marched out of the tiny fort and home to Virginia. Now the entire Ohio Valley was in complete possession of the French, who ravaged and plundered English trading posts and settlements along the frontiers.[145]

Was it luck or Divine Providence that saved George Washington's life at the Great Meadows? Over one third of his men had been killed in the battle. Why did De Villiers not seek personal revenge for the "assassination" of his brother at the hands of Washington? Why did the French restrain their Indian allies from a wholesale massacre during the battle, after the surrender, and more important, during Washington's march through the wilderness back to Virginia? My sense is that these events were acts of Divine Providence. This was a teaching moment in God's overall plan for George Washington and in the fulfillment of his destiny.

Washington Resigns and Returns to Mount Vernon

Moses was educated in a civilization unmatched by any other at the time. His training was designed to prepare him for positions of authority, or even the throne of Egypt. He became familiar with life at Pharaoh's courts and the pomp and grandeur of Egyptian religious worship. He witnessed the administration of justice. When he was forty years old, Moses became angry at an Egyptian taskmaster who was beating a Hebrew slave. Moses killed the Egyptian and buried him in the sand. When this became known, however, Moses feared for his own life and fled from Egypt to the desert land of Midian. There, he married a daughter of Jethro as part of an agreement to tend Jethro's flocks.[146]

After about forty more years, God spoke to Moses from a bush that was on fire but didn't burn. God sent Moses back to Egypt to lead the Hebrews out of slavery, and into the land promised to Abraham.[147]

Washington, too, had a similar experience working within the British colonial system. His relations with Lord Thomas Fairfax, William Fairfax and Governor Dinwiddie could compare with that of Moses and Pharaoh's court. Washington's story is similar to the Exodus story in which Moses murdered the slave taskmaster and gave up his position in the royal court. Washington resigned his commission,

---

144   Ellis, 17.

145   Barton, 17-18.

146   Logan Marshall, "The Story of Moses, the Child who was Found in the River," *Bible Hub*, 2017, www.biblehub.com/library/marshall/the_wonder_book_of_bible_stories/the_story_of_moses_the.htm. (January 19, 2017).

147   Ibid.

Mount Vernon

gave up his position in the Virginia Militia, and returned to his farm at Mount Vernon after the murder of Jumonville and his surrender at the Great Meadows. But after a time he was invited to return to military service to help achieve victory over the French.

The aftermath of Washington's first military campaign had been grievously disappointing to him. The Virginia Regiment he had commanded was divided into ten independent companies, each commanded by a captain. For Washington, this would have meant an insulting demotion from his previous colonel's rank.[148] He did not desire to serve at a lower rank than before. When offered a commission he replied, "I think, the disparity between the present offer of a Company, and my former Rank, too great to expect any real satisfaction or enjoyment in a Corps, where I once did, nor thought I had a right to, command."[149] Washington resigned his Virginia command to Governor Dinwiddie in October 1754 rather than tolerate a blow to his standing. He returned to private life to concentrate on his farm.

Acquires Mount Vernon

Since the death of his brother, Lawrence III, George had known he had an outside chance of someday becoming lord of Mount Vernon. If Lawrence's widow, Ann, and daughter Sarah predeceased him, he would become Mount Vernon's heir by default. Then, in yet another of the improbable transformations of Divine Providence that eerily propelled his life ever upward, the occupancy of Mount Vernon came unexpectedly within his grasp. Six months after Lawrence's death, Ann had remarried and moved to Westmoreland County. Two years after that, on December 10, 1754, Ann's daughter, little Sarah Washington, died. A week later Ann rented Mount Vernon to George along with its eighteen resident slaves. By the

148   Chernow, 50.
149   Mount Vernon, Washington and the French and Indian War.

terms of the lease, Washington was required every Christmas to ship his sister-in-law fifteen thousand pounds of tobacco, packed in fifteen hogsheads. This deal placed George under considerable pressure to manage the estate profitably.[150]

British Intervention

Across the Atlantic, the British Cabinet saw that a war with the French was unavoidable. Unfortunately for English military planners, the American posed no significant military threat to the French. In fact, not only was there no actual military force in America but the colonies had never before even taken meaningful measures for their own defense. They were unable to undertake the costly task of building forts and maintaining an army.[151]

The British Ministry, seeking a way to fortify the Americans and obstruct the French in the Ohio Valley, directed the colonies to cultivate the friendship of the Six Nations, renewing their treaty with the Iroquois Confederacy, the most powerful of their Indian allies. The Ministry also encouraged the separate colonial authorities to band together for their common defense and undertake some sort of joint action against the French. The individual colonies agreed to these directions and unanimously resolved to form a united alliance for their own protection and preservation.[152]

Preparations for war between the French and the British moved rapidly forward, even though there had been no official declaration of war. First, King Louis XV of France sent three thousand soldiers to reinforce the French army in Canada. The British responded by ordering British General Edward Braddock to sail to America with two full regiments of English regulars to forcibly oust the French from the Ohio Valley.[153]

Braddock was an experienced officer, over sixty years old with forty years of military experience. He was a well-thought-of officer within the British military community but he despised the American colonies and colonists. He also knew he had no military support in America. Before sailing for America he was heard to proclaim the he was "going forth to conquer whole worlds with a handful of men, and to do so must cut his way through unknown woods." Braddock was the first British general to conduct a major campaign in a remote wilderness. He had neither the historical precedents he needed nor the experience himself. He also had no one to guide him.[154]

---

150   Chernow, 52.
151   Barton, 19.
152   Ibid.
153   Ibid, 22.
154   Ibid, 22-23.

Campaign Plans and Washington's Return to Arms

On February 20, 1755, Braddock and his force arrived in America and dropped anchor in Hampton Roads, Virginia. The American colonists were overjoyed by his arrival. This was the first substantial body of British regular soldiers ever to land in America. The British force was augmented by the enlistment of one hundred Virginians. The colonists were now confident that all that was needed to drive the French from the country was the presence of the formidable and highly respected English army. [155]

On April 14, Braddock met with colonial governors in Alexandria, Virginia and revealed the plans. These included offensives in four separate locations. The first force would be led by Governor Charles Lawrence of Nova Scotia, who would secure that province. The second force would be led by General William Johnson of New York, who would recruit and pay a force of volunteers and Mohawk Indians to capture the French post at Crown Point on Lake Champlain, due north of New York City. Governor William Shirley of Massachusetts would lead the third force, equipping a regiment to drive the French from their fortress on the Niagara River, near present-day Buffalo, New York. The fourth and most important campaign would be personally directed by Braddock. He would first lead his two regiments against Fort Duquesne and afterwards drive the remaining French from the Ohio Valley.[156]

In March 1755 Washington wrote Robert Orme, Braddock's chief of staff, and offered his services to the general for the campaign. Braddock had heard numerous favorable reports about Washington, and in April, despite his poor opinion of colonials in general, he invited Washington to join him as his military aide. Also, to solve the problem Washington had with rank, he was offered his previous rank of colonel.

Washington was eager to study military tactics under a professional soldier of such high standing as Braddock. He accepted the invitation and joined the general's swelling entourage of horses, wagons, and men at Frederick, Maryland, in early May 1755.[157] As it was with Moses and his return to Egypt, Washington too was returning to service to free his people.

Defeat and Miracle on the Monongahela

Braddock's mission was doomed to failure before it commenced. There are many reasons for this. The principle reason was Braddock's own self-confidence and arrogance. He was not deficient in courage or military skill but was totally unacquainted with the style of warfare necessary for the American woods. Confident

155   Ibid, 25.
156   Ibid, 25-26.
157   Ellis, 20.

in his own British soldiers, he saw no need for Indian warrior allies. Thoroughly skilled in the tactics of European warfare, he mistakenly believed that battles could be fought in America as they had long been fought in Europe—that soldiers would march directly against their opponents on an open field of battle just as if both were on a military parade ground. Braddock generally held suggestions from Americans in contempt.[158]

The second reason was that Braddock completely sealed his own fate at a meeting with a delegation of Indian chiefs. The general told them their historic claims to land in the Ohio Valley were rubbish and that British troops had no need for assistance from savages. That prompted most of the tribes in the region to side with the French. As Braddock saw it, he commanded the largest and best-equipped military force ever assembled on the North American continent, making victory inevitable.[159]

Lack of Horse Power

Lastly, Braddock was almost forced to cancel his campaign because the Americans were slow to provide the horses, teamsters and wagons necessary to carry his large army's provisions. His main force of more than two thousand men needed to be fed along the route, his heavy cannon needed to be pulled by horses, and all the food for men and horses needed to be carried on wagons. This required horses—about twenty-five hundred in all—plus wagon masters. If the British could not move their equipment and supplies, they could not move their army.[160]

Benjamin Franklin came to the British army's rescue. Serving as colonial postmaster-general, Franklin used his good name and influence with the farmers of Pennsylvania, who provided the necessary wagons and horses.

Braddock Starts his March for Fort Duquesne

Braddock commenced his march to Fort Duquesne from Alexandria, somewhat behind schedule, during the latter part of April 1755.[161]

This cumbersome cavalcade, stretching out over six miles, had to cut its own road through more than one hundred miles of wilderness land that Washington knew to be almost impassable and that even Braddock acknowledged "would occasion great Trouble and retard me considerably." After stepping off at a brisk pace in mid-May from Frederick, Maryland, Braddock's column ground to a near halt once it hit the Alleghenies in June.

He used an advance party of seven hundred men to open a path for the army and its wagons over the rugged forested land. In that vanguard were several guides,

---

158   Barton, 37.
159   Ellis, 19.
160   Ibid, 20.
161   Barton, 28-35.

followed by 350 soldiers under the command of Lieutenant Colonel Thomas Gage, who would later confront George Washington in a very different context. Following Gage was a working party of 250 axmen. One of those axmen was a very young Daniel Boone, who later became a famous frontier trailblazer, scout and pioneer. The latter part of the advance party was composed of the tool-wagons, cannons and a rear guard.[162]

Washington Senses Disaster

Washington began to sense disaster at this time, writing his brother that "this prospect was soon clouded & all my hopes brought very low indeed when I found . . . they were halting to Level every Mole Hill, & to erect Bridges over every brook; by which mean we were 4 Days gttg [sic] 12 miles." Stragglers were also routinely being killed and scalped, a sign that the Indian intelligence network was fully aware of their location and destination. Washington warned Braddock that the expedition's ponderous pace virtually assured that it would be marooned in Indian country once the snows began in the mountains. That would make any advance at all impossible.[163]

With progress so slow, Braddock feared the French at Fort Duquesne would use the additional time to entrench and strengthen themselves. Considering it essential to move ahead rapidly, surprise the French, and cut off additional relief forces, relying on Washington's advice, Braddock placed himself at the head of thirteen hundred select troops and proceeded by more rapid marches toward Fort Duquesne. Beginning this advance on June 19, he carried only the equipment that was absolutely necessary. He left behind the heavy baggage wagons with an escort of six hundred men to follow as best as they could.[164]

Washington Falls Ill

As it turned out, Washington could not pause to savor his influence in the general's decision to detach an advanced "flying force," for in mid-June he was "seized with violent fevers and pains in my head." He proved the latest victim of an epidemic exacting a horrible toll on Braddock's forces, dysentery. This infection of the digestive system produces violent diarrhea, and Washington also suffered cruelly from hemorrhoids. At first the enduring young aide tried to conceal his disorder, but soon found it so devastating he had to travel lying down in a covered wagon. This soon left him so weak he had to accompany the slower-moving forces in the rear. The young aide was so upset at being left behind that Braddock solemnly pledged he would be brought forward before the attack on Fort Duquesne. As Washington's

162   Ibid, 35.
163   Ellis, 21.
164   Barton, 36.

condition worsened, he found it agonizing to lie in the wagon as it jolted along the crude roads hacked through near-impassable woods that the historian Douglas Southall Freeman dubbed the "Shades of Death." Even though by July 8 he had recuperated sufficiently to rejoin Braddock a dozen miles from Fort Duquesne, Washington was still so weak that when he mounted his horse the next morning, he had to strap on cushions to ease his painful hemorrhoids.[165]

Crossing the Monongahela

Early on the morning of July 9, Braddock's advance force, which had grown to some fourteen hundred men, began to ford the Monongahela River in three groups, near present-day Braddock, Pennsylvania, a Pittsburgh suburb. Each group was led by an officer who was to reappear during the American Revolution some twenty years later. The first to cross was spearheaded by Lieutenant Colonel Gage, the son of a viscount, an officer Washington much admired. Gage's group consisted of 350 men and two six-pounder cannon. The second group was led by Captain Horatio Gates, said to be the illegitimate offspring of a duke's housekeeper. His group consisted of 250 carpenters and pioneers and their wagons. The last group to cross, in the early afternoon, was the 750 man contingent led by Braddock himself, but escorted by the weary Washington. In Braddock's group were most of the vehicles, the pack animals, the cattle to be slaughtered for food, and the greater part of the artillery—four twelve-pounders, four howitzers and three Coehorn mortars. [166] All three groups crossed the river without the slightest hint that an enemy force of nearly nine hundred from Fort Duquesne lay poised to attack on the other side.[167]

Ambush

The French were not willing to give up their fort without a fight. They had been receiving reinforcements for two months but they were still unevenly matched against Braddock's much greater numbers. Having been kept apprised of Braddock's progress by daily reports from their scouts, the French decided that an ambush would be their best defense. The night before the battle, the French commander of Fort Duquesne with great difficulty persuaded the loosely allied Indians to join the ambush. The next morning, a combined force of seventy-two French regulars, 146 Canadian militiamen, and 637 Indians (a total force of 855) set out from Fort Duquesne to harass and annoy the 1,400 English. They did not intend to face the British in serious battle. The French picked an ambush location that was seven miles from their fort.[168]

---

165   Chernow, 57.
166   Douglas Southall Freeman, *George Washington* Volume II, *Young Washington* (New York: Charles Scribner's Sons 1948), 65.
167   Chernow, 57..
168   Barton, 42.

"The British gentlemen," one provincial officer wrote afterward, "were confident they would never be attacked and would have laid any odds that they never should be until they came before the fort." Careful British officers realized, of course, that their column's advance might be disputed at one ford or the other. Even soldiers of cautious mind felt that if the troops, the artillery and the wagons could get across the Monongahela unmolested, the remainder of the campaign would be easy.[169]

Disaster

As the rear of the column cleared the curve in the road near Frazier's Trading Post and started northwestward, Washington rode forward with Braddock and the staff. All spirits were high. Gage and his group was then about three-quarters of a mile beyond the ford. Their thinking was that if the French had intended to resist, they would have done so in the early morning, and at the fords, not beyond on the direct way to the fort.[170] After crossing a second ford at Turtle Creek, Gage and his group were at the head of the British column, Gates with his pioneers in the center and Braddock with his main force in the rear.

It was almost one o'clock in the afternoon, and Colonel Gage's forward detachment was progressing up an incline with a few guides and some small flanking parties in the advance. The French and their Indian allies practiced a terrifying form of frontier warfare that unnerved the British. Letting loose a series of shrill, penetrating war whoops— "the terrific sound will haunt me till the hour of my dissolution" a shaken British soldier later said—the Indians appeared from out of nowhere. They swooped down suddenly, and opened fire on the startled British. Before the infantrymen could fire an answering volley, the enemy had melted nimbly into the woods. For a short interval, it seemed they had disappeared. Then it became clear that they had split into two wings and encircled the British, releasing a hail of bullets from behind trees and well-protected, elevated positions. The red-coated regulars standing in ranks were conspicuous targets. Volley followed volley in rapid succession, and the ground became littered with the British dead and dying. The horses, many wounded but all in a frenzy, reared and plunged and tore along the road, dragging wagons after them, trampling the living and the dead. The British ranks were in utter confusion. In the rear, both Braddock and Washington heard the ensuing panic, which neither could see. The vanguard of the British troops, Washington recollected, "were so disconcerted and confused" by the unfamiliar hallooing and whooping of the enemy that they soon fell "into irretrievable disorder." The British soldiers had never encountered this North American form of fighting. "If we saw five or six of the enemy at a time," said one soldier, "it was a great sight and they were either on their bellies or behind trees or running from one tree to

---

169   Freeman, Volume II, 64.
170   Ibid, 68.

another almost by the ground." Even as officers tried vainly to subdue their men's hysterical fears, the soldiers threw down their muskets and fled helter-skelter. All the while, Indians scalped and plundered the British dead in what became a veritable charnel house by the river.[171]

As Braddock and Washington rode toward this scene of helpless slaughter, panic-stricken redcoats streamed back toward them. After Braddock sent thirty men to climb a hillside and secure a high position, British troops fired at them in the smoky chaos under the mistaken assumption that they were French, while British officers fired at them thinking they were deserters. Between the enemy and the friendly fire, all thirty men were killed.[172]

Washington's Shield

Braddock gave Washington two orders: to send another party up the exposed hill and to retrieve two lost cannons. The events surrounding the young colonel during the two hours of the battle provide compelling evidence not only of God's care but also his direct intervention on Washington's behalf.[173] With exceptional pluck and cool-headedness, he was soon riding all over the battlefield. Though he must have been exhausted, he kept going from sheer willpower and performed magnificently amid the horror. Because of his height, he presented a gigantic target on horseback, but again he displayed unblinking courage and miraculous immunity in battle. When two horses were shot from under him, he dusted himself off and mounted horses whose riders had been killed. One account claimed that he was so spent from his recent illness that he had to be lifted onto his second horse. By the end, despite four bullets having torn through his hat and uniform, he managed to emerge unscathed.[174] One eyewitness exclaimed: 'I expected every moment to see him fall. Nothing but the superintending care of Providence could have saved him!" Following the battle, the Indians confirmed that they had explicitly singled out Washington and repeatedly shot at him, but without effect. They therefore became convinced that he was protected by an invisible power and that no bullet could harm him. Indeed, even though hundreds of victims fell around him, shielded by God's hand, he escaped without a scratch, untouched by bullet or bayonet, arrow or tomahawk.[175]

Confused and Panic Stricken British

Braddock came forward to reinforce Gage but with Gage's men in full retreat the two groups of men collided, throwing them into more confusion. The British soldiers, with their officers and comrades falling around them with each discharge

---

171   Chernow, 58.
172   Ibid.
173   Barton 48.
174   Chernow, 59.
175   Barton, 49.

from the woods, were so panic-stricken that they became disoriented. They were uncertain where to go or what to do. Therefore, in keeping with their tactical training, they remained stationary, huddled together in frightened groups in the midst of a ravine, some facing one way and some facing another, firing at unseen targets but all exposed without shelter to the bullets that pelted them like hail. It was butchery rather than a battle.[176]

Washington Is Spared

Braddock, however, was a lion in combat. Although showered with bullets and having five horses shot from under him, he continued undaunted, but his reckless courage did not turn the tide. As the battle raged for over two hours, nearly every member of his staff—including his secretary and two of his military aides—were shot down. Washington, the only uninjured member of Braddock's staff, rode over every part of the field carrying the general's orders.[177] Consequently, every mounted officer except Washington was slain.[178]

Wounding of General Braddock

After two hours Braddock was finally shot in the side and sank to the ground. When Braddock was wounded, his troops swiftly fled the scene. It became a rout—a race for life by every man whose legs could still work. Everything—the wagons, guns, artillery, cattle, horses, baggage, and provisions—was abandoned to the enemy. Braddock, unable to mount a horse, was hurried from the field in a litter and was a mile from the battlefield before his rescuers stopped to dress his wounds.[179]

When the retreating British troops reached the group in the rear of the column, Washington took charge of the remaining Virginia Militia companies. Their duty was to cover the panicked flight of the once glorious British army. [180] Washington then rode forty miles on horseback to warn the British supply column far in the rear, before finally collapsing from sickness and exhaustion.[181]

Death of Braddock

General Braddock lingered in great pain for several days during the retreat. Braddock finally died near the Great Meadows a mile west of Fort Necessity. That night by torchlight, Washington conducted the funeral service of the Anglican Church. To ensure that the body of his mentor General Braddock was never discovered and mutilated by their French and Indian enemies, he had him buried on

---

176   Barton, 46-47.
177   Ibid, 48.
178   Ibid, 50.
179   Ibid.
180   Ibid.
181   Barton, 42.

Site of Braddock's Burial in Washington's Military Road
Photo by John Meyer

Braddock's Grave after Reburial in 1904

Washington's French and Indian War Campaign
Courtesy of Mount Vernon Ladies' Association

the road of retreat and allowing the remaining wagons, horses, and men to march over the grave, leaving it undetectable.[182]

French Celebrate—British Escape

The French and Indians did not pursue their prey. So elated were the Indians over their unanticipated success, and so eager were they to secure the rich spoils left by the British, that instead of pursuing the retreating British army and perhaps totally destroying it, they remained on the field celebrating; they had never before known such a rich harvest of scalps and booty.[183]

The brutality of the battle was indicated by the number of casualties: of the over 1,400 British soldiers, 714 were killed or wounded; and of the eighty-six officers, sixty-two were killed or wounded. The losses of the French and Indians were slight, amounting to only three officers and thirty men killed, and as many other wounded.[184]

War's Conclusion

Six weeks after the massacre, Washington accepted a position as colonel of a Virginia Militia regiment, which shielded Virginia's exposed western frontier. By 1758 he had attracted the favorable attention of the newly appointed British commander, General John Forbes. Washington was given command of a brigade consisting of the troops from four separate colonies and made a brigadier general.

---

182   Chernow, 60.
183   Barton, 51.
184   Ibid, 51.

With his knowledge of the area and its terrain, it was Washington who wrote the plan of advance on Fort Duquesne that Forbes adopted. Washington's brigade would lead the new expedition.

During the march to Fort Duquesne, Washington's force got split up and somewhat disoriented. Also, being nervous after the Braddock affair, they panicked and began firing wildly upon any intruder they sighted in the wilderness. They mistook each other for the enemy. Washington saw immediately what had happened, rode out in the middle of the crossfire and with his sword knocked his soldiers' rifles upward so the bullets shot harmlessly into the air. Fourteen men were killed and twenty-six wounded by friendly fire. Again, Washington emerged untouched, despite the fact that he was the most exposed to the exchange of fire.[185]

Facing the size of the approaching enemy and sure defeat, the French burned the fort and withdrew before the arrival of Forbes' overwhelming force.[186] The Indians were no longer interested in fighting for French causes. Everywhere on the continent, the British defeated the French: Pennsylvania, New York, Quiberon Bay, Quebec.[187] Although the war was financially costly for the British government, it emerged triumphant when the French signed the Treaty of Paris on February 10, 1763.

Post Battle Stories

As time has passed since the great Battle of the Monongahela, several previously unknown facts surfaced. These not only give a better perspective to the drama that surrounded Washington during the battle but also provide further convincing evidence of the remarkable extent to which God had directly intervened in his behalf.[188] A famous Indian warrior who was a leader in the attack was often heard to testify:

> "Washington was never born to be killed by a bullet! I had seventeen
> fair fires at him with my rifle, and after all could not bring him to the
> ground!"[189]

When one considers that a rifle aimed by an experienced marksman rarely misses its target, his utterance seems to have been prophetic and confirms that an Invisible Hand had indeed turned aside the bullets.

Mary Draper Ingles's Story

Another story was provided by Mary Draper Ingles, who was kidnapped by a band of Shawnee Indians on July 8, 1755, and carried away into the Ohio Valley. She

185   Hart, 232.
186   Chernow, 20.
187   Hart, 233.
188   Barton, 63.
189   Ibid.

recounts an occasion during her captivity when the French arrived and held a council with their Indian allies. The Frenchmen were talking excitedly and gesturing wildly. Mary listened to their conversation, which was about George Washington. She began to inquire more specifically about Washington. The French trappers related the account given them by Red Hawk, an Indian chief integral to the victory at the Monongahela, who told of shooting eleven different times at Washington without hitting him, and because his gun had never before missed its mark, Red Hawk ceased firing at him, convinced that the Great Spirit protected him.[190]

Doctor James Craik's Story

The facts, as articulated in the opening paragraph of this chapter, are another example. In 1770, fifteen years after the defeat, Washington and Doctor James Craik were traveling toward the western territories to explore uninhabited regions near the border of what is now Ohio and West Virginia. They were approached by a company of Indians. Led by their old chief, the Indians relayed the story of how they had tried in vain to kill Washington during the battle, without success. They thought Washington was protected by a Great Spirit.

Sermon by Samuel Davies

Washington's escape from the numerous perils to which he had been subjected during the battle was so obviously miraculous that special mention was made in a famous sermon preached by the Reverend Samuel Davies only weeks after the battle. Davies was considered the greatest pulpit preacher in America, was an active leader in the American revival known as the Great Awakening. He later became president of the College of New Jersey, now Princeton University University. In his 1755 sermon, Davies commended the military qualities the Virginia provincials displayed during the fight and then added:

> "I may point out to the public that heroic youth, Colonel Washington, who I cannot but hope Providence has hitherto preserved in so signal a manner for some important service to his country."[191]

Davies' expectant hope for the young George Washington proved to be quite accurate, and twenty years later it was apparent that God had indeed selected Washington, like Moses, for an "important service to his country." Our nation, like the Israelites, benefited as a result.

---

190   Ibid, 64.
191   Ibid, 65-66.

Chapter 4

Prelude to a Revolution

And the Lord said unto Moses, Pharaoh's heart is hardened, he refuseth to let the people go.[192]

Exodus 7:14

Like Pharaoh's heart, England's King George III too, had a hardened heart. The Book of Exodus tells how God brought freedom to the Israelites and formed them over time into a nation. An interesting aspect of the story is the part played by the Egyptian monarch. In spite of repeated appeals from Moses and repeated demonstrations of God's power through a series of plagues, Pharaoh would not let the Israelites go. In America's story, George III and his ministers played this role. King George III's stubborn character, and his view that the American colonies must be obedient to royal and parliamentary authority, led his county to war despite the many appeals and warnings from his American subjects. Like Israel, America would never have come into existence as a single nation without enduring many misfortunes together. Like the Exodus, the path had to be difficult, to forge unity from thirteen independent colonies. Unity that had never before existed in America. The mistakes on the part of the British king had to be egregious to produce the strong reactions required to overthrow the existing political order.[193]

Tensions with England

Some argue that war between England and its American colonies was inevitable, based on a history that existed long before the circumstances that led to the Revolutionary War. And just as God used Moses, the Egyptian Pharaoh, George Washington, King George III, and the British Parliament as instruments for his agenda of freedom for humanity; God also used the Puritans who settled in New England to establish an American ideology that was in conflict with the concept of government that was demanded by the rulers of England. Some argue that the disagreement over the role of government initially started some 150 years prior to the Revolutionary War. The argument was religious in nature and the Puritans were at the center of it all.

---

192   Bible, 130.
193   Spivey, 59-60.

American Ideology

Religion in the American Revolution was extremely important. Even King George III once joked that the Revolution was a "Presbyterian War"—and he was principally right. New England, the most thoroughly Patriot region, was two-thirds Congregationalist and Presbyterians. These churches were not naturally revolutionary, but their core belief was that kings must exercise their power righteously or risk rebellion by God's Chosen. Their beliefs compelled in them a natural sympathy for the American cause.[194]

Many of the American colonies, New England in particular, were founded specifically as a refuge for those unable to live and grow spiritually under the conditions existing in Europe. Calvinist separatists, or "Pilgrims," came to Plymouth from England via Holland in 1620 inspired to find a place where they could worship freely. Waves of "Puritans" fleeing repression in England came during the 1630s and 40s. The second Lord Baltimore established Maryland in 1634 with specific guarantees of religious toleration, first attracting Catholics and then various other Christian groups. William Penn founded Pennsylvania in 1681 as a "holy experiment" and a haven for all forms of religion, attracting large numbers of Quakers and other minority Christian groups from many European countries.[195]

Some who came to America were not religious dissidents. The English religious establishment, also, came to America. Anglicans came to bring the Church of England first to Virginia and then to the other colonies, predominantly in the South.[196]

Due to the physical separation from England and the existence of a wide variety of churches, the religious establishment in the colonies was not as uniform as that in the Old World. However, the tendency to mix church and civic power remained strong. Religious ties to governmental authority not only continued, but seemed to increase in many areas over time.[197]

Puritans of New England

The Puritans of New England, which included Congregationalists, Baptists, and other dissenting Protestant groups, put into practice the governmental compact theory, dating back to the founding of Plymouth under the Mayflower Compact. Massachusetts, Connecticut, and Rhode Island were established by people voluntarily covenanting together to form a "civil body politic." Under the covenant conception, government's legitimate and proper function was to protect the inalienable rights of man, as granted by God, such as the rights of life, liberty, and property. Their compact

194 Alexander Rose, *Washington's Spies, The Story of America's First Spy Ring* (New York: Bantam Dell 2006), 81.
195 Ibid, 8.
196 Ibid.
197 Ibid, 9.

also provided for government's authority only from the consent of the governed as expressed in the covenant, compact or constitution.[198] These dissenters and their children shared the tendency to constantly tear away at authoritarian structures, to undermine hierarchy, and to decentralize. They shunned human authority in favor of Scripture. The Bible was their manifesto of dissent, a revolutionary document that could and had successfully toppled popes and monarchs. The Bible was wielded by Oliver Cromwell against King Charles I, toppled his reign, and indirectly established the Washingtons in America.[199] The Bible was also used by Samuel Adams and his New England Patriots to initiate the American Revolution against King George III.[200]

British Treatment of the American Colonies

England could accept much of the thought of the Puritans' social compact, but not the part about rulers serving at the whim of the ruled. The lesson of the Puritan and Glorious Revolutions under Oliver Cromwell, to most British, was that only under the direst circumstances could the people dissolve an existing regime. Additionally, to England the American colonists were second-class citizens within the British Empire. The colonists were British subjects, not citizens, and British policy reflected this perspective. The colonies, in England's view, were Crown possessions. Even though Americans had been governing themselves for most of their colonial history, the sovereign political authority still rested with London.[201] Throughout the French and Indian War, the British had also treated the colonial militia with disrespect and had abandoned the American theater when it no longer suited their purposes to remain there, thus leaving the American colonists to confront the savagery of the French and Indians on their own.[202] Over this sovereignty issue, King George's "heart was hardened."

British Trade

How the British managed trade with their American colonies was another example of "the second-class citizen" treatment. To England, the colonies were useful only so far as they were profitable. The colonies were entangled in Britain's mercantile commercial system, which was designed to finance Britain's war machine. The arrangement was essentially as follows: the colonies were to provide raw materials that British industry would turn into finished products that could then be sold back to the colonies. England looked with favor upon colonies that fit into the system. Virginia was considered London's favorite colony. It produced tobacco

---

198   Hart, 235.
199   Under the Puritan Revolutions and cleansing of the Church of England, Lawrence Washington was removed from the Anglican Church and lost his estate. His son John Washington (George Washington's great-grandfather) came to America and established the Washington family.
200   Ellis, 59.
201   Hart, 236.
202   Ibid, 236-237.

and other agricultural products that did not compete with British industry and that could be loaded onto British ships and exported all over the world for considerable profit. In addition, Virginia did not have advanced industry, and so its people bought many products from England. Clothes, linens, shoes, cooking utensils and farming equipment were all items bought by Virginians from British stores.[203]

New England, however, was not a satisfactory trading partner from England's perspective. The colonial Puritans discovered that it was more economical to produce finished products at home than to pay the cost of importing them from England. Also, the New England products were often superior to those of British industries, which had grown somewhat complacent under the protection of monopoly trade laws. The Puritans were building and sailing their own ships that were faster and better than the British vessels, and they had no reservations about poaching into British markets. In response Parliament began to pass a series of irksome laws, directed at New England, such as the Sugar Act of 1733, which interrupted the Puritan rum business by placing a stiff tariff on molasses from the French and Spanish West Indies. Not only did this law punish the Puritans, but two of England's long-term enemies, the French and Spanish. Puritan merchants simply ignored the law, smuggling the molasses past customs officials and trading for it in the black market.[204]

Anglican Church

Another irksome British policy was the continual efforts to bring America's Protestant dissidents into the standards of the English Church. From the beginning, New England had no desire for any part of the British religious system. Its settlers had traveled to the New World specifically to remove themselves from it. The Puritans also had no desire to help finance the British Empire. The Crown was constantly threatening to install bishops in the colonies to administer their churches according to acceptable English ways. The Society for the Propagation of the Gospel in Foreign Parts, originally established in 1701 for the purpose of converting the Indians, had by the middle of the eighteenth century become an instrument for bringing America's Protestant dissidents into communion with the Anglican Church.

Congregational, Presbyterian, and Baptist ministers would reply to every rumor of London imposing bishops on them with flurries of emotional sermons, scathing editorials in colonial newspapers, and penetrating pamphlets denouncing the proposal. When Jonathan Boucher, an Anglican rector from Annapolis, returned to England in 1775, he said the issue of bishops was the backbone of the revolutionary cause. At least one historian argued that "the efforts of the Episcopalians to push their plan [to install bishops in America] was at least one of the causes tending to accentuate the

203   Ibid, 237.
204   Ibid.

growing alienation between Great Britain and her colonial subjects beyond the seas, which prepared the ground for revolution soon to follow." [205] It was in New England that the sentiment for revolution was most enthusiastic. The ministers and civil leaders of the towns along the Eastern Seaboard made it clear very early that they did not want taxes and they did not want bishops. Was it Divine Providence that the Puritans drove the Washington family to America where a Washington descendant led the American Revolution, and descendants of these same Puritans in Massachusetts provided the initial dissent that started the American Revolution?

Effects of the French and Indian War

The conclusion of the French and Indian War in 1763 produced an outpouring of patriotic enthusiasm in the American colonies. After the peace settlement was signed, a longer lasting effect of the war was something quite apart from what the British and French negotiated. Rather, it was the effect the war had on the American colonies. The cost of the French and Indian War and that of controlling their newly acquired territories were both huge for the British. The national debt of Great Britain, inflated by military spending, had swollen to a stupendous 130 million pounds, with annual interest payments of 4.5 million pounds. This absorbed more than half the national budget.[206] The British government looked for new revenue sources to help pay those expenses. The long spiral of events that led to the American Revolutionary War began as the British government looked to its American colonies as that new revenue source to pay for the cost of the French and Indian War. [207]

Washington the Country Squire

Nobody exceeded the influence and impact on George Washington's life that was attributed to his half-brother Lawrence III and his mentor William Fairfax. But nothing he ever did personally had a greater influence on the shape of his life than his decision to marry Martha Dandridge Custis. Her huge dowry from her first marriage immediately catapulted Washington into the top tier of Virginia's planter class as the master of Mount Vernon.[208] This marriage, conducted on January 6, 1759, came at a critical moment in the life of Washington, who went from a young officer at the mercy of the British military establishment to a prosperous planter who didn't have to answer to anyone. He had married up in the world, as had Martha before him, and they both had inherited a huge chunk of the Daniel Custis fortune. Once again, an untimely death contributed immeasurably to Washington's increasing wealth. Martha's money made her new husband one of Virginia's richest men, enabling him to issue his own declaration of independence. The marriage brought eighty-five

---

205   Ibid.
206   Chernow, 136.
207   Russell, 89.
208   Ellis, 40.

dower slaves under his control, doubling his labor force. Dorothy Twohig, an editor of the Washington Papers, notes:

> "With his marriage, he was now in control of one of Virginia's largest and most profitable estates, including property in six counties amounting to nearly eight thousand acres, slaves valued at £9,000 Virginia currency, and accounts current and other liquid assets in England of about £10,000 sterling."

Washington Acquires Mount Vernon

Then two years later, on March 14, 1761, Ann Fairfax Washington Lee, the widow of George's half-brother, Lawrence III, died. Because Ann had no surviving child, George Washington suddenly moved up from a renter to full-fledged ownership of Mount Vernon, including another five slaves. These sudden windfalls gave Washington new social standing and considerable freedom to maneuver.[209]

Life of a Virginia Aristocrat

The next sixteen years Washington devoted his energies to perfecting the elegant lifestyle of a Virginia aristocrat, making his military experiences into memories, but eventually worrying himself sick that he and his fellow Virginia planter class dignitaries were trapped in a grand economic network designed to reduce them all to bankruptcy and ruin. Initially, Washington's motivation for the American Revolution centered on that economic system, not religion, taxes, or lack of representation in government, as was the case in New England.[210]

This period between the French and Indian War and the Revolutionary War was the most settled period of Washington's life. The physical centerpiece of his newfound stability was Mount Vernon. He expanded both the mansion and the property. He added a full second level to the mansion home. Though not in the same league with brick mansions like the Fairfaxes' Belvoir or Thomas Jefferson's Monticello, the enlarged and embellished interiors of Mount Vernon and its stucco simulated-brick-over-wood exterior, were designed to make a statement. By 1775 Washington had more than doubled the size of Mount Vernon, from about three thousand acres to sixty-five hundred, through buying adjoining parcels of land when they became available. He more than doubled the size of his slave population to a total of over one hundred, much of that number acquired through a single purchase of forty-six new slaves.[211]

---

209   Chernow, 98.
210   Ellis, 40.
211   Ibid, 41.

Martha Dandridge Custis
Courtesy of Mount Vernon Ladies' Association

Raising Martha's Children

The emotional center of gravity of Washington's world was his wife Martha, who came to the marriage complete with two young children, Jackie (four) and Patsy (two). As a stepfather, Washington was dutiful and engaged, especially when it came to Jackie. He wanted the boy to receive the kind of education he had missed. Jackie was raised with all the advantages and freedoms that his stepfather had been denied: his own personal servant; a private tutor, who resided at Mount Vernon; the newest toys and finest clothes, all ordered from London; and his own horses and hounds for fox hunting.

George deferred to Martha on all final decisions concerning the children. He was their guardian; she was their parent. He was to provide, but not to decide. So off Jackie went to King's College (now Columbia) in New York; the local College of William and Mary in Williamsburg appeared to be not good enough for him. Jackie lasted only a few months at King's College. At age nineteen he married Eleanor Calvert, the daughter of Benedict Calvert, a descendant of Maryland's founding family. The new couple were established on one of the inherited Custis estates, where Jackie failed at managing his inherited plantation. He died in 1781 while visiting his stepfather, General George Washington, who was conducting the siege of British General Cornwallis at Yorktown.[212]

Patsy had a more troublesome life than Jackie's. Even as a little girl she began to experience seizures that only worsened with time. These eventually took the form of what would now be called grand mal epilepsy. She received the latest dolls and toys from London every year along with medicinal potions that included a medieval iron ring with allegedly magical curative power. Even with trips to several doctors and health spas, despite all their efforts, nothing worked. Patsy died after having one of her seizures in 1773 at the age of seventeen.[213]

Pastimes

George's favorite pastimes were fox hunting, dancing, horse racing, and gambling. According to his diary, he spent between two and five hours a day for forty-nine days in 1768 on horseback pursuing the elusive fox. He enjoyed these activities, especially after 1765, when he hired Lund Washington, a distant relative, to assume many of the estate's managerial duties. His travels to Alexandria, Annapolis, and Williamsburg to participate in horse racing were conducted using a chariot, custom made in London, with leather interiors and his personal crest emblazoned on the side. His personal records reveal that between the years 1772 and 1774 George played cards some twenty-five times per year and that he just about broke even. Washington's favorite wine was Madeira and he purchased it by the butt (150 gallons) and by the pipe (110 gallons). He enjoyed the attention of two manservants: Thomas Bishop, a white servant who had been with him since the Braddock campaign; and Billy Lee, a mulatto slave, who started serving in 1768 and who remained with Washington the remainder of George's life.[214]

212 Ibid, 43.
213 Ibid.
214 Ellis, 44.

Washington's Distillery

Farming and Diversification

During this period Washington experimented with different farming techniques and the growing of different varieties of tobacco. Always receptive to innovation, he studied agricultural publications and experimented with oats, wheat, and barley. He planted in soil from various corners of his property. He eventually recognized the folly of staking his fortune on tobacco. The soil at Mount Vernon, he eventually understood, had "an under stratum of hard clay impervious to water," which was washing away the thin topsoil and leaving behind "eyesore gullies."

Besides poor topography, Washington also had to contend with fluctuating tobacco prices—under imperial law, all sales went through England—and he never knew what his crops would bring until he heard from London.[215] After several seasons of drought or heavy rain, George realized that he needed to diversify.

He answered that need by starting a fishing enterprise on the Potomac. He also built a distillery and mill that remains at Mount Vernon to this day. The combination of his slaves with those of Martha exceeded Mount Vernon's labor requirements, so George hired his slaved labor force out to his neighbors.[216]

Most of Washington's plantation workers were African slaves, with indentured servants the other labor category. At this stage of his life, there is no evidence he felt

215   Chernow, 109.
216   Russell, 55.

Washington's Grist Mill

any moral anxiety about owning other human beings. Later in his career, after his experience in the American Revolution exposed him to a broader set of opinions on the matter, Washington developed a more critical perspective on the institution of slavery. Like most Virginia planters, Washington talked and thought about his slaves as "a Species of Property" very much as he described his dogs and horses. When they ran away, he posted notices for their recapture and rewards for return. His one concession to the humanity of his slave workers, and an attitude shared by Jefferson and many of the wealthier Virginia planters, was that he would not sell them without their consent if the sale broke up the slaves' families. He was also attentive to their health, warning overseers not to overwork them during periods of bad weather and taking personal charge if disease broke out in the slave quarters. There were trusted slaves who enjoyed considerable freedom of movement and personal discretion, like his servant Billy Lee, and a favorite messenger empowered to make minor business transactions named Mulatto Jack. Most of the slaves who worked his farms, however, he treated as cattle and referred to only by their first names.[217]

Early Public Offices

In 1758 George's celebrated military reputation helped him win an election for Virginia's House of Burgesses from Frederick County, where he owned land. Seven years later he was elected to the same office from his home county of Fairfax.

217   Ellis, 46.

In October 1762 Washington became vestryman of Truro Parish, a post he held for twenty-two years. The twelve-man vestry oversaw the temporal affairs of the church at Pohick, which formed part of the Anglican, or "established," Church. During the next decade Washington performed standard vestry duties, such as helping to pay the minister, balance the church budget, choose a site for a new church, oversee its construction, and select furnishings for the communion table. When the new church was completed, he bought two pews and contributed funds to buy gold leaf for religious inscriptions emblazoned across the altarpiece. Washington also served three terms as churchwarden, a post in which he helped to care for the parish's poor people and orphans.

Because Mount Vernon sprawled into Fairfax Parish, as well, Washington bought another pew at Christ Church in Alexandria and joined the vestry there, too.[218] This same Christ Church in 2017 voted to remove the George Washington memorial plaque from its sanctuary because "it creates a distraction to our worship space and may create an obstacle to our identity as a welcoming church . . . ."[219] Washington's extensive church activities taught him self-government and provided him with plenty of administrative experience.

Washington and the British Imperial Mercantile System

During the 1760s and 1770s, England's initial American agenda focused on budget deficits and revenue. When resistance to new taxes flared in the colonies, the government's attention shifted to a search for more palatable forms of taxation. Continued resistance led to frustration and anger in London. Eventually, enforcing obedience to royal and parliamentary authority became the focus of all concerned. New Englanders, upset over the escalating tensions with England, saw King George III and his ministers George Grenville, Charles Townshend, Frederick, Lord North, and Parliament as the faces behind their deteriorating relationship with the British Empire. George Washington saw a completely different face. He saw the face of Robert Cary.

Cary was Washington's man in London. He was the head of Cary and Company, one of the City's principal and most successful mercantile houses. The Cary connection was another legacy of the Custis estate, since the firm had represented the business of Martha's first husband, as well as her own during her brief time as a widow. Since Washington now was entrusted with the patriarchal responsibility of Martha, Jackie, and Patsy, he also was responsible for the Custis estate. This included three plantations totaling eighteen thousand acres spread out along the York River. These lands were worked by more than two hundred and eventually three hundred slaves. Mount Vernon may have been Washington's signature statement as a new

218   Chernow, 130.
219   Lori Aratani, "Historic Alexandria Church Decides to Remove Plaques Honoring Washington, Lee," *Washington Post*, October 28, 2017.

member of the planter class, but the Custis plantations in the Tidewater, devoted almost entirely to tobacco, produced the bulk of his cash.[220]

It was the size of his annual tobacco production that made Washington eligible for Cary's services. Smaller growers—by the middle of the eighteenth century the majority of Virginia planters—sold their crops to domestic buyers and bought most of their consumer goods locally. But the planters with the largest estates, those at the very top of the social order, preferred the consignment system, whereby they entrusted the sale of their crop to a mercantile house in England, using their extensive credit for the necessary funds to tide them over until crops were harvested and sold. In theory, this arrangement assured the highest price for one's crop. For many, the greatest advantage of the consignment system was the access it offered to London's shops and stores. By consigning his tobacco crop to Robert Cary, Washington was joining the elite within the Virginia elite, who could wear the latest English fashions and, in their own world, consume just as conspicuously as members of polite society back at the empire's metropolitan center in London.[221]

Surviving accounts give insight to the spending frenzy going on at Mount Vernon when Washington was expanding and furnishing the house during the five years starting in the early 1760s. These reveal that in an average year he would order from Cary goods valued at the equivalent of two to three million 2019 dollars.[222]

Estate Running in the Red

Eventually, it began to dawn on Washington that he was running through his entire Custis inheritance. In 1763 he rejected a request for a loan from an old army buddy, Robert Steward,[223] explaining that his Mount Vernon expenses had "swallowed up before I knew where I was, all the money I got by marriage nay more." He was truly stunned the following year when Cary apprised him that his account was more than £1,800 in the red, a debt that was only going to increase once Cary began charging five percent annual interest on the principal. Washington was caught in a trap that was snaring so many other Virginia planters that Thomas Jefferson, another victim, described it as the chronic condition of indebtedness. That then became "hereditary from father to son for many generations," Jefferson said, "so that the planters were a species of property annexed to certain mercantile houses in London."[224]

Washington's initial reaction to Cary's horrible news was the farmer's perennial lament: bad luck and bad weather. Then he began to question Cary about the tobacco market. He understood that markets fluctuated, almost by definition. But why was it

220   Ellis, 48.
221   Ibid, 49.
222   Ibid.
223   Chernow, 139.
224   Ellis, 50.

that swings in the market always appeared to go against his interest? Why was it that the price he received for his tobacco stayed low while the prices he paid for Cary's shipments kept going up? He also complained about both the quality and cost of the imported goods. He accused Cary of selling him inferior products and hiking up the prices by twenty percent because he was a mere American colonist, too ignorant to know the difference.[225]

After much thought, Washington concluded that no amount of diligence on his part, no good fortune with weather, no favorable fluctuation in the tobacco market, could combine to pull him out debt, because the mercantile system itself was a conspiracy designed to assure his dependency on people like Cary. [226]

There is no evidence that Cary actually overcharged Washington for goods or that he failed to provide Virginia planters fair value for their tobacco. History has shown that Virginia's planter class did struggle to grow tobacco as a cash crop due to the dwindling fertility of the soil. Also, vagaries of the tobacco market in Europe were being manipulated by cheaply produced Spanish tobacco that drove prices down. Also, social historians have targeted the planters' lavish lifestyles, which combined a blissful obliviousness to their bottom line with an apparently irresistible urge to imitate the styles and consumption of the English gentry.[227]

From Washington's point of view, the consignment system, by its definition, placed his economic fate entirely in Cary's hands. It provided the London merchant with total control over the price Washington got for his tobacco, the cost and quality of all the goods he received in return, and the debits and credits to Washington's account. Cary's reach, Washington believed, extended to the separate accounts he kept for Jackie and Patsy based on their Custis inheritance. All the risk of weather, spoilage, market fluctuations, and shipping mishaps fell on Washington's side of the ledger. All the leverage lay with Cary. Every time one of the invoices from Cary and Company arrived at Mount Vernon, it served as a stark reminder of Washington's dependence on invisible men in faraway places for virtually his entire way of life. If the core economic problem was tobacco, the core psychological problem was control. That would prove to be the highest emotional priority for Washington, which once threatened, set off internal alarms that never stopped ringing.[228]

Stamp Act

Just as Washington was grappling with the bad news from Cary, in the fall of 1765 Parliament's much-despised Stamp Act was scheduled to go into effect in Virginia. This was England's first effort to impose a direct tax on the colonies to help defray the costs of managing its expanding empire. The Stamp Act taxed printed

225   Ibid.
226   Ibid.
227   Ibid.
228   Ibid, 51.

material: legal documents, newspapers, almanacs, and even playing cards.[229] The stated purpose of the tax was to help pay for British troops stationed in North America after the victory in the French and Indian War. The response from the colonies was immediate and full-throated in its militancy. The Americans protested, as there were no foreign enemies on the continent, and declared that it was a violation of their rights as Englishmen to be taxed without their consent.[230] The American slogan "No taxation without representation" was coined, and petitions sent to Parliament and the king.[231]

The first colonial protest groups, mostly merchants and landowners, established connections through Committees of Correspondence. These created a loose coalition that extended from New England to Maryland.[232] A new secret organization called the Sons of Liberty was created and its protests often turned violent and destructive.[233] In retaliation for the tax, the thirteen colonies agreed upon a boycott of British manufactured goods.

While those in New England would make the legal arguments about taxation without representation, Washington's thinking was based on his personal experience with the British Empire's practical operation. He moved instinctively to the much more palpable issue of economic independence.[234]

After only one year, Parliament revoked the act. But still needing money, Britain looked for other ways to tax Americans.

Washington's Personal Rebellion

Washington, in addition to supporting the boycott of British manufactured goods, chose to act in a direct and personal fashion to recover his independence from Cary and Company. Starting in 1766, he abandoned tobacco as his cash crop at Mount Vernon and instead began growing wheat. He built a mill to grind it into flour, and sold the flour in Alexandria and Norfolk. He built a schooner to harvest herring and shad from the Potomac River and sold the fish locally and in the Caribbean. Washington eventually bought a ship, which he christened *The Farmer*, to carry his flour, fish, and corn to such distant markets as Lisbon. He developed a full-scale spinning and weaving operation at Mount Vernon to produce linen and wool fabric for workers' clothing. He continued to produce tobacco on his Custis plantations—so Washington was not completely free from Cary until 1774—though his purchases were significantly smaller.[235]

229　Chernow, 137.
230　"Stamp Act," *History.com*, www.history.com/topics/American-revolution/stamp-act (March 18, 2017).
231　Ibid.
232　Ibid.
233　Ibid.
234　Ellis, 52.
235　Ibid.

Land Speculation—Looking West

Washington also spent this time diversifying through land speculation. Like many other Virginians of the eighteenth century, he believed the Potomac River extended westward to the Mississippi or even the Pacific Ocean. He regarded Virginia as the gateway to the West. In 1762 he joined several organizations for improving navigation on the river's upstream sections. He chaired meetings of the Potomac Company at which fifty "Negro Men" were hired to dredge the river. His efforts yielded few practical results. The natural water route to the interior did not exist, and the man-made version that did ultimately connect the Atlantic Seaboard to the Midwest turned out to be the Erie Canal, in New York.[236]

Great Dismal Swamp Investment

Another land opportunity in which Washington was a participant began in May 1763. He joined nine other investors in a plan to drain the Great Dismal Swamp in southeastern Virginia, extending from current-day Norfolk into North Carolina, and turn it into lucrative farmland. Washington and his syndicate hoped to bypass royal regulations that limited grants of Crown lands to one thousand acres per individual. To circumvent this limit, they manufactured 138 fake names when they submitted their land petition in Williamsburg. Like every economic activity in Virginia, the Dismal Swamp project relied on slave labor, and Washington contributed six slaves to do his share of the draining and dredging.[237] Nothing much came of the venture to drain the forty thousand acres the partners acquired, though Washington held on to his four thousand acres until 1795.[238]

Ohio Country—Confused Policies

In Washington's mind the big prize lay over the mountains. His several initiatives to acquire tracts in the Ohio Country overlapped in unclear patterns of speculation, and the jurisdictional problem created by border disputes between Virginia and Pennsylvania, the overlapping claims of different Indian tribes, and the shifting policies of the British government all enhanced the confusion. But at the bottom line lurked a basic conflict about the Ohio Country's future: Washington believed it was open to settlement; the British government believed it was closed; and the Indians believed it was theirs.[239]

The strength of the Virginia economy, combined with increased population, ensured unstoppable westward expansion. On September 9, 1763, Washington

236　Ibid, 54.
237　Chernow, 137.
238　Ellis, 54.
239　Ibid, 55.

and nineteen other entrepreneurs banded together to launch the Mississippi Land Company, which hoped to claim 2.5 million acres of land in the Ohio Valley. This enormous chunk of real estate would include sections of what later became Ohio, Indiana, Illinois, Kentucky, and Tennessee. The British preferred to save the fur trade with the Indians, and by a royal proclamation on October 7, 1763, banned settlers from regions west of the Allegheny Mountains. Its effect was to make the region from the Great Lakes to the Gulf of Mexico and between the Mississippi and the western slope of the Appalachians an Indian reservation. The Crown rationalized this policy by saying it was easier to defend its subjects in the seaport cities. In a colony infatuated with real estate speculation, it was a disastrous political blunder to confine settlers to the Eastern Seaboard. Fearful that his western bonanza might evaporate, Washington condemned the proclamation. "I can never look upon that Proclamation in any other light than as a temporary expedient to quiet the minds of the Indians," [240] he said. For Washington, what he considered an infamous decree was doubly damaging because it interfered with the bounty claims of veterans from the Virginia Regiment who had served in the French and Indian War. To nobody's surprise, settlers from Germany, Ireland, and elsewhere continued to spill into the Ohio Valley in a resistless tide.

In 1765 the Mississippi Land Company hired an agent to lobby the British Privy Council on behalf of its proposal to create a feudal kingdom in the Ohio Valley, with the settlers as serfs and the owners as lords. The British ministry rejected the proposal, claiming that such a grant would violate the treaties recently signed with the Iroquois and Cherokee, but then in 1770 it approved a similar request for 2.5 million acres by a group of English investors to create a new colony called Vandalia in the same region. Two years later, Washington wrote off his investment as a loss, eventually describing the experience as clear evidence of the British government's "malignant disposition towards Americans."[241]

French and Indian War Patents

Washington's only victory in land speculation took thirteen years of multifaceted dialogue and was largely a product of his status as a veteran of the French and Indian War. During the worst days of that war, when colonial recruits were in greatest demand, Virginia's Governor Dinwiddie issued a proclamation making available two hundred thousand acres of "bounty land" on the east side of the Ohio River to Virginians who answered the call. Moreover, the infamous Proclamation of 1763 included one vaguely worded provision that granted five thousand acres each to former officers who had served the cause. Relying on these two proclamations, Washington was relentless in pressing this claim. He organized the veterans of the Virginia Regiment and led the political fight in Williamsburg to obtain patents on plots

240   Chernow, 137.
241   Ellis, 56.

of land over the mountains. These bordered the Ohio and Great Kanawha Rivers in what are now southwestern Pennsylvania, southeastern Ohio, and northwestern West Virginia.

In the fall of 1770 Washington personally led an exploratory surveying excursion to the Ohio and Great Kanawha, and the following year commissioned the completion of that survey. As governors in Virginia and ministries in London came and went, the interpretations of British policy toward the American interior changed. The core issue was the Proclamation of 1763. In one interpretation, it rendered all of Washington's western claims invalid, and all his time and energy wasted, because London had declared that the entire Ohio Country was forbidden to settlement.

Washington regarded this version of British policy as a massive delusion that was also wholly unenforceable. The British monarch could proclaim whatever he desired, but the practical reality was that thousands of colonial settlers were flooding across the Alleghenies every year, establishing their claims not by legal appeal to colonial or British authority, but by the physical act of occupying and cultivating the land. Possession was nine tenths of the law. Washington believed there was a race going on for the lands of half the continent. If he were to play by British rules, which refused to recognize the race was even occurring, others who ignored the rules would claim the prize. His solution was to regard the restrictive British policies as superfluous and to act on the assumption that, in the end, no one could stop him.[242]

In 1774 Washington learned that Wills Hill, the Earl of Hillsborough, who was secretary of state for the American colonies, had ruled that the promised land grants to veterans of the French and Indian War would be restricted to British regular soldiers only. Washington viewed this with contempt: "I conceive the services of a Provincial officer as worthy of reward as a regular one," he observed, "and can only be withheld from him with injustice." And since Hillsborough's decision was "founded equally in Malice, absurdity, & error," [243] Washington felt no obligation to obey it. As far as the American West was concerned, Washington was already declaring his independence.

Clearing his Debts

Despite the results through land speculation, crop diversifying, and the lingering London dependencies, he remained in debt. Washington's preferred course after 1765 made it clear that he was determined to defy the cycle of indebtedness that had swallowed up so much of the Virginia planter class. He was hell-bent on freeing himself from the clutches of Robert Cary.[244] Washington shaved his debt in

242   Ibid, 57.
243   Ibid, 58.
244   Ibid, 56.

half by 1770.[245] In retrospect, he was already in personal rebellion against the lavish seductions of the British Empire. [246]

The Townshend Acts

Having failed to learn its lesson with the Stamp Act, Great Britain again provoked colonial discontent in 1767 with the Townshend Acts, which placed taxes on paint, glass, paper, and tea, and bolstered the power of royal officials by freeing them from relying on colonial assemblies for money.[247] The Townshend Acts also established the American Board of Customs Commissioners with headquarters in Boston, where resistance to the Stamp Act had been the fiercest. Five officials were appointed to exercise control of American customs, enforce trade acts, and collect duties.

British Enforcing Trade in America

In order to reinforce the power of the new custom commissioners, new admiralty courts were created in Boston, Philadelphia and Charleston.[248] Hardening its stance toward the restive colonists, the Crown dispatched the HMS *Romney* to Boston, where in May 1768 colonial radicals had a chance to ponder the political message carried by its fifty guns.

That year, the new customs officers stationed at Boston had seized a sloop called the *Liberty*, owned by the wealthy Patriot John Hancock. The sloop was carrying a cargo of Madeira wine and was seized because Hancock had not paid the required taxes. The customs officers seized the sloop and towed it under the guns of the warship *Romney*. The outraged Patriots of Boston could not recapture the *Liberty* but they managed to seize one of *Romney's* boats, which they carried to Boston Commons and burned in a bonfire. Hancock was charged with smuggling but was acquitted.[249]

In September 1768 British warships disembarked two regiments of soldiers in Boston. The troops were ordered to protect the customs officers due to civil unrest. They marched through town to the beat of fife and drums and then pitched tents on the Common in a show of strength designed to intimidate local protestors.[250] Much like Egypt's Pharaoh, the British king's "heart was hardened."

245   Chernow, 139.
246   Ellis, 53.
247   Chernow, 143.
248   "1767 – Townshend Acts," *History.com*, March 19, 2018, www.stamp-act-history.com/townshend-act/townshend-acts/. (April 20, 2019).
249   Ibid.
250   Chernow, 143.

Washington Joins the Taxation Argument

One could easily argue that the events of the winter of 1768-69 converted George Washington from a rich, alienated farmer into a confirmed militant against British policies. Had he died before that winter, he would have left no real record of distinction, aside from his youthful bravery during the French and Indian War. That winter changed everything, and he began to develop into the Washington known to history. Like Moses, had Washington seen his burning bush?

Moving beyond the disputes over self-advancement that had preoccupied his younger, insecure self, Washington suddenly seemed a larger figure in the evolving fight against British injustice. All his boiling frustration in his unsuccessful quest for a royal commission during the French and Indian War; all his vocal disaffection with Robert Cary; and all his dismay over British policies that handicapped him as a planter and real estate speculator—these enduring grievances now crystallized into splendid wrath against the Crown.[251]

Protest and Boycott

Protests spread throughout the colonies against the new Townshend taxes. Parliament grew so frustrated over the colonial protests that it proposed (though never executed) that the dissident leaders be caught, shipped to England, and tried for treason. Washington received a packet of documents from Doctor David Ross of Bladensburg, Maryland. It contained news of associations being set up in Philadelphia and Annapolis to boycott nonessential British imports as long as Parliament persisted in imposing unfair taxes on the colonies. The packet contained plans for a similar Virginia association, drawn up by a nameless writer. Washington sent the packet to his friend and neighbor George Mason, who turned out to be its original author.[252]

On April, 5, 1769, Washington delivered to Mason a letter that gave both his private and his public reasons for supporting a boycott of British goods. Doubtless thinking of his own predicament, he said a boycott would break the burdensome cycle of debt that trapped many colonists, purging their extravagant spending.[253] In other words, a collective decision to stop buying British commodities would enforce a level of discipline and austerity on the Virginia planter elite that most of its members—and truth be known, Washington himself—had shown themselves unable to achieve voluntarily. While such a scheme risked a collision course with the British Empire, it reduced the risk that so many Virginia planters were running by remaining on a collision course with bankruptcy.[254] In the letter, Washington made

251 Ibid, 144.
252 Ibid.
253 Ibid.
254 Ellis, 60.

clear that his opposition to arbitrary taxation had much to do with setting a precedent against further mischief. Just as the British assumed the right to taxation, so "they may attempt at least to restrain our manufactories, especially those of a public nature." Striking a militant tone, Washington suggested that he had moved beyond petitioning the king and now preferred direct action, although not yet military. He suddenly found a clear, spirited voice of protest, one that spoke of abstract rights instead of just personal advancement or economic necessity.[255]

In many ways, Washington's letter to Mason foretells the success of the American Revolution: he tried to be law-abiding, endorsed incremental change, and favored violence only if all else failed. The American Revolution started as a series of measured protests by men schooled in self-government, a long, exhaustive search for a diplomatic solution, before moving toward open rebellion.[256] It could be viewed that God's ten plagues in Egypt were

Raleigh Tavern—Williamsburg, Virginia

similar, measured protests perpetrated on the Egyptian population to influence Pharaoh to release the Hebrew people from slavery.

Royal Governor of Virginia Dissolves House of Burgess

On April 30, 1769, Washington headed to Williamsburg to present George Mason's boycott plan to the House of Burgesses. Until this point Washington had been a minor, often absentee, legislator, too reserved and standoffish to emerge as a major political force. One observer characterized him as "too bashful and timid for an orator." Some may argue that up until this point Washington had a similar disposition as Moses did when God, at the burning bush, ordered him to go "unto Pharaoh, that thou mayest bring forth my people the children of Israel out of Egypt."[257] Moses initially made excuses because he felt inadequate for the job God had asked him to do. But God was not asking Moses to act alone. God provided assistance from his brother Aaron and from God himself. Moses rose to the task.

Now fired up with a newfound sense of leadership with George Mason's help,

255   Chernow, 144-145
256   Ibid, 145.
257   Bible, Exodus, 3:7-11.

Washington too rose to the occasion. He served on three standing committees, signifying an unforeseen elevation in Virginia politics.[258] By May 1769, the Burgesses approved the Virginia Resolves, which contended that only they had the right to tax Virginians. They also insisted upon the right to petition the Crown for grievances and restrict trials for treason and other crimes to the colony itself.[259]

Upon hearing of the work of legislature, Norborne Berkeley, Lord Botetourt, the king's appointed governor, promptly dissolved the House of Burgess.[260] After Botetourt's decree, Washington and his fellow burgesses recognized how little real authority they wielded. They weren't the colony's ultimate source of power, which was given sparingly at the whim of the Crown. Washington and many other fellow burgesses retired to the Apollo Room of Williamsburg's Raleigh Tavern to ponder "their distressed situation."

Here Washington introduced the boycott scheme that he and Mason had developed. The dissident burgesses formed a committee, including Washington, that accepted the plan for a nonimportation association. The next morning the burgesses reconvened to the Apollo Room and affixed their

Apollo Room of the Raleigh Tavern

signatures to the plan, which called for a boycott of any British goods subject to taxes in America. This Virginia Association would remain in force until the Townshend Acts were repealed.[261] This was an important moment in Washington's public career, for he now became an acknowledged leader in the resistance movement within Virginia's planter class.[262]

In late July Washington informed Robert Cary and Company that he was "determined to adhere religiously" to the new boycott agreement. In submitting a list of goods he wanted, Washington apprised his agents that nothing should be sent to him that appeared on the roll of products taxed by Parliament "as I have heartily enter[e]d into an association bound to boycott such goods."[263]

---

258   Ellis, 145.
259   Ibid.
260   Ibid, 146.
261   Ibid.
262   Ellis, 61.
263   Chernow, 146-147.

John Hancock by Sanford Mason

The Boston Massacre

The Massachusetts General Court also denounced the Townshend Acts. It stated that the Acts violated the principle of no taxation without representation. The

76

Massachusetts House of Representatives sent a petition to King George asking for the repeal of the Townshend Revenue Act. In February 1768 Samuel Adams of the Massachusetts House of Representatives drew up the Massachusetts Circular Letter to the other colonial assemblies. It asked them to join the resistance movement and oppose the new taxes. The British government ordered the Massachusetts House to recall the letter. The legislators refused and the House was dissolved by the royal governor of Massachusetts just as Botetourt had done to Virginia's assembly. [264]

After the civil unrest in Boston concerning the seizure of Hancock's sloop *Liberty*, and the subsequent occupation of the city by some four thousand British soldiers, matters became extremely edgy. The soldiers' very presence was a constant reminder that Britain was attempting to dominate the American colonies. On March 4, 1770, Boston Patriots clashed with British troops at John Gray's Ropewalk in the Fort Hill district of Boston. The altercation involved dozens of soldiers and ropemakers. One of the British soldiers involved in an argument at the Ropewalk was Private Matthew Kilroy. His argument was with a colonial, Samuel Gray.

The next evening, a British soldier was on guard duty at the sentry box in front of the

Site of the Boston Massacre

Boston Customs House on King Street. A British officer, Captain John Goldfinch, standing near the sentry, was being taunted by several citizens for not paying a barber's bill. Private Hugh White, who had been involved in the previous day's skirmish at John Gray's Ropewalk, stuck a teenager with the butt of his musket for insulting Captain Goldfinch. A crowd of over fifty quickly grew and began harassing the two redcoats. The soldiers called for reinforcements and eight additional British soldiers led by Captain Thomas Preston quickly arrived. The citizens continued to harass the soldiers and the crowd grew to over two hundred.

The redcoats soon found themselves being pelted by snowballs, ice, coal, and oyster shells. When Private Hugh Montgomery was hit in the face, he became enraged, raised his musket and fired into the crowd, instantly killing Crispus Attucks. Other soldiers, thinking that they had heard the order to open fire, also began to shoot into the unarmed crowd.

---

264   *History.com* ,"Stamp Act."

Private Kilroy killed Samuel Gray, with whom he had argued at the Ropewalk the day before. Three other colonists would die from the volley: Patrick Carr, Samuel Maverick, and James Caldwell. Six additional citizens were wounded. [265]

Privates Kilroy and Montgomery were found guilty of manslaughter but avoided the death penalty by having the letter "M" branded on their thumbs with a hot iron. Both were discharged from the army and sent back to England. Nevertheless, Patriots such as Samuel Adams and Paul Revere used what came to be called the Boston Massacre as a calculated piece of political propaganda, designed to rouse antagonism toward the Crown in all the colonies.[266]

Partial Repeal of the Townshend Acts

Parliament repeated its backpedaling pattern just as it had with the Stamp Act. On April 12, 1770, all the Townshend taxes were cancelled except the tax on tea. [267] The tea tax was to remain as a symbol of British authority to tax the colonies. Most colonial observers, Washington included, believed the crisis had been averted.[268]

The Tea Act of 1773

After the partial repeal of the Townshend taxes, the only remaining tax was that on tea. However, colonists continued to boycott tea. As a result, England's East India Company soon had literally tons of tea in its London warehouses and was on the verge of bankruptcy. To keep the East India Company solvent, the British ministry under Lord North proposed that the company could ship tea directly to America from China. That would avoid the tax on goods first sent to England, as required by previous legislation, which they believed the colonials would appreciate. Under the proposal, Americans could pay considerably less tax on tea, three pence per pound as opposed to twelve pence if the tea had been shipped through England before arriving in America. That meant Americans would pay less tax on tea than residents of England. However, the Americans rejected the Tea Act, refusing to accept the idea of paying any British import tax. The colonists had not forgotten their outrage at the Stamp Act of 1765, and their successful efforts have the hated act repealed.

The American colonists in the ports of Boston, New York, Philadelphia and Charleston had time to consider the implications and impact of the Tea Act before ships laden with tea arrived in their harbors. The colonies used the press to spread the political discussions. Circulars and handbills were printed and distributed. The Sons of Liberty, the secret society formed to protect the colonists' rights, organized public demonstrations against the British government. In Philadelphia, a public

265   "The Boston Massacre," *Land of the Brave*, March 20, 2018, https://www.landofthebrave.info/boston-massacre.htm. (April 20, 2019).
266   Ibid.
267   "The Townshend Acts," *Land of the Brave*, March 19, 2018, https://www.landofthebrave.info/townshend-acts.htm. (April 20, 2019).
268   Ellis, 61.

Boston's Customs House

meeting was held and agreed unanimously that anyone who aided in "unloading, receiving, or vending" the tea was an enemy to his country. Colonists resolved to prevent the landing and sale of the tea. They wanted it sent back to England.[269]

The Boston Tea Party

In the winter of 1773 three East India Company tea ships arrived in the ports of New York, Philadelphia and Charleston. The consignees refused to accept the shipments and ordered the tea to be returned. In Boston, the consignees would not allow the tea to be returned. Those consignees were two sons of the Royal Governor, Thomas Hutchinson, and his nephew, Richard Clarke. They were not going to submit to the demands of the colonists.[270] The tea ships *Dartmouth, Eleanor,* and *Beaver,* owned and operated by the East India Company, arrived separately in Boston harbor between November 28 and December 15, 1773. They moored at Griffin's Wharf, a few blocks away from the Old South Meeting House. Each ship was about eighty feet long with a crew of eight to twelve men, who aside from the captain slept in the cargo hold.[271]

---

269   "The Tea Act," *Land of the Brave*, "The Tea Act," March 19, 2018, https://www.landofthe-brave.info/tea-act.htm. (April 20, 2019).
270   "The Boston Tea Party," *Land of the Brave*, March 21, 2018, https://www.landofthebrave.info/boston-tea-party.htm. (April 20, 2019).
271   Ibid.

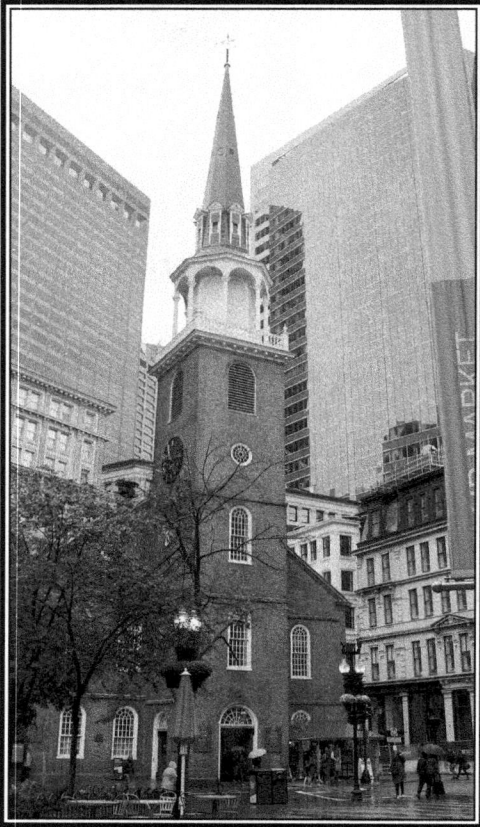

Boston's Old South Meeting House

The law required the tax to be paid the instant the tea was unloaded. Armed guards of Patriots were posted at the wharf to prevent the cargo from coming ashore. The absolute deadline for payment of the Tea Tax was twenty days after a ship's arrival. If the tax was not paid within the twenty days, the authorities would seize the cargo. During the twenty days following the arrival of the first ship, *Dartmouth*, meetings occurred on a daily basis throughout Boston to discuss what was to be done about the shipments of "detested tea." Samuel Adams, John Hancock, and Paul Revere organized one of these on November 29, 1773, the day after the *Dartmouth's* arrival. Over five thousand citizens of Boston attended, so the meeting had to be moved to a larger hall, the Old South Meeting House.[272]

At the meeting on November 29, it was decided to demand that the tea be sent back to England with the tax unpaid. It was also decided to have the ship's owner, Francis Rotch, ask Governor Hutchinson, for permission to sail out of Boston and back to England. On December 16, 1773, at another large meeting at the Old South Meeting House, Patriots were told the governor, had refused their demands. The people of Boston and the Sons of Liberty agreed that their only course of action was to destroy the cargo.[273]

The Sons of Liberty quickly moved into action. Over two hundred men volunteered to participate. The volunteers organized into three groups, one per ship, with a scheduled start time of 7 p.m., December 16, 1773. The destruction of the tea would be risky business. It would be considered an act of treason, punishable by death. A shop owner named John Crane allowed his store to be used as a staging point. It was in this store that Sarah Bradlee, a member of the Boston Daughters of Liberty, thought of using a Mohawk Indian disguise to cover the Patriots' identities.

272   Ibid.
273   Ibid.

Boston's Old South Meeting House—Interior

They would carry hatchets, or tomahawks, which they would use to break open the crates during the raid.[274] One of the participants, George Robert Twelves Hewes, said:

> "To prevent discovery we agreed to wear ragged clothes and disfigure ourselves, dressing to resemble Indians as much as possible, smearing our faces with grease and lamp black or soot, and should not have known each other except by our voices."[275]

The three groups of Patriots made their way to Griffin's Wharf where the three ships were berthed. The leaders of each of the groups of Patriots requested that each captain unlock the hatches to the cargo decks. The Patriots then hoisted the tea crates onto each ship's main deck where the crates were smashed open and thrown into the water. The captains of the three ships and their crews stood by impassively watching the events of what would be referred to as the Boston Tea Party. The surrounding British warships did not fire their cannons.[276] The only casualty during the entire event was one John Crane. A tea crate fell on his head, knocking him out. His fellow Patriots thought him dead so they hid his body in a pile of wood shavings in a nearby carpentry shop.[277]

---

274 Ibid.

275 Ibid.

276 Ibid.

277 "John Crane," *Boston Tea Party Ships and Museum*, March 20, 2017, https://www.boston-teapartyship.com/john-crane. (April 20, 2019).

The Patriots took three hours to dump over forty-five tons of tea into the water. The ships were not vandalized nor was any other cargo stolen. The crews of the *Dartmouth, Beaver* and *Eleanor* confirmed that the protestors had swept the decks clean afterwards.[278] Samuel Adams later stated that the event

> ". . . was not the act of a lawless mob, but a principled protest and the only remaining option the people had to defend their Constitutional rights."[279]

Again, King George's heart was hardened. He was quoted afterwards: "The die is now cast. The colonies must either submit or triumph."[280]

The Coercive Acts (Intolerable Acts)

Following the colonists' defiant display at the Boston Tea Party, people in England were surprised, bewildered, and angered by the colonists' actions. The king and many members of Parliament were becoming ever more antagonistic toward their rebellious American "subjects." After much debate in Parliament, King George III continued to "harden his heart." He assumed an active role in deciding punishment for the disobedient colonists by personally advising Frederick, Lord North, Britain's prime minister. This resulted in the "Coercive Acts," passed in March 1774, which were intended to quell the Massachusetts colonists and force them into submission.[281]

The most severe of the acts was the Boston Port Bill, which closed Boston Harbor to all commercial ships, enforced by a naval blockade. In addition, the Quartering Act enabled British troops to commandeer civilian homes, food, and possessions for their own purposes. Also passed was the Massachusetts Government Act, which made the colony's council positions Crown appointments, rather than elected by the local population. Judges on the colony's Supreme Court would also be appointed by the king. Meetings could be held only with the governor's permission and juries were to be selected by the governor, thus ensuring any court cases would be decided favorably to British aims. As if this were not enough, Parliament asserted the right to abolish at will all rights and liberties protected by the Massachusetts charter.[282]

Additional British troops were dispatched to see that the laws were enforced, bringing the total in Boston to six regiments. The closing of Boston's port to commercial ships raised the greatest anger, because it was clear that the intent was to starve the colony into submission.[283]

---

278   Land of the Brave, "The Boston Tea Party."
279   Ibid.
280   Ibid.
281   "The Intolerable Acts," *Boston Tea Party Ships and Museum*, March 23, 2017, https://www.bostonteapartyship.com/the-intolerable-acts. (April 20, 2019).
282   Hart, 258-259.
283   Ibid, 259.

Reaction from Massachusetts

The British military controlled Boston, but Samuel Adams had organized the Committee of Correspondence that controlled the countryside. It had been organized in 1772 as a shadow government that supplemented the activities of the Sons of Liberty. The Committee established lines of communication, which would bring order and effectiveness to what, until then, had been primarily spontaneous mob uprisings. Each colony would eventually create Committees of Correspondence to communicate with the committees in other colonies. These committees proved effective in binding the revolutionary leaders together in a common cause, and helped form the nucleus of a shadow government.[284]

Unfortunately for England and King George III, his plan did not succeed in its purpose. Instead the colonies became more united through their common hatred of the British. The new laws were referring to as the "Intolerable Acts."

Committees of Correspondence formed in virtually every New England town, and had control of almost all the local governments. The committees dominated the town assemblies and pulpits, and controlled the newspapers. Fiery sermons from Presbyterians, Congregationalists, and Baptists roused the people to action. By the fall of 1774 the Committees of Correspondence had isolated the British authorities in Boston, and except for the occupied city, Massachusetts was practically self-governing.[285]

Samuel Adams by John Singleton Copley

From all over colonial America, supplies of relief poured into Massachusetts. Virginia sent eighty-six hundred bushels of wheat and corn. That included fifty pounds from George Washington, his initial contribution to the starving Bostonians.

First Continental Congress

The committees favored convening a Continental Congress in Philadelphia in the fall of 1774. In August, George Washington found himself in Williamsburg at the Virginia Convention. That body had been called to select seven delegates to that First Continental Congress. After the votes were counted, Washington came in third, just behind Richard Henry Lee and comfortably ahead of Patrick Henry. The vote

---

284   Ibid.
285   Ibid.

was a measure of his growing stature as a determined, cool-headed leader of the protest movement in Virginia.[286]

On September 5, 1774, fifty-five delegates representing twelve of the thirteen colonies gathered in Carpenter's Hall in Philadelphia. The First Continental Congress was the most illustrious group of American men ever to meet in one place. In addition to the Virginia delegation of Lee, Washington, Henry, Edmund Pendleton, and Peyton Randolph, it also included: the learned lawyer John Jay from New York; William Livingston from New Jersey; John Adams and his cousin Samuel Adams from Massachusetts; Roger Sherman from Connecticut; John Dickinson from Pennsylvania; John Rutledge and Christopher Gadsden from South Carolina; and the Presbyterian minister Doctor John Witherspoon of New Jersey.[287]

As one of his ablest biographers put it, Washington's fellow burgesses knew that Henry could be counted on to say the magnificent thing, whereas Washington could be counted on to do the right thing. Washington performed according to script: silent during the debates but thoroughly dedicated to opposing the Intolerable Acts and supporting a rigorous Continental Association against British imports.[288]

On October 14, 1774, the Continental Congress issued a Declaration of Rights, which enumerated specific colonial grievances against the Crown and Parliament. "Whereas, since the close of the last year, the British Parliament, claiming a power, of right, to bind the people of America by statutes in all cases whatsoever," the Declaration began, it went on to proclaim the Intolerable Acts as "impolitic, unjust, cruel, as well as unconstitutional, and most dangerous and destructive of American rights." As a consequence of England's tyrannical behavior, the Continental Congress declared that it had taken the necessary steps to defend America's "religion, laws, and liberties." On October 20, 1774, the fifty-two delegates formed an Association of the United Colonies under these words: "We do for ourselves, and the inhabitants of the several colonies whom we represent, firmly agree and associate under the sacred ties of virtue, honor, and love of country." This established a "league of the continent," in the words of the historian Benjamin Hart, that "first expressed the sovereign will of a free nation in America."[289]

Restraining Act

In response to America's "Declaration of Rights," Parliament passed the Restraining Act, which forbid the four colonies of New England from trading with any other nation but England. Four more regiments were then dispatched to Boston under the command of General Thomas Gage. He was the same Thomas Gage

286   Ellis, 64.
287   Hart, 261.
288   Ellis, 64.
289   Hart, 263-264.

who fought alongside Washington at the Battle of the Monongahela during the French and Indian War. Gage was instructed to find the leaders of the Massachusetts rebellion and arrest them as traitors.[290]

Virginia Readies for War

During the winter of 1774 and spring of 1775, county militia units, calling themselves "independent companies," were organized throughout Virginia. As the colony's most famous war hero, Washington was the obvious choice as commander, and by March 1775 five independent companies had invited him to be their leader. Then in March, a second Virginia Convention was called, this time in Richmond.[291] On March 23, 1775, Patrick Henry stood up before the delegates and sounded an American battle cry:

> "There is no room for hope . . . If we wish to be free, we must fight! An appeal to arms and to the God of Hosts is all that is left us! . . . Three million people, armed with the holy cause of liberty and in such a country, are invincible by any force which our enemy can send against us. We shall not fight alone. God presides over the destinies of nations, and will raise up friends for us. The battle is not to the strong alone; it is to the vigilant, the active, the brave . . . Is life so dear, or peace so sweet as to be purchased at the price of chains and slavery? Forbid it Almighty God! I know not what course others may take, but as for me, give me liberty or give me death!"[292]

The Convention ordered that the Virginia colony "be immediately put into a posture of Defense." This marked the moment when military preparation replaced political argumentation as Virginia's highest priority. With that change, Washington succeeded orators like Henry as the most critical figure. In balloting to select delegates to the Second Continental Congress, Washington received 106 of the 108 votes cast.[293]

It was obvious to Washington from the evidence that King George III's heart had been hardened and that the king intended to make Massachusetts an object lesson of where sovereign power resided within the British Empire. Washington believed that war had become a probability. When Washington departed Mount Vernon on May 4, 1775, for Philadelphia's Second Continental Congress, he took his military uniform.[294]

---

290   Ibid, 266.
291   Ellis, 66.
292   Hart, 266.
293   Ellis, 66.
294   Ibid, 67.

Lexington and Concord

Under the presidency of John Hancock, the Provincial Congress of Massachusetts, based in Concord, also began to make preparations for war. It appointed its own treasurer to collect taxes, selected a Committee of Public Safety to train militia, and stored munitions.

Informed by Loyalist spies of the arms and ammunition being collected in Concord, about eighteen miles from Boston, the British General Thomas Gage decided that the seat of New England's revolutionary government would be an excellent place to administer a sound thrashing to the rebels. The Patriots were planning to adjourn their Provincial Congress on April 15 in order to send delegates to the Second Continental Congress, scheduled to meet in Philadelphia in early May. General Gage knew he had a short window in which to strike.[295]

On April 18, the Patriot Joseph Warren learned from a source inside the British command that redcoat troops would march on Concord that night. Warren dispatched two couriers, the silversmith Paul Revere and the tanner William Dawes, to alert residents of the surrounding towns. The Patriots used lanterns in the towering steeple of the Old North Church to signal the British advance.

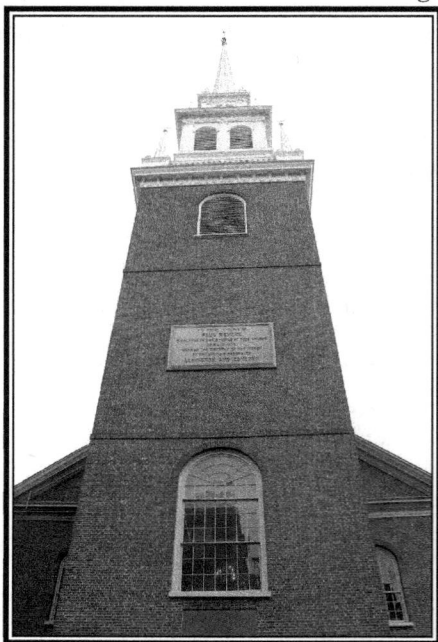

Old North Church

Revere and Dawes traveled by different routes to Lexington, a few miles east of Concord, where revolutionary leaders Samuel Adams and John Hancock had temporarily found refuge in the home of Reverend Jonas Clarke. Having persuaded those two leaders to flee, a weary Revere and Dawes then set out again. On the road they met a third rider, Samuel Prescott, who alone made it all the way to Concord. Revere was captured by a British patrol, while Dawes was thrown from his horse and forced to proceed back to Lexington on foot.[296]

Gage launched his night raid in the early hours of April 19, hoping to surprise the Patriots while they slept. In all, about eighteen hundred British regulars out of

295   Hart, 267.
296   "Battles of Lexington and Concord," *History.com*, A+E Networks, https://www.history.com/topics/american-revolution/battles-of-lexington-and-concord. (March 26, 2019).

Paul Revere by John Singleton Copley

Paul Revere and Old North Church

a total Boston garrison of thirty-five hundred would be dispatched along various routes. This was to be a major attack.[297] At dawn on April 19, some seven hundred British troops arrived in Lexington. They came upon seventy-seven militiamen gathered on the town green. A British major yelled, "Throw down your arms! Ye villains, ye rebels." Heavily outnumbered, Captain Jonas Parker ordered his band—Patriot farmers serving as militiamen—to disperse. Before that could happen, a shot rang out. To this day, no one knows which side fired first. The British subsequently released several volleys before Major John Pitcairn could restore order. When the smoke cleared, eight Patriot militiamen lay dead and nine were wounded. Only one redcoat was injured.[298]

Major Pitcairn was joined by troops commanded by Lieutenant Colonel Francis Smith. The combined force proceeded to Concord to search for arms. The vast majority of the weapons had already been relocated. The British decided to burn what little they found, and the fire got out of control. Hundreds of militiamen occupying the high ground outside Concord incorrectly thought the whole town would be torched. About a thousand Patriot militiamen hustled to Concord's North Bridge, which was being defended by three companies of British soldiers. The British fired first but fell back when the colonists returned the volley.[299] The British prepared to return to Boston but were impeded by almost two thousand militiamen—known locally as "Minutemen" for their ability to be ready at a moment's notice. At first, the militiamen simply followed the British column. Fighting started again soon after the retreat began, however. The militiamen fired at the British from behind

---

297   Hart, 267.
298   *History.com*, "Battles of Lexington and Concord."
299   Ibid.

trees, stone walls, houses, and sheds. Before long British troops were abandoning weapons, clothing, and equipment in a panicked, every-man-for-himself sprint back to Boston.[300]

When the British force reached Lexington during its retreat, it ran into an entire brigade of fresh redcoats that had answered a call for reinforcements. That did not stop the colonists from resuming their attack, which continued all the way through Arlington and Cambridge. In the evening a contingent of newly arrived Patriot Minutemen from Salem and Marblehead, Massachusetts, had a chance to cut off the redcoats and possibly finish them off, but the British were able to reach the safety of Charlestown Neck. There they had the support of their naval fleet. [301]

The Patriots had soundly defeated a British force of 1,800 men, among the best trained and most experienced in the Imperial Army. In all, the British suffered some 273 casualties. By contrast, forty-nine Americans were killed, and forty-one wounded. The numbers were not especially large, but the British had rarely suffered such a humiliating defeat. [302]

Second Continental Congress

When the Second Continental Congress gathered on May 10, 1775, the War for Independence was already well under way. Many of the delegates selected to attend still hoped to restore harmony between America and the mother country, but to do so would be to desert the Patriot army in Boston, which had succeeded in blockading General Gage's forces. There was also amazing news from the western frontier. Two small bands of irregular troops, one led by Benedict Arnold and another, eighty-three Green Mountain Boys led by Ethan Allen, had captured Fort Ticonderoga in early May. John Hancock arrived from Massachusetts to preside as President of the Congress. News also came that England planned to strengthen its army, rebuild its navy, and devote all of its attention and power to suppressing the revolt around Boston. No longer could this be a mere conference of delegates. This assembly had to transform itself into a governing body with executive powers. It voted to issue paper money and to meet British encroachment with force. What was needed was a leader, someone who could transform a part-time militia of farmers, merchants, and preachers into a disciplined army.[303] Washington, who had been given no committee assignments during the First Continental Congress, was asked to chair four committees charged with military readiness. He was the only delegate to attend in military uniform.[304]

300   Ibid.
301   Ibid.
302   Hart, 269.
303   Ibid, 272.
304   Ellis, 69.

Washington—Commander in Chief of the Continental Army

John Adams proposed George Washington as the obvious choice to serve as commander-in-chief of the Continental Army. Washington was still remembered and revered for his exploits twenty years earlier in the French and Indian War. He was also a southerner, and thus could help cement a union between North and South. Many southerners, especially Anglicans, viewed the conflict as essentially regional, between New England's religious zealots and mother England. Washington's nomination broadened the war and the cause to include all the colonies, particularly the most populous and wealthiest—Virginia.[305]

Washington was the reluctant warrior, and had slipped out of the convention hall, hoping his name would be overlooked. He was honest and realistic about his qualifications to lead the American army to victory. Though a battle-tested veteran, he had never commanded any unit larger than a regiment. He had no experience deploying artillery or maneuvering cavalry and no background whatsoever in the engineering skills required to build defensive positions or conduct sieges. Compared to the British officers he was sure to face on the battlefield, he was a rank amateur.[306]

On June 16, 1775, George Washington was unanimously selected to lead America into war. He warned his fellow countrymen: "With utmost sincerity, I do not think myself equal to the command I am honored with."[307] He was right. For the larger truth was that no one in America was qualified to lead an American army to victory, because the odds against such an outcome appeared overwhelming. No matter how glorious the cause, the prospects of thirteen disparate and contentious colonies defeating the most powerful army and

John Adams by John Singleton Copley

---

305   Hart, 272-273.
306   Ellis, 71.
307   Hart, 273.

navy in the world were remote and extreme. It would be almost another year before Thomas Jefferson would draft the document, the Declaration of Independence, in which the delegates to the Continental Congress pledged "our lives, our fortunes, and our sacred honor" on behalf of American independence. Washington fully recognized that by accepting the appointment as commander-in-chief that he was making a personal pledge before anyone else in America. If he failed in the high-stakes gamble, his Mount Vernon estate would be confiscated, his name would become a slur throughout the land, and his own neck would almost surely be stretched.[308]

Washington refused a salary but agreed to accept financial compensation only for his war expenses. With that he departed for Boston where the New England Patriots eagerly awaited the arrival of their army's leader.

Was the chain of events that led to Washington's appointment as commander-in-chief of the Continental Army just luck? Was he pre-destined

Thomas Jefferson—1791 by Charles Willson Peale

to lead the American Revolution back in 1653 when John Washington's ship ran aground at Mattox Creek, Virginia? Did he just happen to be at the right place at the right time, or was it an act of Divine Providence? You now have the facts. You decide.

---

308   Ellis, 71.

Samuel Adams's Grave—Boston, Massachusetts

Part II

Forming a Nation Through Sacrifice, Hardship, and Miracles

P art Two is focused on America's Exodus journey. Specifically, the war and nationhood. Similar to the Hebrew Exodus, where God brought freedom to an enslaved people, he also, through the experience of their journey, molded them into a nation. To accomplish his purpose, God worked through great and small men with all their inherent strengths and weaknesses. Along the way, God sustained them by performing miracles.

During the Hebrews' Exodus, God did not make freedom and nationhood an easy course. Their journey lasted forty years. Time after time the Hebrew people came to the end of their resources and to the point where there was nothing left but to rely on God. They became dissatisfied and complained bitterly to Moses about their trek through the wilderness. At each critical moment God worked a miracle to sustain the Israelites.

When trapped against the Red Sea, God parted the waters and allowed the passage of the Hebrew people; then destroyed Pharaoh's army when it pursued. God provided water and food when there was none and protected the Hebrews from their enemies. Through all this time of shared hardship, sacrifice, and danger; a new Hebrew nation was formed.[309]

Like the Hebrew nation, America's own Exodus during the Revolution involved a long war and years of sacrifice and hardship. Freedom did not come easily to America, either. Many of the founders themselves saw God's miracles working to sustain a cause frequently on the verge of extinction. Unity came slowly and painfully over a period of years as the war touched one region after another. The focus of this part is on the historical record of the war and how through timely events/miracles America was sustained, obtained victory, and formed into an American nation.[310]

---

309   Spivey 229.
310   Ibid.

Chapter 5

Siege of Boston

We have nothing my dear sir to depend upon, but the protection of a kind providence and unanimity among ourselves.

George Washington to John Adams
April 15, 1776.

In the spring of 1775, while George Washington was participating in the Virginia Convention in Richmond and the Second Continental Congress in Philadelphia, Massachusetts was busy coming to the support of Boston after the confrontation with the British at Lexington and Concord. Patriot militia poured into the towns surrounding Boston. General Gage estimated that he was surrounded by some fifteen thousand New England Minutemen and an untold number of Patriot sympathizers. Those militiamen assembled around Boston in Roxbury, Cambridge and Chelsea. Due to England's naval superiority and its control of Boston Harbor, the British were able to receive supplies and additional soldiers.[311]

The largest contingent of Patriot soldiers was fifteen Massachusetts regiments, commanded by General Artemis Ward. As more regiments arrived from other areas, these units agreed to place themselves under General Ward. He ordered defensive entrenchments to be built around Cambridge and Roxbury. British troops continued to arrive by sea including three new generals who were added to Gage's forces: William Howe, Henry Clinton, and John Burgoyne.[312]

Gage's naval commander, Admiral Samuel Graves, recommended early on that the high ground around Boston be occupied to protect his fleet. Gage did not approve Graves' recommendation and instead pulled all his forces onto the Boston peninsula. By early June, with the arrival of more British forces and the three additional generals, Gage decided that he was ready for offensive action. He planned to attack Dorchester Heights—today's Fort Point—on June 18 and to continue attacks on Roxbury and Charlestown.

311   Hart, 269.
312   Spivey, 94.

Boston in 1775 was much smaller, hillier, and more watery than it appears today. The Back Bay was still a bay and the South End was likewise underwater.

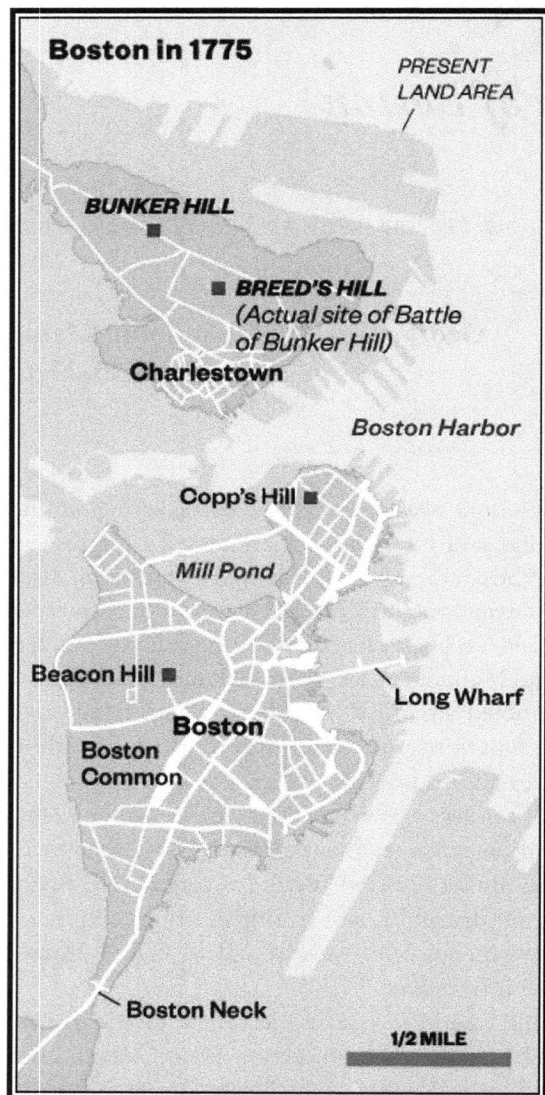

Boston in 1775

PRESENT
LAND AREA
/

BUNKER HILL ■

■ **BREED'S HILL**
*(Actual site of Battle
of Bunker Hill)*
Charlestown

Boston Harbor

Copp's Hill ■

Mill Pond

Beacon Hill ■

Long Wharf

Boston
**Boston
Common**

Boston Neck

1/2 MILE

Boston and Charlestown
Courtesy of Smithsonian.com

Hills were later leveled to fill in almost a thousand acres. Boston was virtually an island, reachable by land only via a narrow neck. Despite the results obtained in the Battles of Lexington and Concord, it remained unclear whether the ill-equipped rebels were willing or able to engage the British army in pitched battle. Leaders on both sides still thought the conflict might yet be settled without full-scale war.[313]

Patriots Occupy the Hill

On June 16, 1775, Ward learned of the British plans for offensive action. Patriot Colonel William Prescott and his Massachusetts regiment of eight hundred men were ordered to march from their positions in Cambridge and to build fortifications on top of Bunker Hill, on Charlestown Peninsula, overlooking Boston. As Prescott arrived in Charlestown in the dark he chose instead to fortify Breed's Hill, which was smaller and closer to Boston.[314] The reasons for the change in locations are confusing. But as Nathaniel Philbrick argues in *Bunker Hill,* it was a "purposeful act, a provocation and not the smartest move militarily." Short

---

313   Tony Horwitz, "The True Story of the Battle of Bunker Hill," *Smithsonian.com*, May 2013, https://www.smithsonianmag.com/history/the-battle-of-bunker-hill-36721984. (April 1, 2018).
314   "Siege of Boston," History.com, 2009, http://www.history.com/topics.american-revolution/siege-of-boston. (March 30, 2018).

View of Boston from Bunker Hill - 2018

on cannons and the know-how to accurately fire those they had, the rebels couldn't do much damage from Breed's Hill. But their threatening position, on high ground just across the water from Boston, forced the British to try to dislodge the Americans before they were reinforced or fully entrenched.[315]

Patriots frantically threw up breastworks of earth, fence posts and stone. The Patriots' position covered an area less than fifty yards square. Although never finished, the works would grow during the night and next day to a height of six feet above the ground. At first light, Prescott realized that his redoubt was exposed to the north. He ordered his men to extend the breastworks another one hundred yards. He later realized a large open area remained beyond the extended breastwork and the Mystic River shoreline. To remedy this gap, Prescott ordered Captain Thomas Knowlton with his two hundred Connecticut troops into the gap. Knowlton took up a position behind a rail fence with a low stone footing, scattering his troops thinly to cover this large expanse.[316] Aside from the problems with his position, Prescott faced other major disadvantages. His troops were both exposed and exhausted. The Americans were a motley collection of militia from different colonies, with little coordination and no clear chain of command.[317]

Colonel John Stark arrived later in the afternoon with his First New Hampshire Regiment. He decided to position his men in support of Knowlton and the thinly defended fence line between the hundred-yard breastwork and the Mystic River. As

---

315   Horwitz.
316   Spivey, 97.
317   Horwitz.

Stark positioned his men, he noticed that his left flank ended on ground above the riverbank and that a lower beach extended to the water. Even at high tide, that beach was wide enough for the enemy to pass through if they elected to flank the Patriots' position. Stark immediately ordered two hundred of his men to build a stone wall across the beach. He placed a stake forty yards in front of the wall and ordered that no one open fire until the enemy reached the stake.[318]

The British Response

As the morning's sun rose over the Atlantic Ocean on June 17, crewmen on HMS *Lively* observed the new activity on Breed's Hill and opened fire on the colonial position. The cannonade increased as the morning wore on.

Gage desired to strike a decisive blow at the rebels by sending a direct assault on the redoubt atop Breed's Hill. A quick rout of the rebels would demonstrate British determination and military superiority. Gage placed Howe in charge of the attack.[319]

While the troops and equipment were being readied for the assault, Gage made his own reconnaissance of the Patriot position. From the Mystic River he observed that the rebels were apparently not defending the northern side of Breed's Hill. His observation probably was made before Knowlton and Stark had joined the Americans and taken up positions north between the breastwork and the Mystic River.

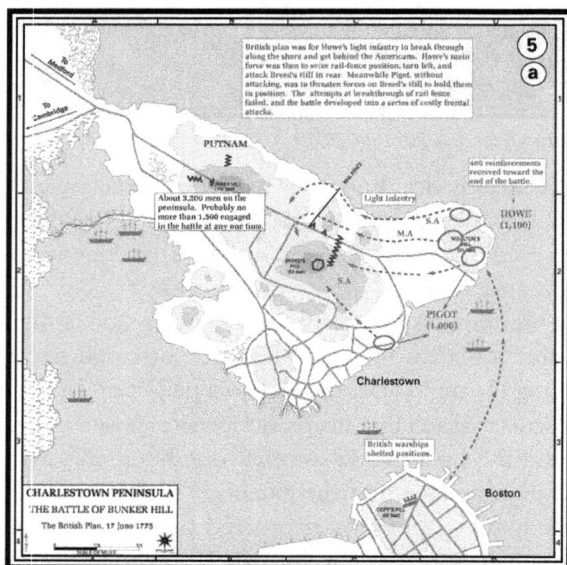

Battle of Bunker Hill
Courtesy of U.S. Military Academy

Howe devised a two-pronged attack. He would send one force directly against the redoubt while another would attack north of the redoubt by flanking the colonial left along the Mystic River. Once around and behind the Americans' lines, Howe's flanking force would cut off the rebel position and open it to destruction from the rear. Howe's attack would be supported by his field artillery of brass six-pounders, a battery of twenty-four pounders on Copp's Hill in Boston, and over two hundred naval guns.[320]

318　Spivey 97.
319　Ibid. 98.
320　Ibid.

As the British ferried their troops across the harbor into a position to attack, Howe observed some of the rebel activity on the north slope of Breed's Hill. It was Knowlton's Connecticut regiment and Stark's New Hampshire regiment moving into position. Instead of changing his plan of attack, Howe called for additional forces. He asked Admiral Samuel Graves to move a ship or floating battery up the Mystic River to support the attacking right flank. Admiral Graves denied the request because the Mystic River had not been charted and its water depths were unknown.[321]

At three o'clock Howe ordered his attack. He had three thousand regular troops in line of battle. General Robert Pigot led the attack on the redoubt with about half of the British force. Howe commanded the flanking column, which he expected to make the decisive breakthrough on the right wing along the Mystic River beach. He assigned the beach attack to his light infantry companies, led by his own regiment, the Royal Welsh Fusiliers.[322]

At this point the town of Charlestown at the base of Breed's Hill was aflame from the constant cannonade from ships and shore batteries.

The British commanders were over-confident. They had a low opinion of their American opposition. They considered the hastily assembled farmers and tradesmen to be ill-equipped, undisciplined, and even cowardly in light of their inclination to hide behind objects like walls, trees, and buildings. On Breed's Hill the rebels seemed to confirm that prejudice by hiding behind hastily prepared defensive positions. But Howe was not an ignorant commander. He designed his flank attack to bypass the strongest defensive point and quickly unravel the rebel positions from the flank and rear. He intended to neutralize the enemy's advantage by using his field artillery on those American positions that were to be assaulted from the front. He had a sound plan. His problem was execution and maybe some interference from a Divine Providence.

The Battle Unfolds

Howe's artillery opened the battle with a fury as planned but within minutes fell silent. A dispatch reached the general informing him that someone had brought the wrong sized cannon shot. Instead of the proper six-pound cannonballs, twelve-pound ammunition had been loaded in the caissons. An enraged Howe ordered that grapeshot, metal balls the size of musket bullets, a large-scale analogue to buckshot, be fired instead. Grapeshot, a short-range anti-personnel weapon, proved ineffective at long range against the Americans' breastworks. Desiring no further delays, Howe ordered his infantry to advance without the support of artillery.[323]

The attackers quickly got some unpleasant surprises. The seemingly open pasture in front of the American line proved to be an obstacle course. The high,

---

321 Ibid.
322 Ibid.
323 Ibid, 100.

Battle of Bunker Hill by John Trumbull

unmown hay obscured rocks, holes, and other hazards. Fences and stone walls also slowed the British.[324]

The Welsh Fusiliers were the first to reach the rebel line. They came in along the beach trotting seven abreast with weapons leveled, expecting an ineffective first volley from any rebels on the beach and a quick bayonet fight, if any at all. They advanced without apparent opposition until they passed Stark's stake in the sand. Suddenly, a firestorm erupted from the American line, decimating rank after rank of Fusiliers. [325] When the rebels opened fire, the close-packed British fell in clumps. In some spots, the British lines became jumbled, making them even easier targets. The Americans added to the chaos by aiming at officers, distinguished by their fine uniforms.[326] The attack dissolved as British survivors pulled back into disorganized retreat. This same scene was replayed before the rail fence and the redoubt. Soon the British troops, momentarily dispirited, were back in the landing area where they had started.[327]

The disciplined British quickly re-formed their ranks and advanced again. This attack advanced only on the high ground without attempting another attack on the

---

324   Horwitz.
325   Spivey, 100-101.
326   Horwitz.
327   Spivey, 101.

beach. It met with the same results as the first; British dead and wounded littering the field.[328]

The Americans were not without their problems. The men suffered from dehydration. Each was near exhaustion after having worked all night building their defenses only to remain in position and fight through the entire day without relief or resupply. Ammunition at this point became critical for the Americans. At this stage of the war the hastily assembled militia units fought with virtually no system of communications or logistics. During the day, Ward had dispatched orders to various units to reinforce the defenders on Breed's Hill. Because many of those orders were misrouted or misunderstood, Prescott received very little support.[329]

With the arrival of fresh troops from General Clinton the British devised a new plan for their third attack. They moved their artillery closer and raked the rebel defenses, particularly the breastwork, with grapeshot. When the British infantrymen attacked the third time, they marched forward in well-spaced columns perpendicular to the Americans, instead of in one broad line parallel to the breastwork.[330] American fire checked the initial advance, but as their ammunition was used up, their firing sputtered and "went out like an old candle," Prescott wrote. His men resorted to throwing rocks, then swung their muskets at the bayonet-wielding British pouring over the ramparts.[331] Prescott and his men had to give ground. Fortunately, Knowlton and Stark continued to hold the fence line. From there, they could support the withdrawal of Prescott's men and prevent their being cut off by the British advance. As the Americans fell back in good order, the redcoats crowded into the redoubt on Breed's Hill, the victors.[332]

In just two hours of fighting, 1,054 British soldiers—almost half of those engaged—had been killed or wounded. American losses totaled over four hundred, including the death of Doctor Joseph Warren, one of the original leaders of the rebel underground.[333] The British had taken the hill but it was a Pyrrhic victory. As Clinton remarked, "another such would have ruined us."[334] Badly depleted, the besieged British abandoned plans to seize another high point near the city.

Divine Providence at Bunker Hill

Bunker Hill should have closed the door on the American Revolution. A clear rout of the rebels on Breed's Hill would undoubtedly have put an end to the rebellion. An undisputed victory would have given a clear message that insurrection

---

328   Ibid.
329   Ibid.
330   Horwitz.
331   Ibid.
332   Spivey, 102.
333   Chernow, 192.
334   Hart, 270.

was pointless. As events unfolded, however, God's hand moved to change the odds in favor of the Americans. He ensured that the rebellion would not be snuffed out and would instead go on to a new level of intensity.[335]

Although the Americans did not win the battle of Bunker Hill, they attained a distinct moral victory by their successive repulses of the attacking redcoats and their orderly escape from capture. General Howe was not able to follow up on his gains and continue to attack the surrounding rebel strongholds due to his losses and the condition of his command. The situation would have been much different if the British had routed the Americans early and easily. There were practically no defenses around Cambridge and the rebel headquarters. If the British had continued to press their attack on this area, the results would have been disastrous and could have collapsed the entire rebel line around Boston.[336] General Howe became excessively cautious after this battle due to the losses he suffered at Bunker Hill. This caution by Howe may have played a role later in the war when he faced similar circumstances: frontal attacks on a fortified defensive position.

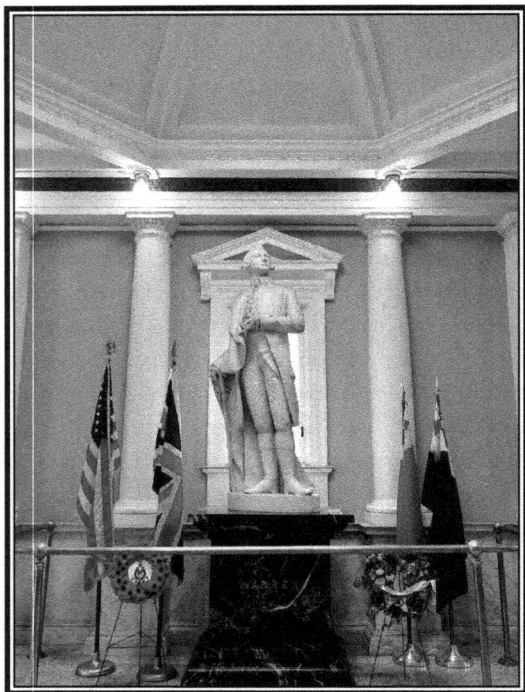

Doctor Joseph Warren

Some will argue that the British were just unlucky at Bunker Hill. I argue that there was more in play at Bunker Hill than luck or British incompetence. God's purpose was accomplished at Bunker Hill when the British were denied a quick and convincing victory. God's providential hand can be seen in the many unusual situations that came together to produce the results. Let's review.

Picking the Wrong Objective

Why Gage desired to drive the rebels from Breed's Hill through a flanking maneuver coordinated with a frontal assault remains a mystery. This tactic was

---

335   Spivey, 103.
336   Ibid.

certainly the quickest solution but proved the costliest in terms of casualties. Clearly, Gage had other options that his staff articulated. Those with military experience believe Clinton's suggestion to attack and occupy key terrain on Charlestown Neck, would have been the best tactical move. The Breed's Hill position was not a serious threat to the British in Boston, especially since the rebels had no artillery or anyone with the experience to use it. By occupying Charlestown Neck, the British forces would have severed the rebel supply and communication lines. That would have forced the rebels to launch their own attack or be annihilated from the rear with no means of escape. The rebels lacked the maturity as a fighting unit to coordinate an attack, so it is likely they would have been forced to surrender without a fight. It was personal pride and their low opinion of the Americans' fighting ability, not sound tactical judgment, that dictated the British course of action. The circumstances presented a chance for open combat, the regulars' strong suit, quite different from the guerilla warfare they experienced on their retreat from Lexington and Concord. Better yet, to Gage, it was an opportunity to teach a lesson. Despite their best military minds being on the scene, the British took a rash approach when they had no need for haste. In so doing, they picked the wrong objective, for which they paid dearly in casualties. They never regained the initiative.[337]

Wrong Ordnance

Howe knew from observation that the rebel line along the rail fence on Breed's Hill's north slope was beyond range of the navy's shipborne artillery and his guns atop Copp's Hill in Boston. He also knew that taking that rebel position was critical for his flanking maneuver. His solution was to use his own field artillery to blast the rebel position. The troops had painstakingly brought their smaller, six pounders across the harbor by small boat and manhandled them over obstructions and up the hill to get them into position. Their fire should have made the rebels' rail fence line indefensible. Support from these artillery pieces was a critical part of Howe's maneuver plan. When he discovered that the wrong cannonballs had been brought over for the battle, it was too late to do anything about it. Howe ordered his infantry into action without his artillery; hoping the rebels would flee at the sight of the British presence on their front and flank. When the rebels elected to stand and fight, the British infantry were relentlessly pounded until the rebels' ammunition was exhausted. Afterwards, a British supply officer was charged with negligence. However, every gunner, ammunition handler, and officer should have shared the blame. How was it possible that not one of these British artillerymen caught the mistake? Think about it. That mistake is equivalent to sending an entire infantry regiment marching into battle carrying their muskets but no bullets.[338]

---

337   Ibid, 105.
338   Ibid, 107.

The Beach

No American commander noticed (or perhaps simply ignored) the fact that the Mystic River's edge lay well beyond its bank, across an extended beach until Stark took his position along the rail fence. Then he noticed the beach from the drop-off at the end of his line. Though Stark got no orders to defend or fortify the beach, recognizing the hazard to his left flank he ordered two hundred men to build a stone wall and defend it. This was the exact location Howe had selected for his Fusiliers to attack in their flanking maneuver. Stark could have elected just to keep the beach under observation or position sentries there, but his decision to fortify it saved the day. The British Fusiliers running down the beach would have easily swept away anything other than a strong force behind good protection. Howe's attack would have been a quick and easy victory.[339]

Naval Support of Howe's Right Flank

Howe did observe the rebel fortification of the rail fence and stone wall on Breed's Hill's north slope, which was exactly where he intended his flank attack to go. That was why he asked for a navy ship to sail up the Mystic River to provide artillery support to his right flank. This would have placed British naval artillery in the rear of the rebels' rail fence and stone wall, resulting in an indefensible position for Stark's First New Hampshire militiamen. Unbelievably, General Howe's request was rejected by Admiral Graves on the grounds that the navy had not sounded the Mystic River. This was incomprehensible. British naval forces had been operating in and around Boston for over six months, yet no one had thought to check this particular area for navigability. That oversight is even harder to understand considering that it was Admiral Graves who early on had recommended that Gage aggressively occupy the high ground around Boston, better to protect his fleet. How could Graves have made such a recommendation without knowing where his fleet could maneuver?[340] Could you imagine the British army operating in and around Boston for six months without any maps of the area, then go into battle without a map? How could the British navy have been so negligent?

Certainly all the mistakes on both sides of the battle could be argued as incompetence or bad luck. But the British were not recognized as incompetent. Both on land and on sea, they were seasoned warriors, the world's finest fighting force. They clearly misread their American enemy. The mistakes of Bunker Hill are incomprehensible and can only be argued as attributed to God's providential hand.

Siege of Boston

Washington was en route to Boston when he received the news of Bunker Hill. It came in a dispatch delivered to him at the home of Leonard Lispenard of

---

339   Ibid, 106.
340   Ibid, 106-107.

Hoboken, New Jersey. The site had been incorrectly labeled as Bunker Hill, an error that would stick. More important, the dispatch revealed that the British had not only forced the American retreat but had also inflicted maximum terror on the supposedly amateurish Americans by incinerating Charlestown, leaving the town a smoking ruin.[341]

As Washington and his party, consisting of Thomas Mifflin, Joseph Reed and Generals Charles Lee and Phillip Schuyler, pushed northward, his mind was occupied with the situation awaiting him in Boston. He felt beleaguered by the myriad of social duties thrust upon him as he passed through an unending succession of towns. He endured ritual greetings from each town's leading citizens. Knowing that people wished to see him astride a horse, Washington would step down from his carriage, drawn by two white horses, and mount a horse before entering a town, turning each arrival into a theatrical performance. On Sunday, July 2, he finally arrived at Cambridge. The next day he assumed control of the Continental Army, which by then had laid siege to Boston and the many redcoats bottled up in the city.[342] Strictly speaking, the Continental Army would not exist until the start of the new year; until then, Washington was commanding a collection of provincial militia units whose enlistments would run out in December. Instead of a hard core of experienced veterans, the Continental Army became a constantly fluctuating stream of amateurs, coming and going like tourists.[343] Washington and Lee toured the lengthy American defensive fortifications that had been built to deter a new British attack. Those works had been thrown up helter-skelter over a ten mile front. They viewed the eerie reality of two armies separated by scarcely more than a mile, enjoying panoramic, unobstructed views of each other.[344] "It is not in the pages of history, perhaps, to furnish a case like ours," Washington complained to John Hancock, "to maintain a post within musket shot of the enemy for six months together . . . and at the same time to disband one army and recruit another, within that distance of twenty odd British regiments." [345]

Instead of the twenty thousand men that Washington expected, his first reports revealed he had less than fourteen thousand, further depleted by sickness and furloughs. From Prospect Hill, Washington could observe the British. What he saw were professional entrenchments supported by navy ships strategically anchored in the harbor. Washington's troops were scattered over many miles with exterior lines, meaning any troops moving to support other American troops could not move on the shortest path but would have to travel via roundabout roads. The British had the advantage of concentrated defenses with interior lines and could easily support one

---

341   Chernow, 192.
342   Ibid, 193.
343   Ellis, 83.
344   Chernow, 194-195.
345   Ellis, 83-84.

another, or move to strike Washington from any location.[346]

Washington immediately began to make improvements to both his forces and his fortifications. He ordered ten thousand hunting shirts to clothe the men and to give them some military appearance. He organized his forces into three divisions, or wings: the right on Roxbury Heights under Ward, the left on Winter and Prospect Hills under Lee, and the center around Cambridge under the command of Putnam.[347]

Of major concern to Washington was his inventory of gunpowder and artillery. At one point an assessment revealed that the entire stock of powder available would supply only nine rounds per man. Word of this situation spread among the ranks, and a deserter eventually informed the British commanders in Boston. The British found this information so farfetched they dismissed it as a rebel trick.[348]

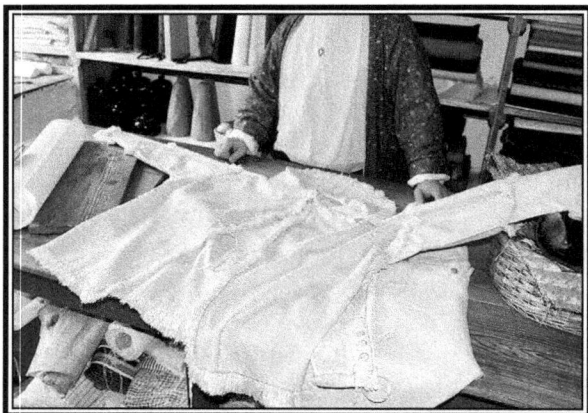

Revolutionary War Hunting Shirt

Washington found himself in a precarious situation. He had to reorganize and discipline the forces available, and at the same time attempt to recruit a new army, largely by inducing the same troops to re-enlist. Clothing, equipment, and money were all in critically short supply. He could not complain about this publicly for fear of exposing his weakness to his enemy.[349] He had to become an expert bluffer, pretending to have military strength he did not possess.

Fortunately for Washington, his opponent was dispirited from the cost of his victory at Bunker Hill. Gage seemed satisfied simply to defend Boston. His subordinate, Clinton, argued against inaction. He proposed to move against Dorchester Heights, to the south of Boston. Such an expedition was planned and organized but cancelled for unexplained reasons. The British continued to improve their fortifications in Boston and on Bunker Hill. Navy ships' positions in the harbor now included the Mystic River, and more troops replaced those lost at Bunker Hill. The British Ministry eventually became dissatisfied Gage's inaction. On October 10, he was replaced by Howe.[350]

---

346   Spivey, 111.
347   Spivey, 111-112.
348   Ibid, 112.
349   Ibid.
350   Ibid, 113.

The story of the siege of Boston can be told in one sentence: Washington's makeshift army kept more than ten thousand British troops bottled up in the city for over nine months, at which point the British sailed away to Halifax. It was more a marathon staring match than a battle, but the smaller details that led to the termination of this standoff pointed to the hand of Providence.

Washington Obtains His Artillery

About November 1775 Washington saw an opportunity to deliver a major military defeat to the British by taking Dorchester Heights. Then unoccupied, the bluff overlooked the British positions from the south. It was the same position the British had canceled their plans to occupy. From the heights, the Patriots could shell the British in Boston and their fleet in the harbor. [351] Such a move would force the British to come out of Boston and fight or evacuate the city.

Could it have been an act of Divine Providence that in one campaign the Americans twice fortified the exact location that the British had plans to attack? First was Stark's decision to fortify the beach on the Mystic River prior to the Battle of Bunker Hill: the exact target of General Howe's flanking maneuver. Now, five months later, Washington made plans to occupy and fortify Dorchester Heights: the same location the British wished to occupy but had failed to do so in a timely manner.

The main problem for Washington was that once his army occupied the hill, he had no cannons or sufficient powder with which to bombard Boston.[352]

It then occurred to Washington that back in May, heavy artillery, gunpowder, and ammunition had been captured by Ethan Allen and Benedict Arnold at Fort Ticonderoga. Henry Knox, a chubby bookseller from Boston, who would become Washington's artillery commander, was ordered to transport Ticonderoga's fifty heavy guns to Cambridge. The movement of these weapons to Boston is one of the great military epics in American history. With winter arriving, Knox and his men had to move sixty tons of ordnance three hundred miles. The task was extremely difficult. In the dead of winter, Knox moved them on sleds, up and down icy, snow-covered hills and across frozen rivers. One cannon fell through the ice, but through enormous effort and ingenuity, Knox retrieved the piece. The completion of this almost impossible but vital job, without complaining, made the 250-pound Knox one of Washington's favorite officers.[353] In late January 1776, Knox arrived with the ordnance that for the first time gave Washington the capability of offensive action.[354]

---

351   Hart 277
352   Ibid
353   Ibid.
354   Spivey, 114.

Occupying Dorchester Heights

On the evening of March 2, 1776, Washington opened a diversionary artillery bombardment of Boston with some of his newly delivered artillery, which had been installed at Lechmere Point, Cobble Hill, and Roxbury. The British were shocked by the large caliber of weapons used against them for the first time. Washington continued the bombardment on the night of March 3, then with even heavier concentration on the night of March 4, when his men were to occupy Dorchester Heights. The cooperation of British artillery batteries, which began to exchange fire, added to the noise and smoke that helped mask Washington's troop movement.[355]

At 7 p.m., Washington ordered General John Thomas to move three thousand men to the base of Dorchester Heights, a very risky operation because the location was in full view of the British. But suddenly a low mist rolled in, perfectly timed to conceal Patriot movements, while at the same time leaving the top of the hill perfectly clear, fully lighted by a bright moon, thus aiding the Patriots who were building fortifications. Boston remained shrouded in fog throughout the night, and the British could not see what was happening across the water. Additionally, the prevailing breeze blew noises made by Patriot engineers away from British ears. At three in the morning, work was completed. The three thousand builders departed and three thousand fresh soldiers moved in. At dawn, the British were amazed to see the Patriot fortifications. The rebels have "done more in one night than my whole army would have done in months," Howe said.[356] Washington's men continued to work on their fortifications, preparing to defend them against the expected British attack.

Henry Knox
Courtesy of Biography.com

355   Ibid, 115.
356   Hart, 277.

The British Response

British artillery batteries opened fire on Dorchester Heights for two hours but soon suspended their cannonade. They could not elevate their guns enough to reach the high American parapets. This cessation of fire encouraged the American men who were already in high spirits and sure they could repel a British attack on their heavily fortified position. Almost simultaneously with the halt in the rain from the enemy's cannon came signs of commotion and confusion in Boston.[357] Howe gave Brigadier General Valentine Jones the mission of driving the Americans off the hill with an assigned force of twenty-two hundred men. By noon on March 5, the Boston waterfront was a beehive of activity. Men and equipment assembled and began moving by small boats to waiting transport vessels. The assault force moved across the harbor towards Castle William. The first phase of the British attack was to be a landing on the point of Dorchester peninsula opposite the castle. From the landing area the British would attack the easternmost rebel fort first, rendering cannon fire from the other rebel batteries unusable. The landing required that troops and equipment be put into small boats for the movement ashore. Although this operation was to take place in generally sheltered waters within Boston Harbor, its success depended on the conditions of tide, wind and surf.[358]

The Storm

According to the historian J.T. Flexner, at this point, "the sky suddenly blackened with what soldiers on both sides considered the most awesome storm they had ever seen." The winds were of hurricane strength, making a British attack impossible. Americans continued to work through the storm, and, when the sky cleared, the Patriot fortifications were so strong as to convince Howe that an attack on Dorchester would be suicidal, similar to what he had experienced at Bunker Hill.[359] Two weeks later the Patriots fortified Nook's Hill, making the British position in Boston untenable. Howe ordered the evacuation of Boston and on Saint Patrick's Day 1776, he and his forces set sail for Halifax, Nova Scotia.[360]

God's Hand at Boston

Washington was able to retake Boston without shedding any blood. He called the storm "a remarkable interposition of Providence." Timothy Newell, a Boston selectman, agreed, writing in a journal entry on March 17:

357 Douglas Southall Freeman, *George Washington* Vol 4 *Leader of the Revolution* (New York: Charles Scribner's Sons, 1951), 37.
358 Spivey, 117.
359 Hart, 278.
360 Spivey, 119-120.

"Thus was this unhappy distressed town through a manifest interposition of Divine Providence relieved from a set of men whose unparalleled wickedness, profanity, debauchery and cruelty is inexpressible."[361]

Washington's success at Boston had many ramifications. Boston was liberated. The Continental Army had suffered no disastrous casualties or defeat. The fire of rebellion survived, just as it had after Bunker Hill. The political ramifications were just as significant as the military. The Continental Congress moved to the irreversible step of independence. The Founding Fathers, praying for God's protection, committed themselves to a course that would lead either to a new nation or catastrophe.[362]

How could the successful American results during the siege of Boston be explained but through the hand of Providence? Twice the Americans fortified positions at the exact spot where British attacks were planned, without advanced knowledge of those attacks, at Bunker Hill and Dorchester Heights.

Twice the weather came to the rescue of the Americans. The mist and favorable wind shielded the Americans from British observation as the Patriots occupied Dorchester Heights. The storm on March 5 made the British attack impossible and allowed time for Washington to complete his fortification of the heights.

Henry Knox's three-hundred-mile winter transport of Fort Ticonderoga's ordnance was a miracle in itself. The arrival of the big guns completed the critical tasks required to allow Washington to take the offensive.

Howe's refusal to accept accurate information about Washington's pitiful supply of gunpowder and his decision to remain passive in Boston allowed for Washington to take the initiative.

Howe called off the expedition to occupy Dorchester Heights in the fall of 1775 because he thought, correctly, that without heavy artillery the rebels could pose no threat from that quarter. He had not reckoned on his enemy's feat in obtaining the heavy guns they needed. Yet when the Americans opened their diversionary fire with their newly obtained heavy artillery on the night of March 2, Howe did nothing but return fire. For two more days he did nothing to take the high ground at Dorchester that could threaten his position.

At about 10 p.m. the night of March 4, a British officer received a report that "the rebels were at work on Dorchester Heights." Brigadier General Francis Smith, one of the leaders of the Lexington and Concord assaults the previous year and not famous for his energy or initiative, got the report but did nothing with it. He took no action to confirm the information nor did he forward this critical intelligence up his chain of command. Smith allowed dawn to come, and allowed Howe to discover the bad news for himself.[363]

---

361   Hart, 278.
362   Spivey, 122.
363   Spivey, 124.

When Washington's troops marched into Boston, amid much cheering and fanfare, they saw that the Old South Church had been desecrated, turned into a riding school for British cavalry. This highlighted the belief of many Patriots that they were fighting not only for political freedom; they were also fighting for God.[364] The events and results of the siege of Boston reveals that God was on the Patriots' side.

Siege of Boston Helped Forge a Nation

Similar to God and Moses leading the Israelites in the wilderness for forty years and, in so doing, forging a nation, the results achieved through the siege of Boston did much to forge an American nation. In early 1776 Congress was still divided between radical and conservative delegates. The radicals seemed to be moving toward independence from England and formation of a new nation. The conservatives were committed to seeking redress of grievances and a return to normal relations with England. The conservatives feared a war and probable ruin and continued hoping for reconciliation. At this point in history most of the deliberations in the Continental Congress had sided with the conservative approach, even to the point that delegates from six colonies were under specific orders to vote against independence.[365]

On March 23, 1776, when news arrived that Washington and the army had forced the British to abandon Boston, the political complexion in Congress completely changed. In April, the delegates from South Carolina, Georgia, and North Carolina received instructions permitting a vote for independence. In May, Congress passed a resolution that individual colonies could assume all powers of government, in effect displacing any vestiges of Royal authority.[366]

On June 7, 1776, Virginia's Richard Henry Lee finally proposed a motion that the United Colonies declare themselves free and independent states. John Adams seconded the motion. On June 11, Congress appointed a committee of five to prepare the formal declaration: Benjamin Franklin, Roger Sherman, John Adams, Robert Livingston, and Thomas Jefferson. Jefferson, being the youngest and the best writer, wrote the first draft.[367]

The adoption of the Declaration of Independence on July 4, 1776 was just an official ratification of what had already occurred. On May 10, town meetings all over Massachusetts had already declared independence. Five days later Virginia also declared independence.[368]

A number of independent governments began to take shape in other colonies. The royal governors were virtually powerless even by the time of Lexington and

---

364   Hart, 278.
365   Spivey, 121.
366   Ibid, 122.
367   Hart, 280.
368   Ibid, 278.

Concord. After hostilities commenced, the Committees of Correspondence had gone a long way toward establishing their own governments with executive powers. Loyalty toward the royal government faded as the population trended toward the Patriots. North Carolina's Governor Josiah Martin and Virginia's Governor John Murray, Lord Dunmore, fled to British warships, and others soon followed. Connecticut's governor switched sides, and was given a leadership position in the Revolution. Massachusetts reestablished its original government charter, which Parliament had suspended. Many states began drafting their own constitutions including Virginia, whose George Mason drew up an eloquent Declaration of Rights. It featured the lines:

> "That all men are born equally free and independent, and have certain inherent natural rights . . . among which are the enjoyment of life and liberty, with the means of acquiring and possessing property, and pursuing and obtaining happiness and safety."[369]

Thomas Jefferson would use these words when tasked to craft the Declaration of Independence.

The Americans were very familiar with the plight of the Israelites, who had failed to keep God's laws even though they were his chosen people. The newly adopted Declaration of Independence continually called on God, the "Creator," the "Supreme Judge of the World," to approve of their separation from England. The document's signers seemed to say that they, too, were fleeing from a pharaoh. But what happened when the pharaoh followed? In the Old Testament, God answered that question at the Red Sea, when he destroyed Egypt's army. The Americans responded to their pharaoh, King George, with revolution. They knew they too would need miracles similar to what occurred at the Red Sea if they were to have any hope of freeing themselves. The Americans had already seen two such miracles at Bunker Hill and Dorchester Heights, and there would be many others.[370]

---

369   Chernow, 236.
370   Hart, 285.

Chapter 6

Long Island

The Americans had been remarkably favored by the sudden rise of a fog which covered the East River. "At this time a very dense fog began to rise. It seemed to settle in a particular manner over both encampments. I recollect this peculiar providential occurrence perfectly well, and so very dense was the atmosphere that I could scarcely discern a man six yards distant;" said Benjamin Tallmadge. To General Howe's astonishment, the entire Continental Army had vanished, as if into thin air.

Benjamin Hart
Faith and Freedom

For the Hebrew nation, the direction of travel through the Wilderness was provided by God's pillar of cloud by day and a pillar of fire by night.[371] George Washington had to rely on his own military instincts, also provided by God, to predict when and where General Howe would return to America. Washington was confident that New York—wealthy, easily supplied, situated between the South and New England, and possessing a superb harbor—would be Howe's target. In this, Washington was correct. Howe and his generals planned to use New York as their base of operations. The Hudson River was New York's great lure. The Hudson led north almost to Lake George. Lake George led to Lake Champlain, which emptied into the Saint Lawrence and Canada. This waterway route suggested an obvious line to be held. The idea of separating New England from the rest of the colonies, dividing the American effort in two, was a prime object of British strategy.[372] New York City also happened to have a very large population loyal to the crown. Controlling New York City would permit the British to march north up the Hudson River, thereby severing the fiery New Englanders from their less hostile brethren in the mid-Atlantic states and South. British control over the region would gradually tighten until the rebellion suffocated.[373]

371 Bible, Exodus: 20.
372 Bruce Bliven, Jr, *Battle for Manhattan*, (Papamoa Press, 1956), 6.
373 Alexander Rose, *Washington's Spies, The Story of America's First Spy Ring* (New York: Bantam Dell, 2006), 10.

On an island at the mouth of the Hudson, surrounded by navigable waters, New York City offered Howe an easily defended base, thanks to the strong British navy. No American navy existed.

Defending New York City

Washington arrived in New York on April 13, 1776, to take charge of defensive preparations that were already under way under Charles Lee. It would have been difficult to imagine a more perfect place for the British army to confront and crush the Continental Army than New York City. The same qualities that made New York a majestic seaport turned it into a military nightmare for its defenders. There was hardly a spit of land that couldn't be surrounded and thoroughly shelled by the British ships that would certainly control the seas. Topographically, it was tailor-made for the kind of amphibious operations that British naval supremacy made possible and Washington's force could contemplate only in its dreams.[374] Lee wrote to Washington:

> "What to do with the city . . . puzzles me. It is so encircled with deep, navigable water that whoever commands the sea must command the town." [375]

The city was most certainly doomed, but Washington and Congress considered it a "post of infinite importance" that would be politically demoralizing to surrender without a fight. The British, with their naval superiority, could strike from anywhere. Washington, with his army of around twenty thousand men and no navy, had to allocate forces to cover each possibility. At the very least the Americans would have to make the British pay severely for the city, as they had made them pay at Bunker Hill.

Washington planned to defend New York City by digging in and making earthworks for gun positions at the Battery, elsewhere on Manhattan, and in Brooklyn. In addition, he intended to build Fort Washington near Manhattan Island's northern tip.[376] To ward off attacks by sea, Washington sealed off the end of every street with a barricade and sank offshore obstructions to British ships. By early June the Continental Army had 121 cannon in Manhattan, on the New Jersey shore, on Governors Island, and in Brooklyn, all ready to bombard the British fleet. [377] The fortifications themselves were well engineered and executed, but the plan was too ambitious. It spread Washington's forces too thin.[378] There was so much to fortify—

---

374   Ellis, 93.
375   Philander D. Chase, ed., *The Papers of George Washington,* Revolutionary War Series, vol 3, 1 January 1776 – 31 March 1776 (Charlottesville: University Press of Virginia, 1988), 339-341.
376   J. Jay Myers, "George Washington: Defeated at the Battle of Long Island," *American History Magazine,* History Net, June 2001. (February 10, 2019).
377   Chernow, 231.
378   Myers.

both sides of both rivers in addition to the key terrain features all over the long, narrow, rocky island of Manhattan—none of the works was first class and most of them were pitifully inadequate.[379]

A considerable part of the effort to prepare New York for the British assault was calculated to frustrate the superior British navy. The Americans hoped to substitute shore batteries for the warships they lacked. They thought the guns on Governor's Island, on the Brooklyn-Queens shore, and on the Manhattan shore, could make the East River too dangerous for British sailors. They also believed the Hudson River could be blocked off by sinking a line of heavily weighted ship's hulls across it just a few hundred yards north of where the George Washington Bridge now stands. The underwater obstructions were supposed to worry the British captains, while gunfire from the American batteries at Fort Lee, on the New Jersey end of the line, and Fort Washington, on the Manhattan side, was to add to their discouragement. The combination might make the British feel that a sail up the river was not worth the risk.[380]

The area known as Brooklyn Heights took on a special significance. These heights lay about a mile east of the Manhattan waterfront across the East River, commanding the river and the port. New York would be untenable if the enemy held this area. The defense of Brooklyn Heights would require a sizable force and a dangerous division of Washington's forces.[381]

Washington placed his largest contingent of troops, initially numbering four thousand and commanded by Nathanael Greene, on Brooklyn Heights. He considered these to be his best soldiers. Facing the Patriots would be Howe and approximately thirty-two thousand soldiers, including some eight thousand Hessian mercenaries. Admiral Richard "Black Dick" Howe supported his brother with the largest expeditionary force Britain had ever dispatched—ten thousand sailors on thirty warships with twelve hundred guns and hundreds of supporting vessels.[382] The British king and Parliament had decided they needed to inflict a devastating blow to regain control of the colonies quickly and completely.

The British Arrive In Force

On June 29, sentries on Staten Island signaled to Washington that forty British ships, the first installment of the fleet, had been spotted off Sandy Hook and would soon glide majestically through the Narrows. When this first wave of 110 warships and transport ships grew visible from Manhattan the sight was impressive, almost dreamlike, to behold. These were the same ships that had evacuated Boston in March, then marked time in Halifax before sailing south to New York. Fortunately for

---

379   Bliven, 9.
380   Ibid, 10-11.
381   Spivey, 128.
382   Myers.

Washington, this advance guard decided not to force the issue immediately. Some ships dropped anchor off Gravesend, Long Island, but no offensive action materialized. British troops began disembarking on Staten Island without opposition. Howe was biding his time until the bulk of the fleet, sailing from England under the command of his brother Richard, could join him in New York.[383]

On July 2 and 3, 1776, the very days the Continental Congress voted to approve American independence and revised the language of Thomas Jefferson's draft Declaration of Independence, the advance elements of Admiral Howe's fleet of seventy warships and four hundred transports began pouring his troops onto Staten Island.[384] It was the largest military force ever assembled on the North American continent and the largest army the British would ever gather in one place during the entire war.[385] About a quarter of the British force was German mercenaries, collectively referred to as "Hessians."

General William Howe
Courtesy of Biography.com

British Test the American Defenses

On the afternoon of July 12th five British ships—the forty-gun HMS *Phoenix* and the twenty-gun HMS *Rose*, along with a schooner and two tenders—sailed toward the Battery on lower Manhattan. In their first test, the American defenses failed miserably. Only half the artillerists manned their guns, and hundreds of soldiers lined the shore transfixed by the enemy ships, as if attending a sporting event. Six Patriots were killed in an artillery company under Captain Alexander Hamilton when their cannon exploded, possibly from defective training or from intoxicated gunners mishandling their ordnance.[386]

Unharmed by steady fire from Patriot artillery on the Manhattan and New Jersey shores, *Phoenix* and *Rose* sailed past the Hudson River obstructions and

383   Chernow, 234.
384   Ibid, 244.
385   Ellis, 93.
386   Chernow, 238.

Admiral Richard Howe
Courtesy of Biography.com

between Fort Lee and Fort Washington. On their way, they pounded the urban population of New York City with a terrifying two-hour cannonade that shrouded the city in smoke and panicked its occupants. The ships continued to sail some thirty miles upstream to Tappan Bay, near Tarrytown. The affair demonstrated the vulnerability to British warships of a town encircled by water.[387]

On the evening of the *Phoenix* and *Rose* bombardment, Washington and his officers noticed that the appearance of a new ship, HMS *Eagle*, had triggered delirious cheers from British soldiers aboard ships and encamped on Staten Island. From that, they deduced correctly that Admiral Howe had arrived.[388]

Howe Brothers Extend a Peace Offering

Still hopeful that their misguided American cousins could be restored to their senses, the Howe brothers came to North America bearing both peace and a sword. On July 17, they extended a parley to discuss restored peace. This offering was dismissed by General Washington as a ruse meant to "distract, divide, and create as much confusion as possible."[389]

British Make Their Move

On August 22, the British made their opening moves. In six hours, Admiral Howe efficiently ferried his brother's troops from Staten Island to Gravesend Bay, at the southwestern corner of Long Island, landing them below Greene's position on Brooklyn Heights. Unfortunately for the Americans, Greene had become seriously

---

387   Ibid.
388   Ibid.
389   Ibid.

ill and Washington replaced him with John Sullivan of New Hampshire. But soon

General Nathanael Greene
Courtesy of Biography.com

dissatisfied with Sullivan's performance, Washington put another New Englander, Israel Putnam of Connecticut, in his place. As a result, Washington had a commander in the field who had little knowledge of the local terrain.[390] As more American militiamen streamed into New York, Washington's army expanded to twenty-three thousand soldiers throughout the New York region, including Brooklyn, Manhattan, and Fort Washington, but many were untrained youths grabbed from shops and farms who would soon confront a highly professional military force.[391]

The American Position in Brooklyn

On Long Island, Putnam organized his position into two defensive lines. The first was on a heavily wooded rise called the Heights of Guan. The ridge ran roughly parallel to the East River, which lay behind the ridge. The heights consisted of a series of low hills running across Long Island at an oblique angle. These hills were easily passable only on four existing roads that cut through passes. After Washington transferred more men to Brooklyn Heights, the Americans defended three of the passes with three thousand men, but in a colossal strategic blunder, Putnam left the one on his left flank, Jamaica Pass, unprotected. That was all the advantage Howe needed.[392]

The Americans' second or main line of defense was manned by four thousand soldiers. This position lay across Brooklyn Heights, stretching almost a mile between Wallabout Bay and Gowanus Bay. Five strong points, forts with interconnecting trench works, anchored this line.[393]

British Attack

The British had devised an ingenious battle plan that envisioned a fantastic triple assault against the American forces. General Phillip von Heister's Hessians kept the American center busy while General James Grant's five thousand troops hit the American right. Then Howe's ten thousand soldiers would flank the American position on the Heights of Guan by marching through the unprotected Jamaica Pass, wrapping up the unprotected left flank of the Americans' first line of defense.

On the night of August 26, the British general personally took charge of the ten-

390   Myers.
391   Chernow, 244.
392   Myers.
393   Spivey, 131.

thousand-man right column, nearly half of his total twenty-two thousand attacking force. With a steady flow of information on the American defenses provided by Tory sympathizers, General Howe executed his battle plan. Under the leadership of Sir Henry Clinton, Lord Charles Cornwallis, Sir Hugh Percy and guided by local Tories, the British force moved through Jamaica Pass so it could fall upon the Americans from the rear. Early on the morning of August 27, cannons signaled the British to begin their attack all along the American front. Through bad intelligence, Washington incorrectly thought the main British assault would come on Manhattan and that Long Island was just a diversion. Retaining the majority of his men in Manhattan, he transferred ten battalions to Brooklyn, bringing total American troop strength to a paltry seven thousand men when the British attacked—with three times the numbers..[394]

Howe's surprise was complete. By 2 p.m. the Americans' first defensive line ceased to exist. To retreat from the ridge to their main defensive line, they had to fight their way through Howe's forces behind them. The Hessians moving in from the front and center attacked especially fiercely—sometimes bayoneting Americans trying to surrender.[395]

Americans Retreat

The day proved to be a disaster for the Americans, but it would have been even worse if not for the action of William Smallwood regiment of four hundred to five hundred men from Maryland, temporarily commanded by a young and capable major named Mordecai Gist. Although inexperienced, they were among the best and bravest troops that day. While under fierce attack, they made an orderly retreat to the Cortelyou House, a stone structure that commanded the Mill Dam Road and bridge, the only escape route across the Gowanus Salt Marsh.[396]

The American General William Alexander, who called himself Lord Stirling, , ordered Gist and his men to hold off the enemy while the other Americans withdrew across the Mill Dam Road. Not only did Gist's men hold off the British, they made six counterattacks before being forced to scatter and make their own individual ways back to the American lines. The British soon backed the Americans into a defensive position two miles across and about one mile deep on the shore of the East River.

Admiral Howe had a multi-part mission during the British attack: he was to sail up the East River, bombard the American position from the rear, provide cover for Grant as he attacked the American right using Gowanus Road along Brooklyn's western shore, keep the two wings of Washington's army divided between Manhattan and Brooklyn, and cut off an American retreat across the East River. Fortunately

394   Henry P. Johnson, *The Campaign of 1776 Around New York and Brooklyn* (Brooklyn: Long Island Historical Society 1878), 154.
395   Myers.
396   Ibid.

for Washington, the winds and current prevented Howe from sailing his fleet up the river to use his great firepower to wreak havoc on the Patriots. The Americans had their back to the river and the British army in their front, ready to pounce. Washington knew what would happen if the wind changed.[397]

The disheartened remnants of American units from the Heights of Guan flooded into the main Brooklyn Heights defenses, closely pursued by advancing British and Hessian formations. Heavy fighting broke out all along the line. The disorganized Americans could only wait for the final assault.[398]

The American casualty toll for the Battle of Brooklyn, also known as the Battle of Long Island, was grim: three hundred killed and another thousand taken prisoner, including, temporarily, Generals Stirling and Sullivan. If Washington stared into the abyss at any single moment of the war, it must have been as he contemplated the vast British force arrayed below him, poised to destroy his army forever.[399] General Howe had the Continental Army at his mercy, pinned against the East River. It appeared the American Revolution was about to conclude in abrupt fashion. Only a miracle could save the American cause—something akin to the parting of the Red Sea.[400]

First Miracle—Howe's Pause

Washington got his miracle. The miracle came in four parts. First, despite the urging of his subordinates who wanted to complete their victory, General Howe stopped his attack. Perhaps he feared a repeat of the costly and bloody victory he had won at Bunker Hill. His after-action report to Parliament reveals that he thought the American army "could be had at a cheap price," meaning he was thinking of a siege. The Howe brothers imagined that they could now deliver the final blow to Washington by slipping warships behind him in the East River, catching him in a vise between royal sailors and soldiers. William Howe's delay helped save Washington's army and the American cause. Historians have criticized Howe for his decision to stop the attack on Long Island. If he had pressed the offensive and successfully taken Brooklyn Heights, he would have destroyed or captured major elements of the Continental Army and most of its leaders, including George Washington.[401]

The American Escape

After the disaster on August 27, Washington remained on Long Island and reinforced his army until he had about ninety-five hundred troops in the Brooklyn defenses. On August 29, he finally began to realistically assess the danger of his

---

397   Ibid.
398   Spivey, 134.
399   Chernow, 248.
400   Hart, 288.
401   Spivey, 134.

New York Campaign
Courtesy of Mount Vernon Ladies' Association

situation.[402] He now called on Colonel John Glover of Massachusetts, who commanded one of the army's crack regiments. Glover's "Marvelous Men from Marblehead" were well trained and were seamen and fishermen, so they were accustomed to shipboard discipline and were quick to carry out orders. It was Washington's order for Glover to evacuate the ninety-five hundred men of the American army from Brooklyn. Glover was to ferry the troops across the East River at night, winding up the operation by dawn on the Manhattan side. Knowing Glover was just the man to get his army out of its desperate situation, Washington ordered every flat-bottomed

---

402   Ibid, 135.

boat and other craft fit for transportation of troops down to New York as soon as possible.[403]

Second Miracle—The Storm

The second miracle was the weather, which was still on Washington's side. Prevailing winds along the New York coast in August are normally from the southeast.[404] This would have been ideal for British naval operations in the East River. Yet a drenching storm with unfavorable northeast winds kept Admiral Howe's fleet out of the East River for two days, providing cover for Washington's boat gathering and escape. The August nights were short. Washington knew that if Glover had miscalculated the required time for the evacuation, he would lose any troops unlucky enough to remain on Long Island at dawn.

Colonel John Glover
**Courtesy of
revolutionarywar
archives.org**

The seamen began their work about ten o'clock at night. The drenched Continentals left their entrenchments unit by unit, moving to the boats in darkness and absolute silence. Each unit was told only that they were being relieved by other units and were going back to Manhattan. They did not know the entire army was doing the same thing. By the time any disloyal soldier discovered the truth, it would be too late for treachery. The quartermaster's men had found only a few sailing craft, so there was much rowing to be done that night.[405] At first the crossing was impeded by rough winds and only rowboats could be used, their oars covered with cloth to mute any sounds. In another piece of deceptive theater, Washington kept campfires going on Brooklyn Heights to conceal the evacuation.[406] Then the winds changed, favorable for swiftly making the round trip to Manhattan, despite darkness and unfamiliar waters. Seamen in the rowboats plied them back and forth without a stop, oars muffled, across the fast East River current.[407]

For several hours the situation looked favorable, but then the wind changed again, blowing in combination with an unusually strong ebb tide. The boats with sails could not overcome the two combined forces. Washington realized that many rearguard troops would still be on the island when dawn broke. Their loss would be a serious blow. At one point a rearguard unit under Edward Hand mistakenly received orders to move out of the defensive line and down to the river. Its movement left a gap in the lines that the British, had they been aware of it, could have used to

---

403   Myers.
404   Donald Barr Chidsey, *The Tide Turns: An Informal History of the Campaign of 1776 in the American Revolution* (New York: Crown Publishers, Inc, 1966), 41.
405   Ibid.
406   Chernow, 250.
407   Myers.

Retreat from Long Island by J.C. Armytage

smash through the American defenses. But the British didn't know, and Washington hurriedly ordered the unit back into position.[408]

Third Miracle—Mrs. John Repelye's Dispatch

During the night danger arose from still another quarter. Mr. and Mrs. John Repelye lived near the Brooklyn ferry landing. They were suspected by the Americans as being Loyalists—supporters of the British cause. The Americans even detained John Repelye to keep him from revealing the army's evacuation. That night, seeing a retreat in progress, Mrs. Repelye dispatched her black servant to inform the British commander or any officer he could find. Carefully working his way through the American lines, the servant was apprehended by a Hessian patrol. The Hessians could not understand English or any of the black man's message. The Hessians kept him under guard until the next morning when, too late, he finally found a British officer to receive his report.[409]

Mrs. Repelye's servant had a 75 percent chance of finding an Englishman during his night foray to warn of the American retreat. Instead he was detained by Hessians. Had he delivered his message to anyone who could understand it, or if the retreat had been discovered in any other way, the British could have easily attacked the thinly held defensive positions and routed the remaining American forces on Long Island.

---

408   Ibid.
409   Spivey, 137-138.

Fourth Miracle—The Fog

In a few more hours, Providence rejoined the Patriots' cause again. With another change of wind, Glover's men could again use their sails to speedily make the crossing and return. The tempo of the evacuation picked up, but the fickle wind had done its damage. As the dim first light appeared in the cloudy, gray eastern sky, part of the rear guard was still on the wrong side of the river. As the sky lightened, however, the fourth miracle presented itself. A dense fog rolled in, obscuring the operation's final movements. Colonel Benjamin Tallmadge was in one of the last units to leave. He stated that the fog was so thick that one could "scarcely discern a man at six yards distance."[410] The fog gave the Americans the additional time needed to remove their remaining forces from Long Island in daylight. When the morning fog began to lift and British patrols warily approached to check on the American breastworks, they found them empty. Washington and the last of the rear guard were aboard the boats and sailing to safety. In about nine hours Glover's men had whisked ninety-five hundred men, their supplies and cannon out from under the noses of the British. Not a single American died in this virtually flawless operation. The Revolutionary cause lived on. Later that day, August 30, ten British frigates and twenty gunboats and sloops finally sailed up the East River. They were too late.[411]

Aftermath

Morale plummeted throughout the colonies with news of Long Island. New recruits and supplies became even more difficult to obtain. The Battle of Long Island encouraged and emboldened Loyalists everywhere in their support of the Crown's advancing forces. However, it was not the total disaster that would end the war, as England had desired. The American army was not destroyed or captured; it lived to fight again.[412]

At this point in the war God seemed to be saying to America that freedom was not going to come easily or without a price. Like the Egyptians in the Exodus, the British were also not going to just let "their" colonies walk away. Some have argued that if England had let America go its own way at this point, there was a strong possibility that thirteen new independent nations would have been the result. That was not God's plan for America. There would be a struggle, and winning it would require unity and commitment to a common cause. God would mold the Americans together through these hardships, just as he did the Hebrew nation.[413]

---

410   Chernow, 250.
411   Myers.
412   Spivey, 139.
413   Ibid, 140-141.

Chapter 7

Trenton and Princeton

The Pennsylvania Militia have just broken in the face of heavy musket fire and grape shot. Suddenly, Washington appears among them urging them to rally and form a line behind him. A detachment of New England Continentals joins the line, which first holds and then begins to move forward with Washington front-and-center astride his white English charger. The British troops are placed behind a fence at the crest of a hill. Within fifty yards bullets begin to whistle and men in the front of the American line begin to drop. At thirty yards Washington orders a halt and both sides exchange volleys simultaneously. An aide, Colonel Edward Fitzgerald, covers his face with his hat, certain that his commander, so conspicuous a target, was cut down. But while men on both sides of him have fallen, Washington remains atop his horse, untouched. He turns toward Fitzgerald, takes his hand, and says: "Away my dear Colonel, and bring up the troops. The day is ours." And it was.

Details of the Battle of Princeton
William Stryker
His Excellency George Washington

U pon entering Manhattan from Long Island with his retreating army, Washington deployed his forces at Harlem Heights on the island's northern edge. There he waited for a chance to attack and if forced to withdraw, try to inflict heavy casualties on the British as he retreated. Many historians have noted that Washington's decision to linger on Manhattan was militarily inexplicable and tactically suicidal.[414] By leaving his army on the island, he was putting it in grave jeopardy. As the British ships HMS *Phoenix* and HMS *Rose* had demonstrated, the British fleet was capable of taking an assault force up the Hudson River to land almost anywhere north and in the rear of Washington's forces. If General Howe made such a move, he could trap the Americans, cutting them off from any possible retreat, and defeat them on his own timetable. By staying on Manhattan Island, Washington risked total disaster.[415]

---

414   Ellis, 96.
415   Bliven, 15.

Yet Washington intended to stay for one horrendously simple reason: he estimated that after their defeat on Long Island his troops were too demoralized to stand another major retreat. Even though his losses had been fairly heavy in the Battle of Brooklyn Heights, they were far less serious than the damage done to the Continental Army's self-esteem. As soon as the troops had escaped Brooklyn to the safety of Manhattan, Washington's militiamen had started to desert. They just vanished, walking out of their camps and departing for their homes. In some cases whole regiments had disappeared, almost as a body. Within a week, for example, the eight thousand men in the Connecticut Militia regiments were reduced to two thousand.[416]

Most of those who had deserted were short-enlistment men, drafted by their states for emergencies of just a few months at a time. The so-titled "Continental Militia" were the most poorly trained soldiers in the army. The deserters said their officers were incompetent, and quite a few of the officers were. They complained about the food, the supplies, and the lack of weapons. They were correct. Washington's procurement and supply system was in wretched shape.[417]

But the war was not quite lost and Washington's army, despite the low state of its morale, was still some distance from breaking up under the weight of disenchantment. The one chance he had to lift his force's spirts was not by a long, demoralizing retreat but by a successful battle.[418]

Howe's Inexplicable Maneuvers

Ultimately, both Washington's army and his life were spared, because General Howe also behaved inexplicably. Some historians have argued that Howe saw himself primarily as a peace negotiator instead of a general. For some unknown reason, despite having Washington on the run and potentially trapped, Howe did not close the trap around the Continental Army.

Battle of Kip's Bay

Most of Washington's generals thought New York City was strategically unimportant and should not be defended. But the commander in chief did not want to give the British such a large city as New York to provide a base of operations in America. Instead, he wanted to burn the city. While awaiting approval from the Continental Congress for that drastic action, Washington split his forces into three groups: one under Putnam in lower Manhattan to defend the city; one under Greene stretched across mid-Manhattan; and one under General William Heath to defend Harlem Heights and the King's Bridge. This crossed the Harlem River on the island's north end, and was the only escape available by land for the Continental Army.

---

416   Ibid, 15-16.
417   Ibid.
418   Ibid, 17.

On September 7, Washington received a response from Congress. He did not have to defend New York, but the city was not to be burned. Washington immediately started planning to pull his forces out of the city and consolidate them on Harlem Heights.

Before he could retreat from the city, on September 15, Howe sailed five ships up the East River to Kip's Bay, which extends between today's East 32nd and East 38th Streets. He also ferried over four thousand British troops across the river from Long Island. The five hundred green American militia defending the bay immediately fled for their lives, putting up no resistance. Howe quickly took the Post Road, which was to have been the route for the retreat of Putnam's lower Manhattan force, now trapped.

With Washington unable to stop the men fleeing from Kip's Bay, all General Howe had to do was march unopposed across the island to the Hudson River side. Washington would have lost all of the more than four thousand soldiers assigned to the city's defense. Instead, Howe established a beachhead and waited for his next wave of troops to cross the East River. While Howe idled, Putnam put his forces on the march and escaped the British trap, reaching the safety of Harlem Heights. Putnam saved his forces but did have to leave behind more than half the American artillery.

Battle of White Plains

On October 12, General Howe sent 150 ships up the East River, slipping through pea-soup fog, and deposited four thousand men on the boggy turf of Throg's Neck, a mainland peninsula on the Westchester shore. This marshy spot lay due east of Harlem Heights. Washington's thoughts again focused on how the British might entrap his embattled army by maneuvering into his rear. He could not take any chances and was forced to march another eighteen miles farther north, off Manhattan Island via the King's Bridge, to the village of White Plains.[419] He left two large detachments at Forts Washington and Lee on the Hudson. Howe followed Washington north and by the end of October they clashed at White Plains. Washington was defeated again, but was surprised that instead of finishing off his army, Howe turned back to take the river forts to his rear.[420] Even though Washington had ordered the evacuation of Fort Washington, near the present-day George Washington Bridge, Greene decided to defend it at all costs. That tactical blunder proved costly. When Fort Washington fell on November 16, all of its garrison, nearly three thousand Americans, were killed or captured.

Washington's Escape from Manhattan

With Howe preoccupied with Fort Washington, the remnant of Washington's army escaped across the Hudson at Peekskill. Unsure of Howe's further intentions,

419   Chernow, 257.
420   Rose, 40.

General Charles Cornwallis
Courtesy of Biography.com

Washington divided his forces. He left fifty-five hundred troops under Charles Lee north of New York City to guard the main routes into New England. Washington then took the remainder of his forces into New Jersey to guard against a British advance south to Philadelphia.[421]

Washington discovered that he now faced over ten thousand British and Hessian troops under the command of General Charles Cornwallis. New Jersey's defense escalated into a full retreat by the Americans .

Not much remained of the Continental Army. When John Hancock wrote Washington to inquire about his military intentions, Washington responded politely: "Give me leave to say Sir . . . that our Affairs are in a more unpromising way than you seem to apprehend . . . Your Army . . . is upon the eve of its political dissolution.'"[422]

Much like the dissatisfaction of the Hebrew nation during its years of wandering in the wilderness, and the people's desire to return to Egypt, more New York and New Jersey colonists were now signing up with the British, and signing British loyalty oaths, than with the American army.

Between desertions, combat losses and impending expiration of short-term enlistments, the old Continental Army was now effectively non-operational. Unless a new army could be raised "with all possible Expedition," Washington warned, "I think the game is pretty near up."[423] From August to November 1776 the strength of his army had fallen from twenty thousand to just three thousand. Half of those men had contracts that would expire at the end of December.[424] And as autumn advanced, Howe's chief lieutenant, Lord Cornwallis, relentlessly pursued Washington's army as it retreated through New Jersey.

Howe's Last Chance to Bag Washington

One of the distinctive customs of eighteenth and nineteenth century warfare was the belief that armies should not fight during the winter due to poor weather conditions. Many roads were impassable during winter months thus rendering the army unable to transport artillery and supplies.

Having botched his chance to trap Washington's decimated army on Manhattan, Howe now proceeded to miss another opportunity to hunt down the crippled residue of the Continental Army as it limped across New Jersey in November 1776. Howe chose instead to place his troops in winter quarters around Trenton, New Jersey while he returned to New York and into the arms of his mistress.[425] He had missed his last opportunity to bag Washington's army.

---

421 Ellis, 96
422 Ibid.
423 Ibid, 97.
424 Rose, 41.
425 Ellis, 97.

Washington's Thinking in December 1776

After retreating across New Jersey, Washington moved his remaining army across the Delaware River to the safe confines of Pennsylvania near Philadelphia. He, by all rights, should have welcomed the opportunity to hibernate in winter quarters like his British antagonists, lick his wounds from receiving four consecutive defeats, and reconstitute his American army. Yet Washington was still thinking offensively. He recognized that the entire movement for American independence was on the verge of extinction and might very well expire on its own over the winter. With over half of his force's terms of enlistment to expire at the end of 1776 and with their low morale, the possibility of raising another army in 1777 seemed an impossibility. He needed to "strike some Stroke."[426] He needed a victory.

Washington's Trenton Opportunity

Across the Delaware from where Washington was camped in Pennsylvania was the New Jersey town of Trenton. There was quartered a British force of some fourteen hundred Hessians under the command of Colonel Johann Rall. Rall had received warnings of Colonial movements, but his men were exhausted from being on round-the-clock alert for over a week.[427]

Washington planned a daring crossing of the Delaware and an assault on this Hessian garrison, starting his movements on Christmas night. He envisioned using his shrunken army of just twenty-four hundred in a three-pronged attack. A nineteen-hundred-man diversionary force under Colonel John Cadwalader would flank the Hessians at Trenton at the same time as a blocking move by General James Ewing's seven hundred men.[428]

Washington's main force would cross the Delaware at McKonkey's Ferry, some nine miles north of Trenton, and would march that distance to strike the Hessians at first light. Colonel Cadwalader would cross the river near Burlington, New Jersey. His role was to harass and prevent British and Hessian units near Burlington from racing north to support the Hessians at Trenton. Ewing's force was to cross at Trenton and take up defensive positions along Assunpink Creek and bridge to cut off a Hessian escape. For attacking a defended position, Washington's force was not overwhelming. Most army commanders would prefer a three-to-one advantage for such an attack. Washington was betting on the Christmas holiday celebrations, darkness, and secrecy. He also received help from some of the worst weather on record, which added a degree of safety, but also untold misery, to the undertaking. No commander in his right mind would attack under such miserable weather conditions.

426   Ibid.
427   Ellis, 98.
428   History.com Staff, "Battles of Trenton and Princeton," *History.com*, A+E Networks , 2009, http://www.history.com/topics/american-revolution/battles-of-trenton-and-princeton. (May 25, 2018).

The Hessians

Colonel Rall's Hessians had fought the Americans at Fort Washington, and witnessed their surrender six weeks earlier. Rall and his troops were self-confident and had an unfavorable opinion of their American enemy. After arriving in Trenton, Rall planned to cross the Delaware River to attack Philadelphia but found the river frozen and impassible. He was constantly fighting small bands of rebels that threatened his lines of communications. Daily, he sent out patrols that encountered and exchanged fire with Colonials. His low opinion of Washington's army led him to ignore his superior's advice to set up fortifications. Rall was heard to proclaim: "Let them come! We want no trenches! We'll at them with the bayonet."[429]

Early Warnings

Rall started receiving reports of rebel activity several days before Christmas. On December 23, Doctor William Bryant, who lived near Trenton, sought out the German, colonel to inform him of a report from a black man who had just crossed the river. His information revealed that rebels were drawing rations and preparing to attack Trenton.[430] On Christmas day, the British General James Grant, who was stationed at Princeton, forwarded an intelligence report warning of an attack that day. Because of extreme weather, Rall downplayed the warning, but did ensure that one of his three regiments was prepared and on alert.

Unforeseen Diversion

Around 7 p.m. on Christmas day, an exchange of musket fire broke out north of Trenton. Rall received reports that his outpost on Pennington Road was being attacked. He immediately assembled the regiment that was on alert and sent out reinforcements. Soon new reports came in that some thirty rebels had attacked the outpost, wounded six of his men, but broke off their attack after the first exchange of fire. Afterwards, Rall's patrols found nothing. Rall rejected subordinates' recommendations for more extensive patrols. Unfortunately for him, he assumed the American attack his intelligence reports had predicted had just occurred. Rall returned to Trenton to continue his Christmas merriment and because of the miserable weather, stood down his troops to quarters. Rall himself joined a Christmas party at the home of one Abraham Hunt, where he played cards and drank well into the night.[431]

Rall's Last Warning

That evening a Tory farmer from Bucks County, Pennsylvania approached and knocked on the door of Hunt's house, where Rall was reveling. A house servant would not allow the colonel to be disturbed, so the farmer proceeded to write

429   Spivey, 151.
430   Ibid.
431   Ibid, 152.

a message. It said the entire American army was crossing the river on its way to Trenton. The servant delivered the message to Rall, who could not read English. He felt no urgency to seek a translator, having already fended off what he thought was the foreseen Christmas attack and the weather steadily getting worse. Instead, he tucked the message into his pocket, unread, and continued playing cards.[432]

Washington Crosses the Delaware River

Completely unaware that the mysterious attack on the Pennington Road and the terrible weather had fooled Rall into thinking no further attack was forthcoming, Washington had commenced his crossing of the Delaware River as darkness fell on Christmas day. He called on Colonel Glover and the same brigade of Massachusetts boatmen who had rescued the army from its trap on Long Island. Their task was to negotiate the ice-filled eight-hundred-foot width of the river. Glover used locally procured flat-bottom freight scows called Durham boats to ferry Washington's troops and artillery to the New Jersey bank. This was through a storm of wind, sleet, and snow that caused immense suffering among the ill-clad troops.[433] Neither Colonel Cadwalader's nor General Ewing's forces were able to make their planned crossings that night due to the river conditions at their locations.

Washington's plan was to have completed the crossing by midnight. That would have allowed for the march to Trenton in time for a pre-dawn attack. This plan fell dramatically behind schedule. His forces weren't all across the Delaware until 4 a.m. Every man was bone chilled, half frozen, completely soaked, and not even certain their muskets would fire. They had also lost the cover of darkness for their march on Trenton.[434] Yet they proceeded on.

The Advance and Attack on Trenton

The nine miles to Trenton proved a distressing ride for Washington. His army was only halfway there when the first sunlight wanly colored the sky at 6 a.m. The advance followed two roads. General John Sullivan's, Division followed River Road to the west of Trenton. Nathanael Greene's, division used the Pennington Road to the north. As both divisions plodded on through a new wave of sleet and swirling snow, a messenger from Sullivan, informed Washington that his men's soaked weapons were now useless. "Tell the general to use the bayonet," Sullivan, said. Washington galloped along the lines, trying to speed the march's pace in the brightening morning light. "Press on," he urged the men. "Press on, boys!"[435]

By eight o'clock on the morning of December 26, the Continental Army started its attack on the city. Strangely, the Americans still enjoyed the element of

432   Ibid, 154.
433   Ibid.
434   Ibid.
435   Chernow, 275.

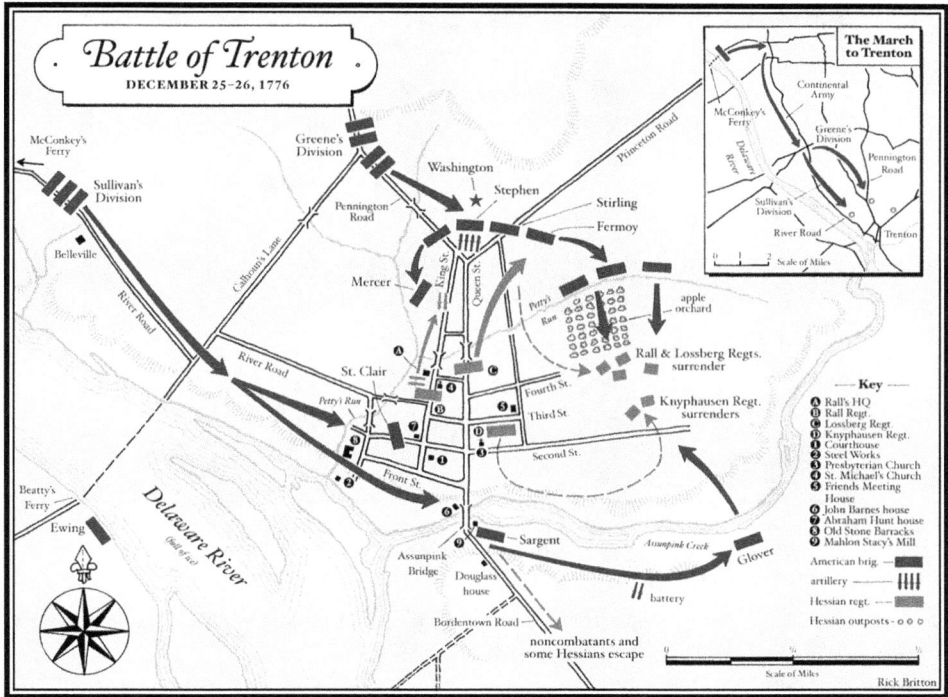

Battle of Trenton
Courtesy of Mount Vernon Ladies' Association

surprise despite the enemy having gotten, and squandered, several accurate warnings, and despite Washington having lost the cover of darkness. As the infantry charged, artillery began to fire and the Hessians awakened, responding in total confusion.

As the German mercenaries began forming ranks for the fight, the Americans entered the city at two points, Sullivan's troops from the west and Greene's from the north. Those Hessians who managed to get organized were able to fight only piecemeal, isolated, engagements.

Andreas von Wiederholdt, a Hessian lieutenant, incorrectly reported to Rall that the Continental Army had surrounded Trenton, leaving no route for retreat. As a result, Rall decided to counterattack rather than withdraw across Assunpink Creek. The American artillery proved decisive, coming into action at the heads of the two main streets. The cannon fire boomed down King and Queen Streets, breaking up the attempted Hessian counterattacks. Washington's forces overpowered the Hessians. Rall, his body riddled with bullets, "reeled in the saddle" before being rescued from his horse and carried to a church, mortally wounded.[436] Many of his soldiers broke ranks, fleeing from the fighting. Rall's normally disciplined regiment was confused and disoriented. Without their commander, the Germans retreated to an orchard

---

436   Ibid, 276.

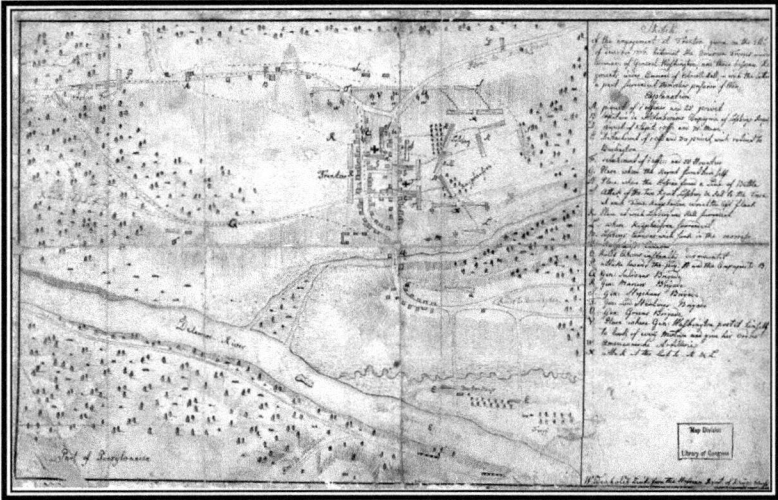

Hessian Andreas Wiederholdt's Trenton Battle Map
Library of Congress

east of town where they were forced to surrender.[437] By nine o'clock, Hessian units were surrendering or fleeing to the south. The battle was over.

Aftermath

In a little less than one hour of fighting the Continental Army captured nearly nine hundred Hessian officers and soldiers, as well as a large supply of muskets, bayonets, swords, and cannons. The Americans inflicted nearly one hundred casualties.[438] Several hundred Hessians escaped before the town was totally encircled. The Patriots also took possession of forty hogsheads of rum. Although Washington ordered the rum to be drained onto the ground, many of his men could not resist the comfort of the warming liquor. Many became intoxicated.[439] The Americans had lost two men frozen during the night. Two American officers and one enlisted man had been wounded. As Rall lay dying, someone found in his pocket the note warning of the American attack that the Bucks County farmer had written the previous evening. When someone informed Rall of its contents he said, "If I had read this . . . I would not be here now."[440] No doubt if he had read the note the outcome would have been dramatically different for the Americans.

---

437   Cody Lass, "Battle of Trenton," *George Washington's Mount Vernon Digital Encyclopedia,* www.mountvernon.org/library.digitalhistory/digital-encyclopedia/article.battle-of-trenton. (May 28, 2018)
438   Spivey, 154.
439   Chernow, 276.
440   Spivey, 154.

Washington's Next Move

After the Hessian surrender at Trenton, Washington focused his attention on his next moves. He assembled his officers to discuss the army's options. Should it attack another British post, hold its current position in Trenton or retreat back across the Delaware River to the safety of Pennsylvania? Washington, recognizing the frigid weather and the wobbly state of his drunken troops, decided the best option was to return across the river to their camps in Pennsylvania.

The Continental Army was exhausted. The men had marched and fought for two straight days through rain, snow, sleet, and hail. Washington knew they needed rest. He also understood that doing nothing was even more dangerous. As a result, once the army was safely back in camp, he shifted his focus to planning another engagement.[441] Headquartered in the "old yellow house" of the widow Hannah Harris, Washington convened a war council on December 27. During that meeting, incoming news forced his hand.

Washington's intelligence indicated that the British and Hessian forces in New Jersey were spread out across the state. He believed that taking up a position in northern New Jersey would encourage recruitment of the local militia and make British positions to the south untenable. He also received word that Cadwalader had finally crossed into New Jersey with eighteen hundred militiamen on the 27th. Despite his doubts about another river crossing, Washington did not want to leave Cadwalader stranded. He also wanted to prove that his previous crossing had not been a fluke. The war council made its decision: to strike Trenton again.[442]

Holding His Army Together

Embarrassed at the Trenton defeat, Howe sent Generals Cornwallis and Grant from New York with superior forces, ordered to attack Washington's army and to stabilize New Jersey.

On December 28, Washington ordered militia units in northern New Jersey to stymie the British and slow their advance by "harassing their flanks and rear." A day later, he started crossing the Delaware again. This time he used some eight crossing points and took twice as many cannon. A fresh sheet of ice slowed the boats, delaying the operation. Washington himself didn't cross until December 30. He stationed his forces on a secure slope behind Assunpink Creek, the narrow but fast-moving stream at the southern end of Trenton.[443]

With enlistments expiring at the end of the year, Washington had to persuade his men to stay on or his army would disintegrate before his eyes. Congress granted him extraordinary powers for six months, allowing him to recruit new troops by

441   Lass.
442   Chernow, 277.
443   Ibid.

paying bounties, to commandeer provisions, and even to arrest vendors who wouldn't accept Continental currency.

By crossing the Delaware and camping at Trenton, Washington made it difficult for his men to decamp when their enlistments ended. He mustered all his hortatory powers to retain his men. On December 30, he ordered an unruly New England regiment to be lined up before him. Sitting erect on his horse, he made an impassioned appeal, asking them to extend their service by six weeks and offering each a ten-dollar bounty. As one sergeant recalled, Washington "told us our services were greatly needed and that we could do more for our country than we ever could at any future date and in the most affectionate manner entreated us to stay."[444]

At first no volunteers stepped forward. One vocal soldier spoke up and recounted their shared sacrifices and how much they had dreamed of heading home. Pulling up his horse, Washington turned around and rode along the entire line of men. He stated:

> "My brave fellows, you have done all I asked you to do and more than could be reasonably expected. But your country is at stake, you wives, your houses, and all that you hold dear . . . If you consent to stay on a month longer, you will render that service to the cause of liberty and to your country which you probably can never do under any other circumstances."[445]

When the drums finished rumbling out the roll call, the Patriot volunteers stepped forward. Washington had held on to more than three thousand men.

The British Movement and Initial Attack on Trenton

Cornwallis had amassed some eight thousand men at Princeton with plans to attack Washington at Trenton. Towards sundown January 2, 1777, Washington spotted the lead elements of Cornwallis' army. From their position on the slope behind Assunpink Creek, American snipers fired at Hessians from Cornwallis' force as they marched through Trenton on King and Queen streets. An advance force of Continental soldiers waded back across the creek; others fell back across a stone bridge.

The British and Hessians made three courageous attempts to take the bridge over Assunpink Creek, but were repulsed each time by American artillery. "The bridge looked red as blood," wrote Sergeant Joseph White, "with their killed and wounded and red coats."[446] Despite the British setback at the bridge, they had discovered a ford

---

444   Ibid, 278.
445   Philander D. Chase, ed., *The Papers of George Washington,* Revolutionary War Series, vol 7, *21 October 1776 – 5 January 1777* (Charlottesville: University Press of Virginia, 1997), 490-491.
446   Chernow, 280.

that led to the vulnerable American right flank. This made the American position untenable. Washington was outnumbered and had no escape strategy. As daylight drew to a close, the British conferred about whether to postpone their main attack. "If Washington is the general I take him to be," Sir William Erskine said, "he will not be found in the morning." An overly confident Cornwallis disputed this assertion. "We've got the old fox safe now," he supposedly said. "We'll go over and bag him in the morning."[447]

Washington was now worried that the superior British force might encircle his men. Again it appeared that he, like Moses, was trapped with his back against the "Red Sea." Any attempt to escape across the ice-choked Delaware River could be costly.

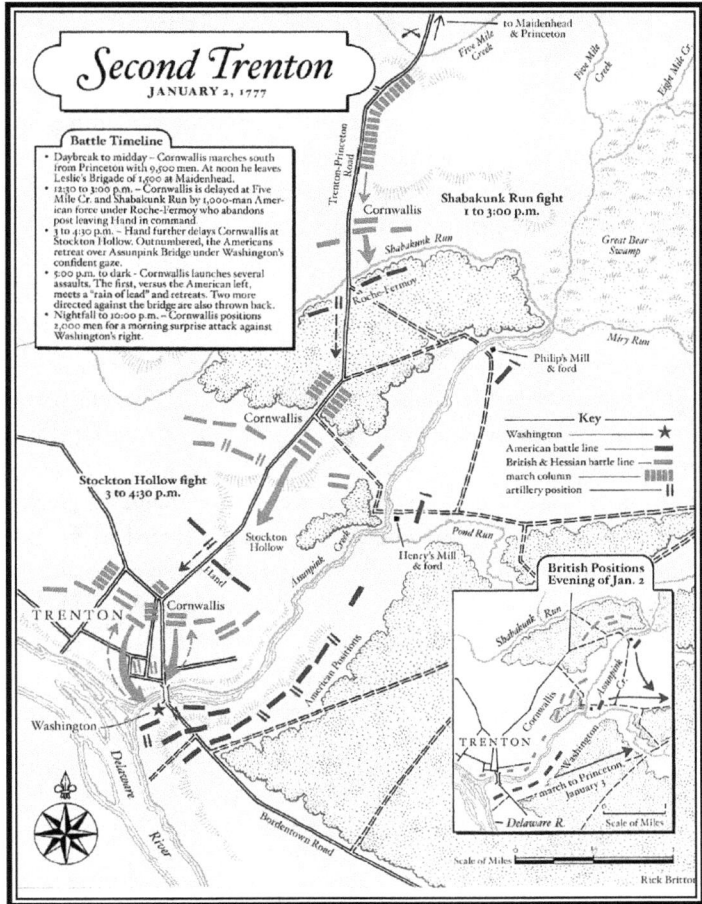

Second Battle of Trenton
Courtesy of Mount Vernon Ladies' Association

Washington's Escape

Washington decided to slip away during the night. But instead of retreating back across the Delaware or to positions farther south into New Jersey and away from the British threat, he would advance around the British left flank on rarely used roads. That would allow an attack on the British forces that had remained behind to

---

447   Ibid.

secure Princeton. This was both daring and brilliant. Daring, in that the risky strategy meant penetrating deep into enemy territory, possibly to be trapped there. Brilliant, in that Washington's strategy turned a defensive maneuver into an offensive one unexpected by the British.

Washington's movement was parallel to the British lines, leaving it susceptible to detection. To conceal his nighttime advance on Princeton, Washington used the same methods of concealment and trickery he used at Brooklyn. He left behind a rear guard of five hundred soldiers to keep campfires burning throughout the night. This left the British with the impression the army had settled in for the night. Washington's "rear guard" also made loud noises to reflect the routines of an army in camp. They chopped down trees, as if creating obstructions; dug into the ground, to create the impression of entrenching; and banged pots and pans, as if cooking and serving rations. Washington's march started after midnight. The wheels of his artillery were wrapped in cloth to deaden the sound. Torches were extinguished. Officers enforced strict noise discipline among the troops. No talking or commands were allowed above a whisper.

As the army prepared to move out, a major obstacle to Washington's plan disappeared. Early in the evening, the wind shifted to the northwest, which helped conceal the noise of a moving army. Also, the temperature began to fall, freezing the roads hard. The wagons and artillery could move easily again, making good time. The weather was a mixed blessing. The wind and temperature added misery for the troops. Marching the twelve miles from Trenton to Princeton during the night and early morning, Washington's men were pushed almost beyond human endurance.

> "It was a long harrowing march down dark country lanes congealed with ice. The weary men wrapped in a numb trance, some barely awake, padded against stinging winds; many fell asleep standing up whenever the column halted."[448]

Seeking Enemy Intentions

To learn the enemy's intentions, Washington had ordered Cadwalader to send out patrols and seek information on British forces and plans. "Spare no pains or expense to get intelligence of the enemy's motions and intentions . . . Every piece of intelligence you obtain worthy of notice, send it forward by express . . . ."[449]

Cadwalader's efforts bore fruit in the form of a detailed, handwritten map of the British deployments around Princeton. Washington received this map while on the march. Cadwalader had drawn it from information reportedly obtained by

448   Chernow, 280.
449   "10 Facts about the Battle of Princeton," *George Washington's Mount Vernon*, www.mountvernon.org/george-washington/the-revolutionary-war/ten-facts-about-the-revolutionary-war/10-facts-about-the-battle-of-princeton/. (May 30, 2018).

an unnamed Princeton college student who had observed the positions around the town. The information passed to Washington indicated that the British had established defensive lines on the west side of town, but the east side was open to attack. His plan was to march his army and strike the town using roads below a bluff to the south of Princeton.

When Washington arrived at Princeton shortly after dawn, the temperature was 21 degrees Fahrenheit with "shin deep snow." His troops immediately set to repairing a bridge over Stony Brook to the south of town. He divided his forces into two groups: Sullivan's Division veered northeast while Greene's moved north.

Battle of Princeton

The first engagement almost did not happen. British Lieutenant Colonel Charles Mawhood was in the process of marching two units, the 17th and 55th Regiments of Foot, to Trenton to support Cornwallis, when to his surprise he spotted the Americans approaching Princeton.

Colonel John Cadwalader's Princeton Battle Map
Library of Congress

Mawhood immediately turned his forces around and engaged the Americans under General Hugh Mercer, part of Greene's Division. Mercer had been sent on a mission to destroy a bridge that led to Trenton on the Continental Army's left. Mawhood ordered a bayonet charge from his position on the William Clark farm's orchard. The charge staggered Mercer's men. Mercer himself was knocked off his horse and given a merciless bayonet stabbing while he lay on the ground. The British had mistaken the handsome and well-dressed Mercer for Washington and

Death of American General Hugh Mercer at Princeton by John Trumbull

mauled him repeatedly, carving seven gashes, until he lay near death.[450] Mercer was a physician from Fredericksburg, Virginia and a personal friend of Washington. This was a disturbing preview of what would happen if Washington should be captured. Mercer would later die from his wounds.

After Mercer's men began their retreat before the British bayonets, Greene directed the Pennsylvania Militia into the battle to stem the British onslaught. They too panicked amid Mercer's fleeing men and "a shower of grapeshot."[451] Washington himself stopped the panic by riding to the front and exhorting his rattled men to stand and fight. "Parade with us, my brave fellows!" he exclaimed, while waving his hat. "There is but a handful of the enemy, and we will have them directly."[452]

Washington rallied the men with an act of incredible bravery. He reined in his horse, faced the enemy directly in front of the American forces, and simply froze. While the British entrenched beyond a hillside fence, Washington strengthened and lengthened the American line and instructed his men not to fire until ordered to do so. He then led his forces up the hill, halting only when they had pushed to within thirty yards of the British. As he gave the command to fire, Washington on his white horse was the largest and most visible target on the field. Washington's aide, Colonel John Fitzgerald, clapped his hat over his eyes to conceal from his sight what he was sure would be the general's mortal wounding. But when the smoke cleared from the fusillade of bullets, Fitzgerald saw Washington, untouched, sitting commandingly

---

450   Chernow 281.
451   Ibid.
452   Ibid.

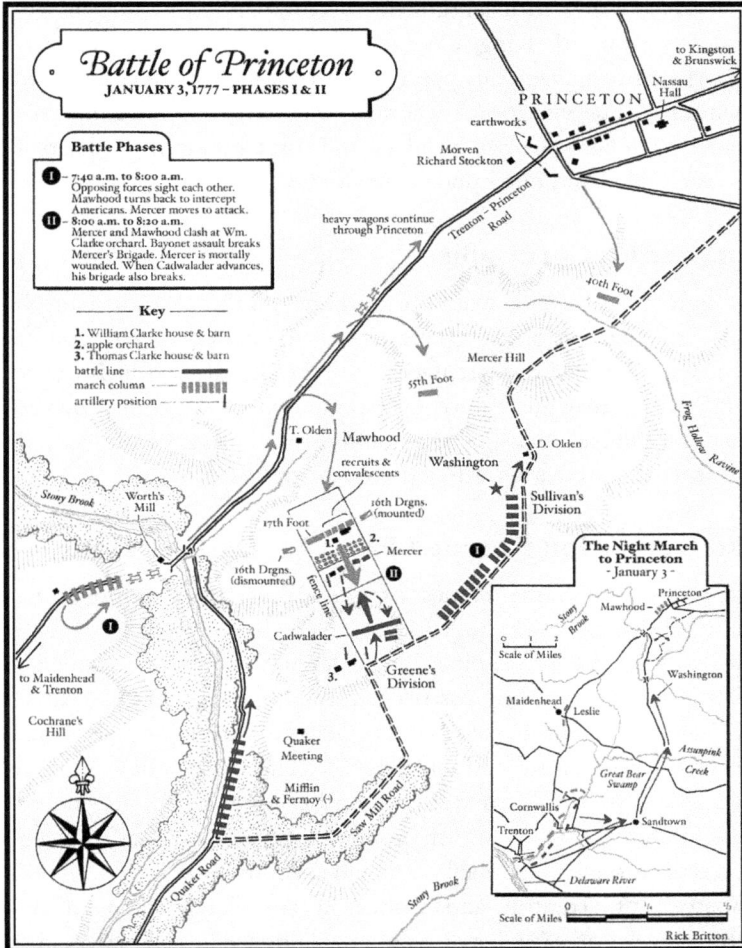

BATTLE OF PRINCETON—FIRST PHASES
COURTESY OF MOUNT VERNON LADIES' ASSOCIATION

atop his horse. "Thank God, your Excellency is safe!" Fitzgerald said to Washington, almost weeping with relief. Washington, unfazed, took his hand fondly. "Away, my dear colonel, and bring up the troops. The day is our own!"[453] In the heavy fighting, American units drove the British back, splitting their force. Some of the British retreated toward Trenton while others moved toward New Brunswick.

In the battle's final phase, two hundred British troops fortified the principal building of the College of New Jersey, Nassau Hall. Firing from this strong point, the British intended to hold off the Americans until a relief party arrived. The Americans positioned cannon around the building and soon began firing on it and

---

453   Ibid, 282.

its occupants. According to legend, artillery commanded by Alexander Hamilton decapitated a portrait of King George II with a cannonball. Outgunned and surrounded, the British eventually presented a white flag of surrender from one of the hall's windows. The victorious Americans had inflicted more than five hundred casualties and taken between two hundred and three hundred prisoners. Only forty Americans were killed and one hundred wounded.[454]

Outmaneuvering Cornwallis

Knowing that Cornwallis would respond to the threat to his rear, Washington ordered his exhausted troops to march to the wooded hill country around Morristown, New Jersey. Outmaneuvered, Cornwallis arrived in Princeton only to witness the Patriots' rear guard moving out of town. Cornwallis then marched to New Brunswick, thinking Washington would threaten that British base. Washington again had outmaneuvered and outfoxed the British hounds.

American Revolution Rescued From Its Darkest Hour

By December 1776 the flames of the American Revolution were almost extinguished. The states of New York and New Jersey were clearly in the hands of the British. The American capital, Philadelphia, was in panic, expecting a British invasion. The Continental Congress packed up and fled, giving its last instruction: ". . . until Congress shall otherwise order, General Washington shall be possessed of full power to order and direct all things."[455] The Continental Army had all but disappeared and what remained would soon be gone, by the beginning of 1777. Most of the soldier' terms of enlistment would expire by January 1. Many on both sides of the issue thought the rebellion would soon be over.

The battles of Trenton and Princeton completely changed this picture. Suddenly, the citizens of New Jersey were retaliating against the Hessian and British troops who had abused them during their months of occupation. British supply and troop movements were harassed by local militia everywhere. Except for a couple of outposts, Howe had to abandon most of New Jersey.[456] Congress moved back to Philadelphia, recruitment for the Continental Army became easier to sell and commissary officers found it easier to find and collect food for the army.

Washington deserves credit for this amazing turn of events. He exhibited great generalship in these battles and was determined to do whatever was necessary to alter the course of a losing effort. Frederick the Great of Prussia, who had seen his share of near-disasters and miraculous victories, would call the ten days from

454 Spivey, 159.
455 Susie Federer, *Miracles in American History 32 Amazing Stories of Answered Prayer* (Virginia Beach Virginia: Amerisearch Inc, 2017), 51.
456 Spivey, 160.

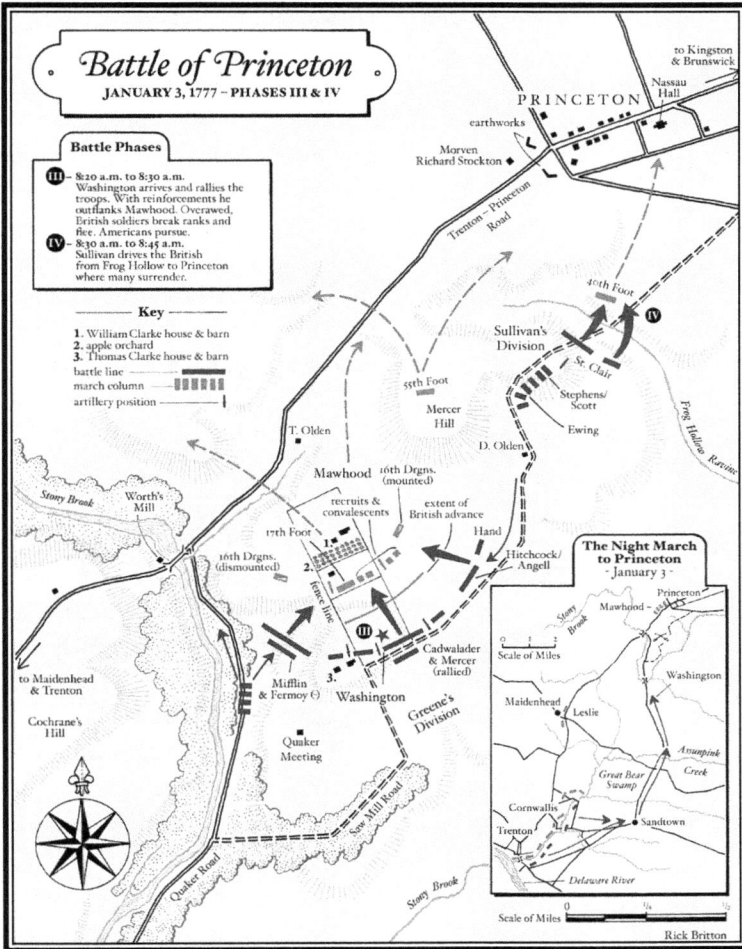

Battle of Princeton—Final Phases
Courtesy of Mount Vernon Ladies' Association

December 26, 1776, to January 3, 1777, "the most brilliant in the world's history."[457] However, Washington took several risks that jeopardized his army. Except for the protection of God's providential hand at critical moments, he would have lost his army and jeopardized the Revolution in 1776. Was this the hand of God driving world events or just plain luck? Consider these events.

Mysterious Attack at Trenton

The Hessians had been warned and were on alert for an attack from the Americans on Christmas day 1776. The seven o'clock attack on the Hessians along

---

the Pennington Road on Trenton's north side was not part of Washington's diversion plan. Washington never ordered such an attack. No one knows for certain who the attackers were or where they came from. Some historians contend that a patrol from a Virginia regiment made that probe. Others surmise it was that local farmers on a rampage over some grievance with the unpopular Hessians. [458] Their identity is not as important as the attack's incredible timing. It caused the Hessian commander, Rall, to respond, and once suppressed, it lulled him into a false sense of security. He thought he had turned away the Christmas day attack that British intelligence had forecast. With the weather deteriorating and the threat subdued, Rall returned his men to their quarters. Washington and all his forces were still on the Pennsylvania side of the Delaware, just starting their crossing. Had the mysterious attack not happened, the Hessians would have remained been on alert and could have easily spotted the American forces as they marched in broad daylight toward Trenton.

The Unopened Warning

Later the evening after the mysterious attack, Rall got another warning of Washington's approach. The Bucks County Tory farmer tried to tell him the rebels were crossing in force. He was denied access to the colonel, who was enjoying his Christmas festivities. Undeterred, the farmer wrote his warning, which was delivered to Rall. Not knowing English, Rall did not bother even to have the warning translated. He placed it in his pocket where it was discovered while he was dying from a wound in the next day's battle. Rall was a professional officer, not considered lazy or inefficient. He had a successful combat record. This unusual lapse can be best understood as another miracle protecting Washington's army during its most vulnerable moment.[459]

Favorable Weather

As at Boston and Long Island, the weather favored the American cause at Trenton and Princeton. Although the terrible weather for Washington's Christmas night crossing of the Delaware subjected his forces to miserable conditions—two were frozen to death—it was also instrumental in giving the Hessian commander a false sense of security. How could any appreciable military force maneuver in such weather? How could any commander order such a maneuver under those conditions? Such questions probably went through Rall's mind. His answer was certainly different than that of George Washington. Rall's actions concerning the readiness of his forces on December 25 and 26 reflected his own thinking, not that of his adversary. That flawed thinking cost him his command and his life.

On January 2, Cornwallis was mired in mud on his slow advance to Trenton.

458   Ibid, 162.
459   Ibid, 162-163.

It was an unseasonably warm day. Where normally frozen roads would be available to easily transport his artillery and supplies, on this day the ice had thawed and the roads turned to mud. If Cornwallis had arrived earlier in the day, Washington's weak position on the Assunpink Creek would have been even weaker. A battle on that day in that place would have been disastrous for the Americans. Cornwallis had already discovered where his men could ford the creek on the American right. Had Cornwallis a couple more hours of daylight, he certainly would not have decided to postpone the attack until the next day. The unseasonable temperatures and muddy roads caused his delay and forced his engagement at the Second Battle of Trenton to begin late in the day. That allowed the opportunity for the Americans to escape—which they did.

When the Americans maneuvered out of their positions behind Assunpink Creek and marched the twelve miles to Princeton, they were not bogged down as the British had been, as the weather again turned in their favor with a dramatic drop in temperature. The roads froze again, and Washington marched away to Princeton. The wind also changed directions, just as it had at Boston, to blow any sounds from his marching army away from his enemies' inquisitive ears. Washington's army made good time in its march to Princeton, with enough time to defeat the British rear guard and depart before Cornwallis could respond. If the Continentals had arrived later in the day, they could have again faced Cornwallis' entire force and a disastrous battle. The weather muddying the roads for the British and freezing them for the American movements played a significant role in the outcomes at both Second Trenton and Princeton.

Princeton Battle Map

While Washington was making his escape from behind Assunpink Creek, he had the great good fortune to have delivered to him a map that showed all the British positions at Princeton. From this map, he knew where to strike—and where not. Had he not received this invaluable intelligence, the outcome at Princeton could have been dramatically different. He might have attacked the fortified British positions instead of their undefended rear. This would have resulted in a stubborn resistance, requiring more time to subdue Princeton's British defenders. That would have given Cornwallis time to arrive from Trenton and to attack Washington from the rear with devastating effect.

Again, Untouched in Combat

Not only did God protect the American army at Princeton, but Washington himself. When Washington, on horseback, rallied his men from retreat and moved them forward to counterattack, he presented himself as the largest target on the field of battle. He personally sat upon his horse between the American and British forces, whose ranks were only thirty yards apart, then gave the order to fire. It is impossible to imagine anyone surviving that exchange of fire. Yet when the smoke cleared, there sat Washington. It was much like the Battle of the Monongahela in the French and Indian War, where every officer on horseback was killed or wounded, yet Washington was untouched—as if the hand of God protected him.

Could all these events be attributed to acts of good fortune? Or was there something else at play: something like acts of Divine Providence? Here is what the president of Yale, Ezra Stiles, stated before the Connecticut General Assembly:

> "In our lowest and most dangerous estate . . . we sustained ourselves
> against the British Army of sixty thousand troops, commanded by . . .
> the ablest generals Britain could produce throughout Europe, with a
> naval force of twenty-two thousand seamen in above eighty men-of-
> war . . . Independence . . . was sealed and confirmed by God Almighty
> in the victory of General Washington at Trenton, and in the surprising
> movement and battle of Princeton . . . Who but a Washington, inspired
> by Heaven, could have struck out the great movement and maneuver of
> Princeton? . . . The United States are under peculiar obligations to become
> a holy people unto the Lord our God."[460]

Just as God sustained and protected the Israelites on their journey in the wilderness, he too sustained and protected Washington and the Continental Army at Trenton and Princeton.

---

460   Federer, 53.

Chapter 8

Saratoga

"The fortunes of war have made me your prisoner," said British General John Burgoyne as he handed over his sword to his American counterpart, Horatio Gates. "I shall always be ready to testify that it was through no fault of your excellency," Gates replied.

Benson Bobrick
Angel in the Whirlwind

The American victory at Saratoga is often seen as the turning point in the war for American independence. Not only did it renew the morale of the American public after its capital, Philadelphia, had been captured, it convinced potential foreign partners, such as France, that America could win the war, and that it might be in their best interest to send aid.

At the beginning of 1777 Washington positioned his army around Morristown, New Jersey. Howe, in command of all British forces in America, remained in New York City with forces that included a naval component able to strike anywhere on the Eastern Seaboard. The British government devised a plan for 1777 to send a strong army down the Lake Champlain-Lake George-Hudson River waterway from Canada into New York, the heart of the rebellious American colonies, to isolate New England. This plan would achieve command of the Hudson River, demoralize the Americans and deter any potential allies, such as the French. The plan would become known as the British Grand Strategy. This had been one of Howe's chief goals, part of his rationale for taking New York City in 1776.

But the Grand Strategy was doomed to failure before it commenced. It failed and became the biggest disaster for the British during the American Revolution, not because it was a bad plan or because of the actions of the British military and their commanders in the field—although they were complicit. This strategy was defeated primarily by the inaction of the leaders in London.

Normal responsibility for such an expedition would have fallen to the governor of Canada, Sir Guy Carleton, who had experience at campaigning in North America. Instead, Lord George Germain, the minister in London with direct control over British war policy, persuaded King George III to appoint Major-General John Burgoyne.

Burgoyne, who had returned to England after fighting in America in the winter of 1776-77, had lobbied specifically for the plan and the opportunity to lead the campaign.

> "I have always thought Hudson's River the most proper part of the whole continent for opening vigorous operations. Because the course of the river, so beneficial for conveying all the bulky necessaries of an army, is precisely the route that an army ought to take for the great purposes of cutting the communications between the Southern and Northern Provinces, giving confidence to the Indians, and securing a junction with the Canadian forces. These purposes effected, and a fleet upon the coast, it is to me morally certain that the forces of New England must be reduced so early in the campaign to give you battle upon your terms, or perish before the end of it for want of necessary supplies," said Burgoyne[461]

John Burgoyne

Burgoyne was fifty-five years old, the scion of an old Lancashire family. He had thirty years of military service and was a member of Parliament. Burgoyne was representative of the upper-class county families who dominated the political, social, and military life of eighteenth-century England. Intelligent, handsome, and humane, he was popular with his troops, who gave him the name "Gentleman Johnny." He also had the less attractive traits of vanity and excessive ambition that, as we will see, were exploited to his detriment during his upcoming campaign.[462]

The Grand Strategy Plan

The plan consisted of three components. First, Burgoyne was to travel down Lake Champlain via boat and recapture Fort Ticonderoga. Then he would advance to the Hudson River via Lake George and progress south to Albany, New York, arriving there before winter weather arrived. Second, a force assigned to Major General Henry Clinton would advance north from New York City, up the Hudson River, to join Burgoyne at Albany. Third, Colonel Barry Saint Leger would advance east down the Mohawk River from Lake Erie with a diversionary force, also joining Burgoyne at Albany.[463]

British Confusion

The plan became somewhat confused when on February 23, 1777, Lord Germain received a letter from Howe, written on December 20, indicating an

---

461   John Luzader, *Decision on the Hudson, The Battles of Saratoga* (Fort Washington, Pa: Eastern National), 2002, 7.

462   Ibid.

463   "Battle of Saratoga," *BritishBattles.com,* https://www.britishbattles.com/war-of-the-revolution-1775-1783/battle-of-saratoga/, (June 5, 2018).

unexpected change of mind. Howe now proposed focusing his main effort for 1777 on Philadelphia, the rebel capital. Referring to the Grand Strategy, he stated, "There may be a corps to act defensively upon the lower part of the Hudson River to cover Jersey on that side, as well as, to facilitate, in some degree, the approach of the army from Canada."[464] In Howe's mind, the northern campaign from Canada would be a secondary operation. His thinking was reinforced later after the defeats at Trenton and Princeton. Was it God's plan to fill Howe with revenge and divert his focus from the Grand Strategy after his defeats of Trenton and Princeton?

Mysteriously, Lord Germain wrote Howe on March 9 giving his approval to the campaign against Philadelphia. A little over two weeks later, Germain issued the orders for the Grand Strategy operation. He gave the command to Burgoyne and called for the "most speedy junction of the two armies." [465]

After Germain approved Howe's plan to capture Philadelphia, Howe wrote on April 2 to propose doing so

General John Burgoyne
Courtesy of BritishBattles.com

by traveling by sea instead of an overland march from New York. This letter did not reach England until early May. Howe's decision had significant consequences. Primarily, it removed Howe's army from a position between Washington and both Howe's remaining force in New York City, under Clinton, and that of Burgoyne. Washington could not abandon the defense of Philadelphia, but he could send troops northward to help stop the British advance from Canada. By taking his army to sea, Howe made it impossible either to cooperate with Burgoyne or go to his assistance

464   Spivey, 166.
465   Ibid.

if needed. The force of thirty-nine hundred regulars and three thousand militia that Howe left in New York under Clinton's command was too small to protect a city with a hundred-mile perimeter and also provide support to Burgoyne. American forces under General Israel Putnam remained a threat within striking distance, in the vicinity of Forts Clinton and Montgomery on the Hudson, about fifty miles north of New York City. [466]

Clearly, Howe believed his obligation to cooperate with Burgoyne was not centered on helping him reach Albany, but to rather help maintain him once he arrived there. While paying lip service to the Grand Strategy, Howe demonstrated little interest in pursuing it.

Thus, a serious ambiguity about the Grand Strategy existed in the mind of the highest-ranking British commander in North America. Responsibility for Howe's half-hearted support can be clearly placed at the hands of Lord Germain. He could have settled the matter with additional correspondence and explicit orders to Howe. He did not do so. For whatever his rationale, he never saw fit to countermand Howe's plans or even to stress the importance of Burgoyne's operation. The continued underestimation of the American enemy is one rationale for this. The British also hoped for an early decisive victory in 1777 to keep the French from entering the war on the side of the Americans. The British did not think it possible for American forces to seriously impede British advances anywhere, even if high-level coordination was imperfect. They should have learned a lesson from the Braddock expedition in the French and Indian War. Could it have been God's plan to place the pride, arrogance and total disregard for American forces into the heads of Lord Germain and General Howe? Such pride and arrogance that they had complete faith that their British forces could conduct two simultaneous American campaigns in 1777 without coordinating either?

Burgoyne Kicks Off the Expedition

By mid-June 1777, Burgoyne's army of over seven thousand British soldiers and German mercenaries set off from the Saint Lawrence River on two hundred flat-bottomed bateaux. The transports were accompanied by a naval force of nine Royal Navy vessels and thirty gunboats. Augmenting the British expedition were a few hundred Canadian and American Tories. Factored into Burgoyne's plan was growing his numbers by recruiting more American Loyalists as his army moved south through New York. Finally, over four hundred Iroquois and Algonquian warriors joined the trip to supply scouting and advance screening. [467]

As his army proceeded southward, Burgoyne drafted and had his men distribute a proclamation that included the statement:

---

466   Luzader, 16-17.
467   Ibid, 19.

"I have but to give stretch to the Indian forces under my direction, and they amount to thousands."

This statement implied Britain's enemies would suffer attacks from Indians allied to the British.

Burgoyne's force was particularly heavy in artillery. Its 138 large-caliber weapons ranged from twenty-four pounders to 4.4-inch mortars. Having been a witness to the action at Bunker Hill, Burgoyne did not intend to be without this military advantage again. Large quantities of ammunition and stores were embarked to support these weapons.[468] The large quantities of supplies were not much of an issue when moving by naval transport along lakes and rivers. The same cannot be said if forced to transport them over rugged, roadless territory.

Burgoyne and his army sailed down Lake Champlain, reaching and capturing his first objective, Crown Point, on June 25. Traveling another ten miles south from Crown Point, Burgoyne reached Fort Ticonderoga on July 1, 1777.

American Opposition

The American, Phillip Schuyler, was appointed to the rank of major general in 1775 and was given command of the Northern Department. This made him responsible for the defense of upstate New York. In early 1777 Schuyler had an inadequate assortment of militia and Continental units available to cover a vast region that included the most likely invasion route from Canada, along Lake Champlain and the Hudson River.[469]

The British Forces

Major General John Burgoyne, commanding
Senior officers: Major General William Phillips, Baron Friedrich Riedesel, Brigadier Simon Fraser and Brigadier James Hamilton

Battalion Companies of Foot:
9th, 20th, 21st, 24th, 29th, 31st, 47th, 53rd, and 62nd.
Hessian units:
Breymann's Jägers, Riedesel's Regiment, Specht's Regiment, Rhetz's Regiment and Captain Pausch's Hesse Hanau Company of artillery

The American Forces

Major General Phillip Schuyler, commanding
Replaced by
Major General Horatio Gates, commanding

Right Wing: Gates in command
Brigadier Glover's Continental Brigade, Colonel Nixon's Continental Regiment, Brigadier Paterson's Continental Brigade
Center:
Brigadier Learned's Continental Brigade, Bailey's Massachusetts Regiment, Wesson's Massachusetts Regiment and Livingston's New York Regiment
Left Wing: Major General Benedict Arnold commanding
Brigadier Poor's Brigade, Cilley's 1st New Hampshire Regiment, Hale's 2nd New Hampshire Regiment, Scammell's 3rd New Hampshire, Van Cortlandt's New York Regiment, Livingston's New York Regiment, Connecticut Militia, Daniel Morgan's Riflemen and Dearborn's Light Infantry

---

468   Spivey, 169.
469   Ibid, 168.

Fort Ticonderoga is at the southern foot of Lake Champlain and just a mile from the northern end of Lake George. Since its capture two years earlier by Benedict Arnold and Ethan Allen, it had been considered an American bulwark against a British invasion from the north. In reality, it was in serious disrepair and garrisoned by a poorly equipped force of only seventeen hundred men.[470]

Schuyler Left to Fend For Himself

In the spring of 1777, Schuyler had asked Washington for ten thousand troops to defend Ticonderoga and another two thousand for the Mohawk River valley. The requests went unfulfilled; Washington had no troops to send. Having never visited Ticonderoga, Washington overestimated its defensibility. He also thought Schuyler's threat would not come from the north but from the south, up the Hudson from New York City.[471]

Capture of Fort Ticonderoga

By July 2, Burgoyne was in a position to attack Ticonderoga. It was his intention to capture the fort and its garrison. The American commander, General Arthur Saint Clair, had to decide whether to stand and fight or evacuate the fort. That choice was essentially made for him when the British occupied a dominating position overlooking the fort called Sugarloaf Hill or Mount Defiance. With British troops and artillery on Sugarloaf Hill, Saint Clair recognized that the fort was indefensible. But he still hoped to delay the British, giving his superior, Schuyler, more time to organize the defense of upstate New York. The longer Saint Clair delayed his evacuation decision, the greater the danger that his exposed forces would be cut off from retreat. He also knew that total dishonor would fall upon him for surrendering what had been termed the "The Gibralter of the North."

On July 5, Saint Clair gave the order to abandon the fort. At night he moved his force south to Fort Edward on the Hudson, which would allow them to fight another day. Burgoyne immediately advanced on the vacated fort immediately and captured practically all the Americans' stores, ammunition, and artillery. But he failed to cut off the American retreat.

When news of the fort's capture reached England, rejoicing erupted throughout the nation. Burgoyne was the hero of the day. His capture of Ticonderoga was the high water mark of his campaign down the Hudson River; events immediately started to turn against him.

Howe Departs For Philadelphia

On July 13, Burgoyne set up his headquarters in Skenesboro at the southern end of Lake Champlain. He paused his southern movement in order to build up

470   Ibid, 169.
471   Ibid.

supplies for his next advance. Meanwhile Howe, with the majority of his British force, prepared to depart New York City, but moving away from Burgoyne. Transported by the Royal Navy, Howe's objective was the American capital, Philadelphia. He had no plans to go up the Hudson to support Burgoyne in executing the "Grand Strategy" and divide the colonies. Howe sailed for the Chesapeake Bay and Delaware River on July 23.

The Jane McCrea Murder and Scalping

While he was headquartered at Skenesboro, a force of about five hundred warriors from the various tribes of the Iroquois Confederation joined Burgoyne. These were fierce fighters, able to play havoc on the Americans retreating from Ticonderoga. However, on July 27 an event occurred that completely changed the American resistance to the British advance.

An Ottawa Indian named Wyandot Panther brutally killed and scalped a twenty-three-year-old woman named Jane McCrea.[472] She had been engaged to an American Tory officer serving in Burgoyne's army. The incident, along with Burgoyne's previous proclamation of "giving stretch to his Indian forces," became a sensation throughout New York and New England. The scalping event was told and published in papers. Some historians today are unsure if her death came at Native American hands or by other means, but the murder of Jane McCrea united Americans against the British and their Native allies. Jane McCrea became a rallying cry, stirring militia units to action throughout the region.

American Forces Grow, British Become Weaker

This was a disaster for Burgoyne, as his plan was to grow his forces by recruiting Tory sympathizers as he moved south. That plan backfired as a result of the Jane McCrea murder. Now, instead of growing, Burgoyne's attacking forces were shrinking the farther he advanced south. His requirement to protect his ever-lengthening supply line from Canada forced him to leave behind a steadily growing number of guard detachments. At the same time, American forces were growing, with the McCrea killing a rallying cry, and because of their retreat closer to their supply base. Another second-order effect of the McCrea murder was the complete loss of the Indians as the "eyes and ears" of Burgoyne's force. After the McCrea incident Burgoyne sought to bring the murderer to justice and rein in his Indian allies to avoid another such event. This alienated his Indian allies, who soon disappeared from his army.

Certainly it was not God that caused the death of Jane McCrea. However, the reaction to this brutal murder that woke the American population to the crisis, some have argued, was the work of God.

472   Ibid, 172.

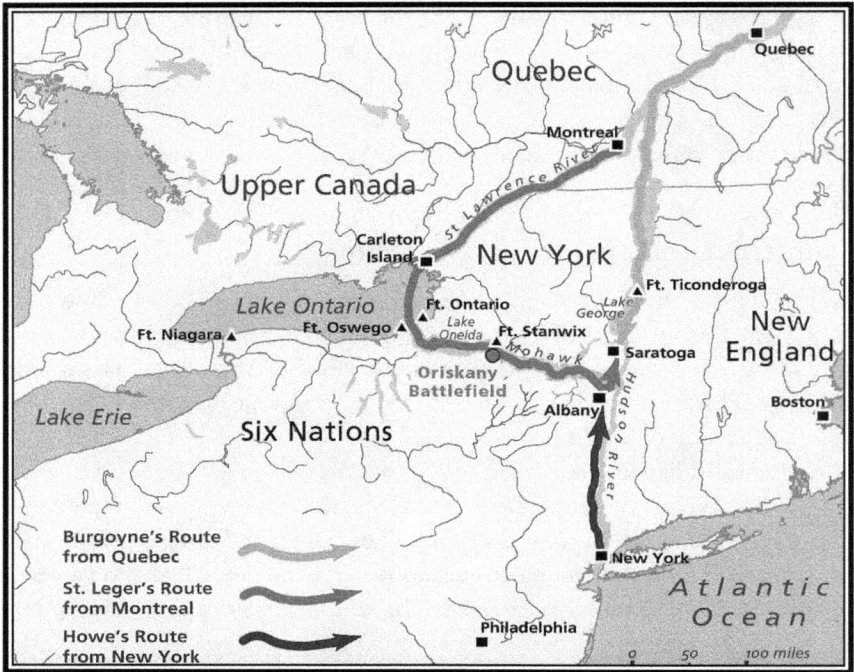

The Grand Strategy Campaign
Courtesy of EmersonKent.com

Burgoyne's Decision on the Direction of Advance

After delaying to consolidate his supplies at Skenesboro, Burgoyne resumed his advance towards Albany. His original plan had been to use his considerable naval contingent to transport his men by water down Lake George to a point where they would disembark and march overland. That leg was a well-traveled route of only ten miles to the Hudson River.

Instead, Burgoyne elected to advance overland due south from Skenesboro through twenty-three miles of dense wilderness.

The Difficult Advance

The forested country, crossed by primitive tracks rather than roads, was difficult for an army having to move massive quantities of supplies and heavy artillery. The advance was made all the more difficult as General Schuyler's Americans helped to impede the British progress, felling trees and destroying any provisions that the British might acquire along this route. The British managed to advance at about one mile per day. This placed additional burden on Burgoyne's supplies and gave the Americans more time to respond to the crisis. By choosing the extended overland route, Burgoyne had placed his army in a perilous position. The presence of his army

152

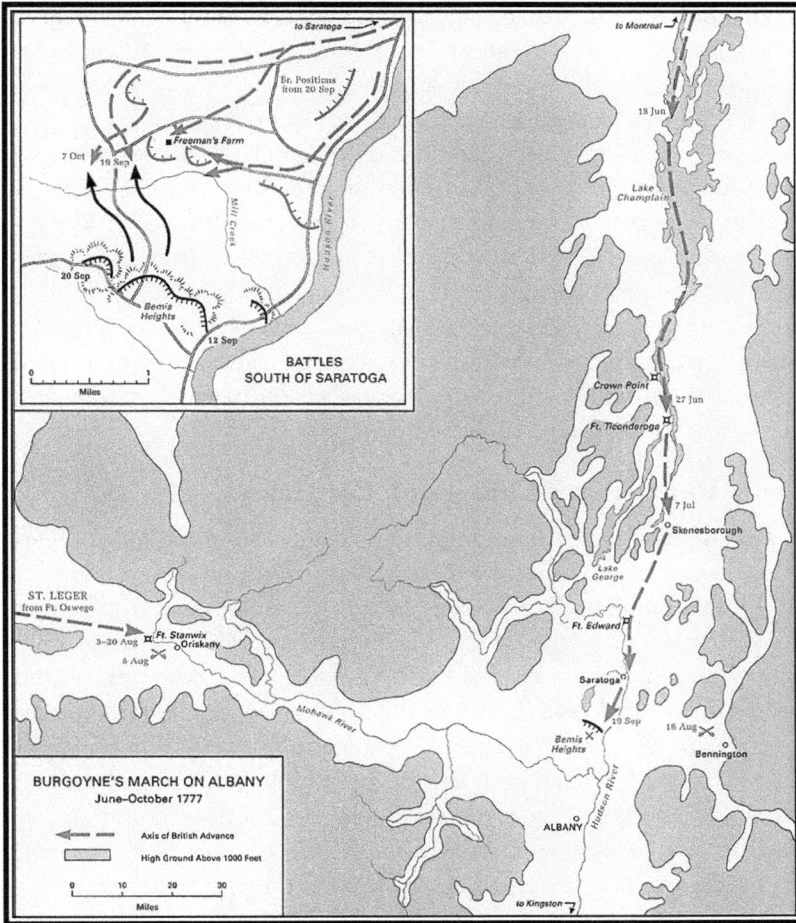

Burgoyne's Advance toward Albany
Courtesy of membersauthorsguild.net

was arousing the local militia in substantial numbers. He was short of food. While the Americans were exchanging territory for time, the British supply problem was growing ever more severe as their line of communications lengthened.

Burgoyne Abandoned His Military Strength

Burgoyne's decision to choose the overland route has puzzled many a military strategist. He threw away the use of his great strength, naval transport, and elected to go where he lacked the capability to advance rapidly. Two factors influenced Burgoyne's choice. First was that Lake George is 221 feet higher than Lake Champlain, and he would have had to drag his artillery, his supplies, and his boats up this rise, through a connecting gorge five miles long. Also, this route between the lakes would have required him to backtrack, heading north on Lake Champlain from Skenesboro before turning to enter Lake George. He feared that route would look like a retreat. He had the initiative and he wanted to keep it.

Why did he think dragging his artillery and supplies over twenty-three miles of wilderness would be easier than five miles uphill? If he worried about the appearance of returning to Fort Ticonderoga and using the Lake George route, then why did he pursue the remaining American forces from Ticonderoga all the way down to Skenesboro? Instead, he could have immediately entered Lake George at Ticonderoga and proceeded to the Hudson River and his objective, Albany? That was especially important, if reaching Albany before winter was his overall objective. Did his personality traits—excessive ambition and vanity—factor into his route decision because he did not want to appear to be seen retreating from the enemy? His decision had to be an act of Divine Providence.

Schuyler's Retreat and Change of Command

Throughout July, Schuyler could muster roughly four thousand Americans who were in various states of disorganization, lacking the means to wage war. The loss of the artillery, ammunition, and stores held at Ticonderoga was a crippling blow for the Americans. Schuyler elected to withdraw to Stillwater, thirty miles north of Albany. While making determined efforts to raise the New England militia, he implemented a scorched-earth policy in the path of the British advance. Schuyler's soldiers were turned into lumberjacks and wrecking crews. They blocked roads and trails with fallen trees and boulders. Streams were dammed and some diverted. Bridges were dismantled or burned. Crops were cut or burned and livestock driven off. Morale among his fighting force was about as low as it could go for men doing such backbreaking manual labor, all the while retreating in the face of the enemy.[473]

On August 10, John Hancock, president of the Continental Congress, relieved Schuyler of command. His replacement was Major General Horatio Gates. Gates was an ex-British officer who had served during the French and Indian War and commanded part of Braddock's ill-fated army at the Monongahela. Now, Gates immediately benefited from major events both east and west of his position. Events he had no control over but would have profound effects on the American defense of the Hudson.

British Supplies Running Short

Burgoyne's circumstances were no better than the Americans'. His army had struggled through the heavy forest from Skenesboro, building a road to carry his artillery and supply carts. As the Americans systematically wasted the country, his army fell short of supplies and reliable transport. The British had so few horses

473   Ibid, 174.

Major-General Horatio Gates by Gilbert Stuart

that the Brunswick Dragoons, a Hessian cavalry regiment, were still on foot instead of mounted. Burgoyne's difficulties proved yet another reminder of the problems of campaigning in the vast forests of North America, difficulties that had been experienced by every British general since Braddock, lessons that should have been learned by 1777.

Burgoyne Learns of Howe's Intentions in Pennsylvania

Burgoyne faced another setback when on August 3 he received a letter from Howe informing him that the main British army was leaving New York City, not to meet him, but to invade Pennsylvania. Burgoyne was dismayed that Howe was not

155

advancing up the Hudson to support him, as envisioned in the original campaign plan as devised and approved by Lord Germain in London.[474]

Much Needed Supplies in Bennington, Vermont

After arriving at Fort Edward on the Hudson in the last days of July, Burgoyne had discovered an answer to his logistical problems. His scouts reported that desperately needed horses and supplies were available in nearby Bennington, Vermont, a short distance to his east. The scouts also reported that American forces were scarce in this region.

On August 9, Burgoyne directed one of his German officers, Colonel Baum, to take a detachment of about eight hundred men to find the necessary horses, cattle, and carriages for his dragoons and for the army's transport, and to collect supplies of food. He also ordered the arrest of anyone "acting" as rebel officers or in rebel governments.

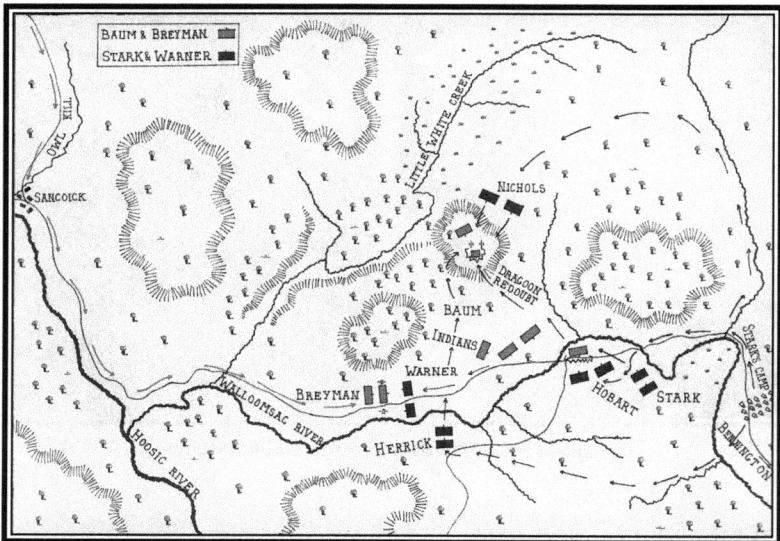

Battle of Bennington
Courtesy of BritishBattles.com

Unknown to Burgoyne was that the New Hampshire legislature, upon learning of his expedition, had raised a brigade of militia during July and given its command to Brigadier General John Stark. Stark was one of the American heroes of Bunker Hill. His fifteen-hundred-man force was tasked with the defense of New Hampshire

474 "Battle of Bennington," *BritishBattles.com,* https://www.britishbattles.com/war-of-the-revolution-1775-to-1783/battle-of-bennington/, (July, 7, 2018).

and its western frontier, which extended into present-day Vermont.[475] Stark marched his men to Bennington, arriving there on August 8.

Battle of Bennington

As the German officer, Baum, advanced on Bennington, his forces ravaged the countryside. On August 14, the Hessians skirmished with a small force under Colonel William Gregg at Van Schaick's grist mill on the Walloomsac River in Saint Croix, now North Hoosick, New York. Baum had received information from a captured American that Stark's forces at Bennington outnumbered his own more than two to one. The German colonel believed the Americans would retreat at the sighting of his arrival. From his position outside the town, Baum sent a dispatch to Burgoyne, saying he intended to give battle to the Americans at Bennington. He requested additional support as it became clear he was substantially outnumbered by Stark's New Hampshire Militia. Burgoyne responded by ordering Colonel Heinrich von Breymann's regiment of 660 men and two six-pound cannons to march the twenty-four miles to Bennington to support Baum. Breymann departed at 9 a.m. on August 15.

The battle commenced before Breymann could join Baum. Breymann was slowed by a heavy rainstorm, which turned the only road to Bennington into a bog. Also, instead of rushing to Baum's support and relief, Breymann seemed possessed with the need to move all his artillery and stores and keep his units in formation. He let precious time pass with frequent stops to close ranks and reorganize. On the march to Bennington, Breymann averaged only about one mile per hour.

Stark pressed his attack on the British on August 16 with a double envelopment, a complete encirclement of Baum's position. With the exception of a redoubt heavily fortified by dragoons, all of Baum's other positions collapsed. Most of the soldiers escaped into the woods. After repeated American attacks, the redoubt finally had to surrender when the dragoons ran low on ammunition and Baum was severely wounded. His force had been annihilated.

About an hour later, Breymann's column approached. Stark immediately attacked Breymann's Germans and forced them to retreat. The Americans pursued and subjected the Germans to a continuous galling fire until night fell. Had Breymann arrived on the battlefield an hour sooner, the results of the battle, and of the campaign, would have been written differently. The British loss of over nine hundred casualties—killed, wounded, and captured—not to mention the loss of their equipment and weapons, can be attributed to the rain, road conditions and Breymann's insistence on an orderly march instead of a quick advance to relieve an overmatched friend.[476] The rain that impeded Breymann's advance to support Baum

475   Spivey, 175.
476   Luzader, 32.

and Breymann's decision to keep his force intact on the march certainly was the work of Divine Providence.

This small but decisive engagement caused Burgoyne to lose nearly a thousand of his best troops. It also failed in the mission to resupply his army with much-needed horses and food during this critical juncture of the campaign.

Fort Stanwix

Almost simultaneous with the British failure at Bennington came another failure on Burgoyne's right flank. Some eighty miles to the west of his position, the fifteen-hundred-man British diversion expedition under Saint Leger, moving down the Mohawk River valley, had reached Fort Stanwix. Called Fort Schuler by

General Benedict Arnold
Courtesy of BritishBattles.com

the Americans, this strong point was defended by 650 American Continental troops who successfully held off Saint Leger's first attacks on August 2. Saint Leger decided to mount a siege against the small fort, which lasted for several weeks.

Before Schuyler was relieved of command, Benedict Arnold influenced him to divide his force and allow Arnold to march to the relief of Fort Stanwix. This part of the Grand Strategy worked as planned. Saint Leger's diversionary campaign down the Mohawk River had successfully divided the American forces when Arnold's detachment left

Schuyler's main body at Stillwater en route to Fort Stanwix.

Arnold departed on August 13. As he advanced to German Flats, some thirty miles east of Oriskany, he captured a number of Loyalists. One of them was a man named Hon Yost Schuyler, a distant relative of General Schuyler. Hon Yost Schuyler was sentenced to death as a spy but was given a reprieve on the condition that he spread the rumor among Saint Leger's Indians that the Americans were advancing in overwhelming numbers. The trick worked. The Indians, who constituted about half of Saint Leger's force, abandoned him and retreated to Canada.

With the loss of his Indians, Saint Leger abandoned his siege of Fort Stanwix and retreated back to Canada. Burgoyne received the news of Fort Stanwix on August 28. Saint Leger's withdrawal left Arnold free to return to the main body of American forces at Stillwater. Had Saint Leger stood his ground and given fight, or allowed Arnold to chase him around the Mohawk River valley, those Americans would not have been available for the Battle of Saratoga. Most important, Arnold would not have been available. As we will soon discover, Arnold played the critical role in the battles around Saratoga. Saint Leger's mission of diversion, support, and ultimately joining with Burgoyne had collapsed. Was it God's plan for him to retreat to Canada instead of facing Arnold—thus allowing Arnold to return and participate in the upcoming battles around Saratoga—the turning point in the American Revolution?

Continued March to Albany

Burgoyne took until September 13 to assemble sufficient supplies to enable his army to continue south. Those supplies had to be dragged through the forests down rudimentary roads that his army was forced to build. Winter was approaching; to camp his army in his current location, far from food supplies, would have been disastrous. He had to either retreat, not an option in his mind, or continue the march south to Albany. March south he did.

Philadelphia Captured – Battle of Brandywine Creek

At the same time, Howe and his army had arrived on the Delaware River, disembarked and were advancing on Philadelphia. Washington blocked Howe's advance by placing his American forces between the British and Philadelphia, choosing a defensive position behind Brandywine Creek. On September 11, Howe used a tactic similar to the one he used at Long Island. He positioned his forces to face Washington's army along the creek and at the same time maneuvered a large force farther upstream, crossing at an undefended spot on Washington's right flank. Howe could now attack Washington's front, right flank and rear. Washington, realizing his critical situation, had to retreat, leaving the road to Philadelphia undefended. Howe captured the American capital on September 26.

Washington's Counter-Attack at Germantown

Washington counter-attacked the British at Germantown on October 4, 1777, and was in a position to win the day, but his forces delayed their pursuit of the retreating British when some 120 British soldiers barricaded themselves in a strongly built stone house called the Chew Mansion. Instead of pursuing the retreating British, the Americans stopped to dislodge the British from the Chew Mansion. That destroyed the attack's momentum and it failed. Philadelphia remained in the hands of the British.

Washington Sends Critical Elements North to General Gates

The Continental Army, beaten but not destroyed, retreated to York, Pennsylvania. The survival of Washington's main force prevented Howe from being able to leave and join forces with Burgoyne. Additionally, realizing that a major battle was shaping up on the Hudson River, Washington sent troops north, specifically Colonel Daniel Morgan and his elite unit of Kentucky sharpshooters. Washington also sent John Glover's Massachusetts regiment that had served with such distinction during the evacuation of Long Island and the crossing of the Delaware before the Battle of Trenton.

Prelude to Battle

With the return of Benedict Arnold and his forces from the Mohawk River valley, the arrival of Washington's reinforcements, and the continued gathering of militia in the Saratoga area, Gates' American forces had grown to over six thousand, approaching parity with his British enemy.[477]

Gates Selects His Defensive Position – Bemis Heights

Having a pretty clear picture of Burgoyne's predicament, Gates correctly surmised that the British would have to either fight or retreat. On September 7, for the first time, Gates ordered his troops to move north instead of retreating. Gates chose an extremely good defensive position blocking Burgoyne's advance at a place known as Bemis Heights. Here a plateau overlooking a narrow bend in the Hudson dominated the road along the riverbank. Artillery could effectively cover the road and the narrow river from this position. It would be suicide to attempt to sail past the American position on Bemis Heights and a frontal attack from the river road would result in significant losses. To approach Bemis Heights, infantry would have to maneuver inland away from the river, over thickly wooded terrain cut by steep ravines and creeks, not ideal terrain for Burgoyne's disciplined formations.[478]

Americans Entrench

The Americans arrived at Bemis Heights on September 12, and began to dig

American Positions on Bemis Heights
Courtesy of BritishBattles.com

entrenchments, block the river road, and fortify the bluffs. Under the supervision of Colonel Thaddeus Kosciuszko, Gates' men laid out fortifications along the crest of the bluffs above the road. They built the main line of entrenchments from a ravine behind the bluffs west to John Neilson's farm on the crest of the heights and extended it southwest for about three-quarters of a mile. The Americans were digging in to block Burgoyne's advance to Albany.[479]

Burgoyne Crosses the Hudson River and Strikes for Albany

Burgoyne's advance continued to progress slowly. His supplies were running low. It became obvious that he would not receive additional assistance from either Howe, Clinton, Saint Leger, Native Americans or American Tories. He was on his

477   Spivey, 177.
478   Ibid, 179.
479   Luzader, 37.

own, but his combat power was largely intact. To defeat his American opponent on the battlefield using his available strength seemed to be the logical and simplest way to advance to Albany. He also knew that his reputation would not survive anything that could be perceived as turning back. Burgoyne decided to cross the Hudson at Schuylerville, about ten miles north of Saratoga, cut himself off from his supply bases and strike directly for Albany.[480] He used a makeshift pontoon bridge consisting of boats lashed together to cross. The bridge was disassembled after all had crossed.

Battle of Freeman's Farm

In the week leading up to his first contact with the enemy, Gates made two wise decisions. First, he allowed Kosciuszko to select the defensive position on Bemis Heights and supervise construction of the fortifications. The site forced the British to maneuver into areas not suited for an assault. Second, he placed his left wing under the command of Arnold, who at this stage of the war had proven himself one of America's most effective field commanders.[481]

On September 19, Burgoyne's army approached the Americans' fortified camp. Some eight thousand men were in lines on the Hudson's west bank, four miles north of Stillwater, at Bemis Heights. The British advanced in three columns, one by the river road under a German officer, Colonel Friedrich Riedesel, the main force in the center commanded by Burgoyne himself, and the third, commanded by Brigadier-General Simon Fraser. Fraser was to make a wide detour around the Americans' left and attack their flank from the west.

Pickets serving under Arnold on the American left soon detected Fraser's flanking movement. Arnold knew his position was at risk if the British could occupy high ground to his west. An attack from this direction would have devastating consequences to the American line.

Gates had no aggressive plan with which to counter the British flanking move. His plan was simply to await attack in his fortified position on the heights. Arnold had no such intention of waiting. He was determined to take the fight to the advancing British and use the advantage his men had in forest fighting. Arnold pressed Gates to attack with the whole army. Gates refused, but finally agreed that Arnold could take his own division forward against the British line.

Daniel Morgan's riflemen advanced in the early afternoon. They were the first to engage the British in and around a clearing known as Freeman's Farm. Morgan launched an assault on a small force of Canadians and Indians, part of Fraser's right wing. Morgan's men were followed by Arnold's division of New Hampshire Continentals. As the Canadians and Indians fell back, Morgan's riflemen rushed on in pursuit but were dispersed by a British counterattack. As a substantial gap

---

480   U.S. Department of Interior, National Park Service, *Saratoga National Historical Park New York*, Washington D.C.: Government Printing Office-2018, 403-332/82045, 2018.
481   Spivey, 180.

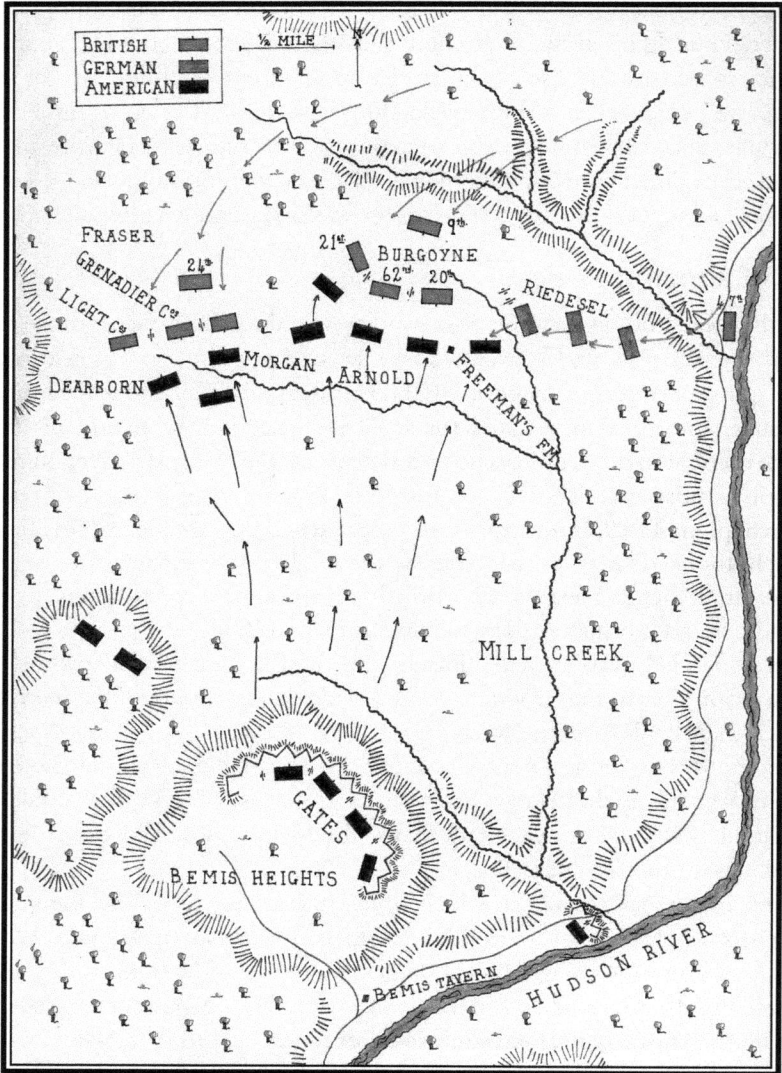

Battle of Freeman's Farm
Courtesy of BritishBattles.com

developed between Burgoyne's center and Fraser, Arnold exploited the breach. He rallied his men to attack the gap between the British center and right wing. To avoid being overwhelmed, Burgoyne's flank regiment was forced to fall back. A desperate battle developed between the attacking Americans and the regiments of the British center. Gates, still on the defensive on Bemis Heights, refused to commit further formations to support Arnold's attack. If he had done so, it is generally accepted that the British center would have been overwhelmed. All afternoon the battle raged back and forth across the field, with neither side able to consolidate an advantage. The hesitancy of each commander prevented many units available to participate in the battle from becoming engaged in the fight.

Riedesel on the British left finally settled the contest. He responded to the crisis with alacrity. Marching his regiments up the hill, he found the British infantry in great difficulty, and without delay, launched a flank attack on the Americans. The fire of his artillery and infantry was sufficient to relieve the pressure on the British regiments and force the Americans to withdraw. By this time night was falling and the Americans fell back to their fortifications.

The British suffered heavy casualties among the regiments that were engaged. Some 600 were killed, wounded or captured. The Americans suffered 350 casualties: killed, wounded or captured.[482]

Technically Burgoyne held the field after the battle, he was credited with a victory, but he realized he had failed in his larger purpose to achieve a breakthrough and open the road to Albany. Burgoyne's senior subordinates urged that the attack on the American position be pressed the next day, September 20. The Americans were in disorder after the failure of Arnold's attack at Freeman's Farm and it may be that an immediate attack would have been met with great success. However, Burgoyne preferred to wait, as his hospital was taxed by the large number of wounded.

On September 21, Burgoyne had his answer to the question whether Clinton was coming up the Hudson to support him. A courier from Clinton arrived and delivered a dispatch dated September 12 that stated in part, "If you think that two thousand men can assist you effectually, I will make a push at [Fort] Montgomery in about ten days."[483] After receiving Clinton's dispatch, Burgoyne surrendered the initiative. As he now anticipated support from Clinton up the Hudson in Gates' rear, Burgoyne would prepare his own defenses and await the arrival of reinforcements. Clearly, it was an act of Divine Providence for this dispatch to arrive at this exact moment to persuade Burgoyne to go over to the defensive and wait—despite his not knowing exactly how long it would take Clinton to arrive. Burgoyne made his decision despite lacking sufficient food to withstand a siege the Americans were sure to provide.

After Freeman's Farm - Battle of Generals Gates and Arnold

After the Battle of Freeman's Farm, not only were the Americans disorganized and critically low on ammunition, but Gates made matters worse by entering into an open and venomous dispute with his primary fighting general, Benedict Arnold.

In his after-action report to Congress, Gates omitted any mention of Arnold's actions during the battle. This led to a bitter argument between the two American

---

482   "Battle of Freeman's Farm," *BritishBattles.com,* https://www.britishbattles.com/war-of-the-revolution-1775-to-1783/battle-of-freeman's-farm/, (July, 15, 2018).
483   Spivey, 183.

leaders. With more and more American militia joining Gates, the American forces grew to approximately twelve thousand men. As Gates reorganized his new and much larger force, he made matters even worse by leaving Arnold without a command.[484]

Burgoyne Waits for Clinton and Builds his Defenses

For sixteen days both armies faced each other without a major attack from either force. Anticipating Clinton's arrival to join his forces, Burgoyne built defensive positions north of Gates's lines at Bemis Heights. Burgoyne's left flank was anchored on the Hudson's west bank where he built a very strong position called the Great Redoubt. That was linked via trench lines to another strong position called the Balcarres Redoubt to the nearby Freeman's Farm. The Balcarres Redoubt was linked via more trench lines to the third strong point, called the Breymann Redoubt, which anchored the British army's right flank. Behind this heavily fortified position Burgoyne would wait for Clinton's arrival.

American Forces Expand While British Ration Their Food

With American forces expanding daily, growing to over twelve thousand, Gates became more aggressive in probing and harassing the British defenses. Gates also sent patrols north of the British position to cut off any movement or resupply efforts from that direction. The Americans captured a British supply flotilla on Lake George.[485] British supplies became critical while Burgoyne waited for Clinton. On October 3, Burgoyne had to order half rations for his command.[486]

Clinton's Advance is Stopped

By October 7, despite considerable success in moving up the Hudson, Clinton was stopped at Livingston Manor, about forty-five miles south of Albany. American militia blocked his march. Clinton would advance no farther in support of Burgoyne. A major British difficulty during the campaign was the lack of communication between Clinton's and Burgoyne's forces. Almost every messenger attempting the journey between the two British forces was caught by the Americans—and hanged.[487]

Burgoyne Sends Out a Reconnaissance in Force

Burgoyne needed to do something, and in his mind, retreating was not an option. He was not convinced he should make a full scale attack. Instead he sent out a reconnaissance in force, a party of seventeen hundred men, to probe the American

484   Ibid.
485   Battle of Freeman's Farm.
486   Spivey, 183.
487   Battle of Freeman's Farm.

American attack on Breymann Redoubt

left and forage for food.[488] If the probing force found favorable conditions, Burgoyne would launch a full attack the next day.

Around noon on October 7, Burgoyne, Phillips, von Riedesel and Fraser marched the British force south along the Quaker Springs road, through the abandoned Coulter Farm, and into the open fields of the Barber Farm on the American left flank. This force was quickly sighted by American pickets near the old Freeman's Farm battlefield and reported to Gates.

Battle of Bemis Heights

The American commander ordered Daniel Morgan's riflemen and the American left wing to advance and attack the enemy. The British were quickly driven back, retreating into their strong points, the Balcarres and Breymann redoubts. Unable to stay out of the fight despite being left without any units to command, Benedict Arnold mounted his horse and charged into the fight anyway. Gates sent messengers ordering Arnold's removal from the battlefield, but they never found him.

Arnold took command of the Americans and ordered an assault on the strongest British position, the Balcarres Redoubt. It did not succeed. Not giving up the fight, Arnold launched another attack, this time on the Breymann Redoubt on the British right flank. At the critical moment of the fighting the British General Fraser was mortally wounded by one of Morgan's riflemen. Some argue that he was personally targeted by Arnold. As Arnold spurred the Americans to continue the attack, he too was severely wounded in the leg. The British and Hessian troops began to collapse after the Breymann Redoubt was captured. Its possession opened the

---

488   Luzader, 53.

American approach to Breymann Redoubt

right and rear of Burgoyne's camp. Under the cover of darkness Burgoyne withdrew the remainder of his force to his last remaining fortified position, the heights of the Great Redoubt overlooking the river road.

The next day, facing overwhelming American opposition and after burying Fraser, General Burgoyne ordered a retreat northward. He had suffered another six hundred casualties and had to leave behind over five hundred sick and wounded. After his retreat, Burgoyne mustered in just thirty-five hundred men fit for duty and an inventory of seven days' provisions.[489]

The American army followed Burgoyne's retreat and enveloped positions the British had built at Saratoga on the Fish Kill, some eight miles north of Bemis Heights. Gates ordered his troops to take positions that would block the British retreat across the Hudson. Recognizing he had no other choice but to surrender or face complete annihilation, Burgoyne opened surrender negotiations with Gates, but delayed the negotiations for days. He still hoped Clinton might arrive and save him. Finally, on October 16, Gates announced a final deadline. Surrender immediately, he warned his adversary, or he would resume offensive action. Unable to postpone any longer, Burgoyne signed the surrender agreement on October 17. The Americans had defeated a brave, well-trained, professionally led army. They witnessed that day the first surrender of a British regular army on American soil.

---

489   Spivey, 184.

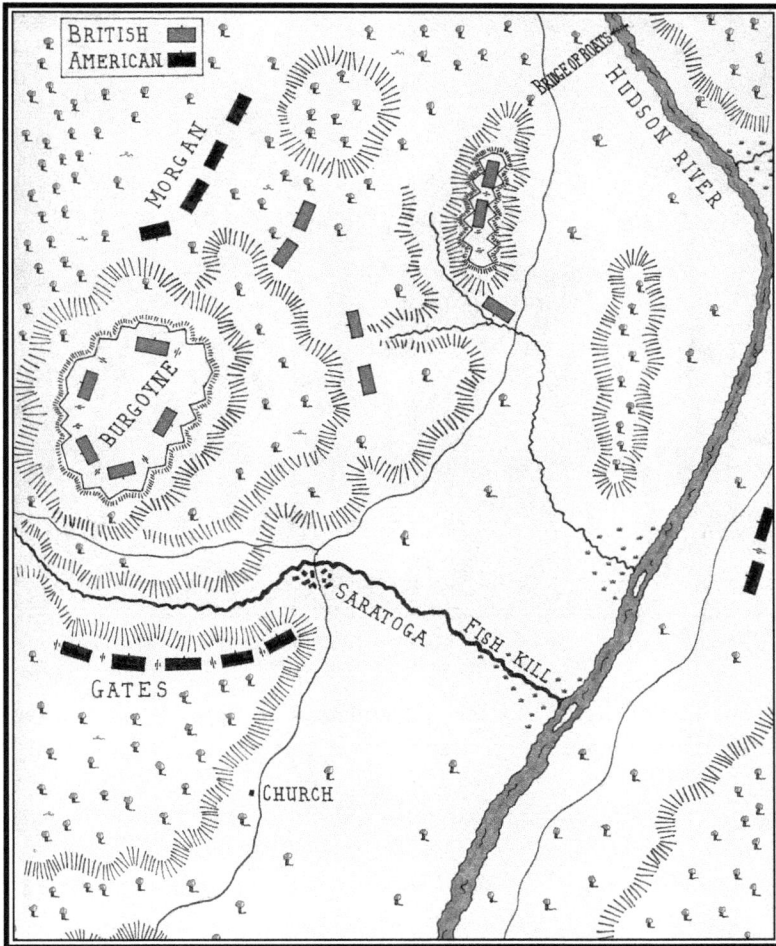

Americans Encircle Burgoyne at Saratoga
Courtesy of BritishBattles.com

On October 26, Clinton evacuated the fortifications that he had captured while moving up the Hudson in his unsuccessful efforts to join Burgoyne. His force returned to New York City. Within two weeks the British garrison at Ticonderoga had abandoned the fort and pulled back to Canada.

Impact of General Burgoyne's Surrender

The victory at Saratoga had wide-ranging implications. Until then, the Revolution's prospects appeared bleak. The American capital was still under British control, and the Continental Congress continued to struggle with an empty treasury

Surrender of General John Burgoyne
Courtesy of BritishBattles.com

and exhausted credit. And so the surrender of Burgoyne's army significantly improved morale among the American Patriots. But the most significant impact of this event was felt in Europe.

Benjamin Franklin was the American commissioner to France. He received the news of the American victory on December 4, 1777, and immediately sent word to King Louis XVI and his advisors. Learning of Burgoyne's surrender, Louis XVI signed an alliance with the United States on February 6, 1778, agreeing to enter the war on the side of the Americans. Spain would sign, too, in 1779.

With the new threat of the French participation in the American Revolutionary War, and the danger of French attacks on British interests around the world, particularly in the Caribbean, Howe had to evacuate Philadelphia, the city he had campaigned and fought two battles to obtain, on June 18, 1778. Howe returned to New York City to consolidate the British forces in America. Washington—or should we say Gates—had recaptured the American capital without firing a shot.

If any of the events as described had resulted differently, the outcome of Saratoga could have been completely different. The American victory was uncertain even up to the last day. Certainly, despite the British flaws in planning and coordination, and the underlying arrogance, it is not hard to imagine Burgoyne reaching Albany in the fall of 1777. There, Clinton's force from New York could have supported him logistically. From Albany, Burgoyne could have conducted a joint operation with

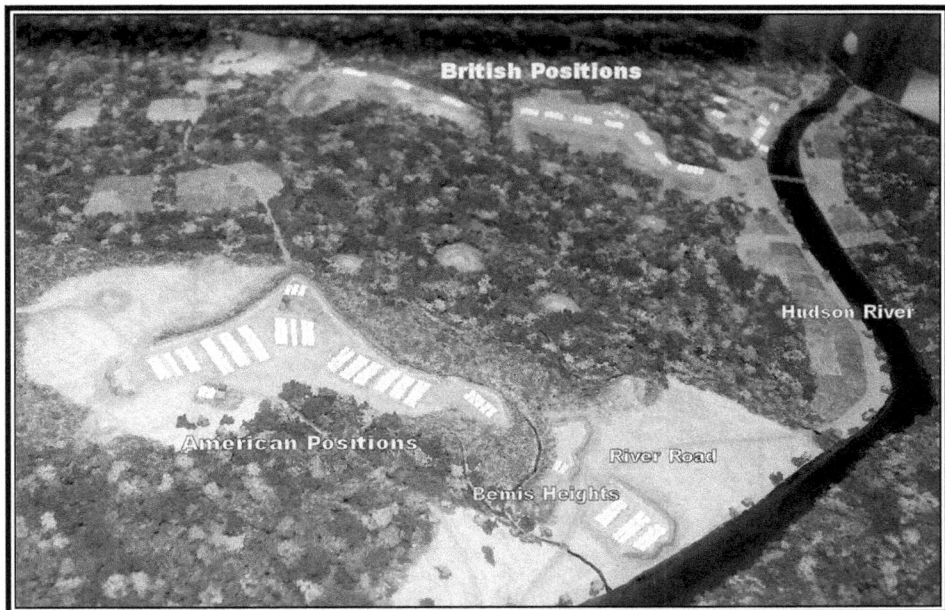

American and British Positions at Bemis Heights

Howe to eliminate Washington's army.

God moved to ensure that this would not happen. It is not my intent to dismiss the sacrifice, courage, and bravery of the Americans who fought and died at Saratoga. They stood and did not run as the British had predicted. It is my desire to present those unexplained factors that were also instrumental in achieving the American victory: those factors that can only be attributed to Divine Providence.

The total British disregard for American resistance and capability as displayed by their leaders, Howe, Burgoyne, and Germain, led to their lack of coordination and operational failure. Burgoyne's decision to proceed to the Hudson River overland through twenty-three miles of wilderness, instead of using Lake George, delayed his advance and accelerated consumption of the scarce provisions needed to carry out the campaign. The rain and muddy road that slowed the British relieving column at Bennington caused the loss of a significant British force and much-needed supplies. The Mohawk River valley operation, despite working perfectly as a diversion, abandoned the field and returned to Canada, allowing Arnold to return to Gates and significantly contribute to the battles of Saratoga. The American reaction to the death of Jane McCrea, which filled the ranks of Gates's army, gave him the strength to attack with overwhelming force when given the opportunity. Clinton's dispatch to Burgoyne, announcing his support mission, led to Burgoyne's decision to go on the defense instead of continuing his attack. Had this dispatch arrived at any other time, Burgoyne would certainly not have relinquished the initiative to his enemy. These are the factors that caused the British defeat at Saratoga. Was it just bad luck or an act of Divine Providence?

As a result of the defeat and loss of an entire army, the entire British force in North America had to go on the defensive until creation of a new "Grand Strategy." This new Grand Strategy, as we will soon discover, had God's hand working again to ensure its failure. With that failure came the birth of a new nation.

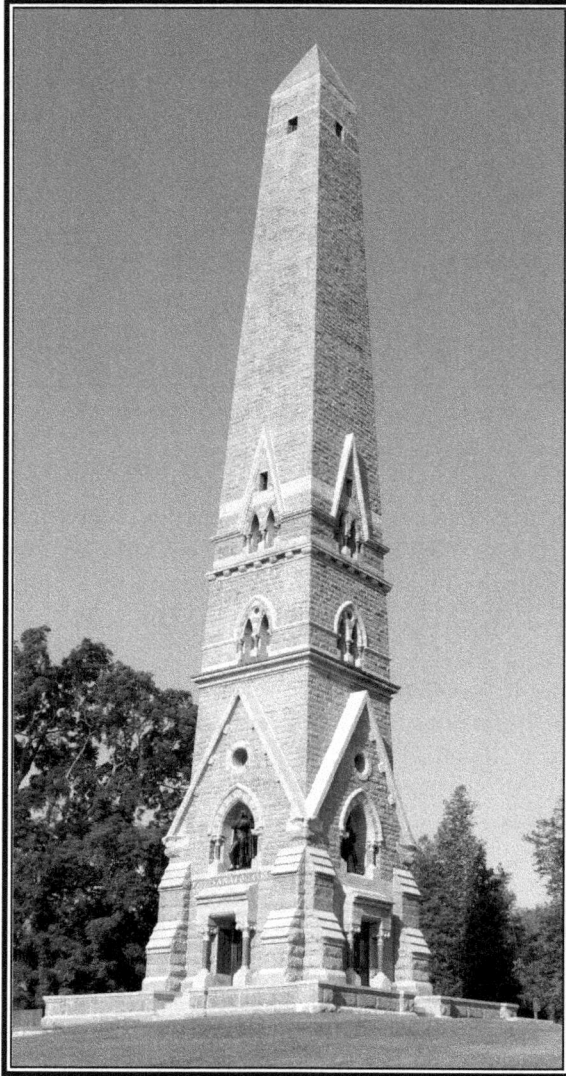

Saratoga Monument

Chapter 9

Southern Campaign – Yorktown

God preserve the United States. We know the Race is not to the swift nor the Battle to the Strong. Do you not think an Angel rides in the Whirlwind and directs this storm?

John Page to Thomas Jefferson
July 20, 1776

God took forty years to mold the Hebrew people into a nation. He accomplished this through exposing them to the adversity, trials, and tribulations associated with roaming in the desert wilderness en route to their promised land. God would not allow the Hebrew people to enter their promised land until they were ready to receive it as a holy nation. While on their journey, God provided for their needs and protected them from their enemies. Time and time again, he tested their faith and through the adversity of their travels, the nation of Israel was formed.

For the first four years of the American Revolution, entire regions were relatively untouched by the fighting. Up to this point most of the fighting had been conducted in the New England and middle colonies. That all changed in 1779 when England looked to the South for aid, believing that this region contained a "silent majority" of Loyalists. Though the rationale for the British campaign in the American South made perfect sense, was it actually God's hand at work, molding an entire American nation just as he did the Nation of Israel?

The chain of events, perfect execution and incredible timing that led to the American victory at Yorktown and the capture of the British army commanded by Cornwallis, cannot be explained other than as an act of Divine Providence. Read on and decide for yourself, but remember to place yourself back in the eighteen century, when coordination and communication between armies and navies was extremely difficult, took months, or was non-existent. For Washington to bring together all the moving parts of his army, the French army and navy to capture Cornwallis at Yorktown was certainly an act of Divine Providence.

1778-1780 War a Stalemate

After the capture of the British army at Saratoga, France and Spain entered into war with England. Now the American colonies became just another theater of war for England's larger global conflict. Of particular interest to the British were their colonies, and those of the French, in the Caribbean. To defend British interests in the Caribbean, the British high command desired to secure a base in America closer to the Caribbean. British thinking at the time concluded that the entire American southern region was less supportive of the "call for liberty" and that the southern Loyalist population would join the British if given the opportunity. Both the desire to acquire a logistical base closer to the Caribbean and that same region's (at least theoretical) loyalty to the Crown led to England's next Grand Strategy: taking the war to the American southern colonies.

At this point in the war for independence, both England and the American states had reached a stalemate. The American defeats at Brandywine and Germantown, Pennsylvania resulted in the British capturing Philadelphia, the American capital. But the American victory at Saratoga and France's entry into the war forced the British to leave Philadelphia and return to New York to support their now global war. The British presence in America had been reduced to a handful of coastal bases, surrounded by hostile countryside. The Americans, however, were in worse shape. The Patriots faced large debts, shortages of all kinds of military materiel, self-interested allies, mutinous rumblings among the troops from at least two colonies, and the general apathy of the population at large.[490] Washington placed his army in New Jersey and New York, to watch the British forces in New York City and to exploit any opportunities. There were no more pitched battles in the North, only raids by the Americans and French against the British in New York and Rhode Island.

General Clinton in Command of British Forces

The British government relieved Howe and replaced him with Henry Clinton as supreme commander in North America. Clinton was ordered to send a portion of his forces to Florida and the Caribbean to defend against the French. Clinton's headquarters remained in New York, where he worked to improve his already strong defensive position. Neither Washington nor Clinton felt strong enough to mount significant offensive operations.

Unfortunately for the British and fortunately for the Americans, the British did not replace their Secretary of State for America, George Germain, after Saratoga. His failures with command and control of two British armies had led to the defeat at Saratoga and in the future would play an instrumental role again at Yorktown, Virginia.

490   Brendan Morrissey, *Yorktown 1781* (Botley, Oxford, England, Osprey Publishing, 1997), 8.

Executing the British Southern Strategy

General Henry Clinton by Thomas Day

In July 1779, General Charles Cornwallis arrived in New York to become Clinton's second in command. In September, Clinton received thirty-eight hundred new troops from England. With these additional troops and Cornwallis as second in command, Clinton was ready to execute his southern campaign.

In December, he set sail from New York with Cornwallis and a fleet of fourteen warships, ninety transports and eighty-five hundred men.[491] They landed on the coast of South Carolina just south of Charleston and joined other British forces that had previously been sent to Georgia and Florida. With total ground forces numbering around thirteen thousand, Clinton was initially successful, much as Burgoyne had been during the early stages of the Hudson River campaign. Clinton first overran Georgia and captured Savannah from a mixed American and French force. He next turned his attention to Charleston.

Surrender of Charleston

Charleston was defended by six thousand American Patriots under the command of General Benjamin Lincoln. This little force had no chance of success against the much bigger, experienced British force that also included a mobile fleet. But under intense political pressure to defend the city, Lincoln unwisely did so, instead of saving his army.

To save his army from combat, and with time being on his side, Clinton laid siege to the city. After experiencing months of this

General Benjamin Lincoln
Courtesy of revolutionary-war.net

491   Christopher Ward, *The War of the Revolution*. Vol 2. (New York: The Macmillan Company, 1952), 696.

siege, on May 12, 1780, Lincoln surrendered his entire force to the overpowering British. It was one of the largest surrenders in American military history. [492]

Cornwallis Assumes Command of British Southern Forces

With Charleston now under British control, Clinton returned to New York, leaving behind Cornwallis with a small force whose mission was to pacify South Carolina and Georgia. The Continental Congress selected Horatio Gates, the victor of Saratoga, to organize the remnants of the Continental forces in the South and counter Cornwallis. But he would experience a stark reversal of his earlier success, perhaps in part because he no longer had such a talented subordinate as Benedict Arnold. (By that point, the disgruntled Arnold had betrayed the American cause and switched his allegiance to Britain.) In one of the most decisive battles of the war, Cornwallis defeated and completely routed Gates at Camden, South Carolina on August 16, 1780.[493]

New Low Point for the Americans

Now the Americans were experiencing trials and tribulations similar to the Hebrews in the wilderness. They had suddenly reached their lowest point in the Revolution since before Washington's decision to cross the Delaware in December 1776. The Continental Army suffered severe shortages of food, clothing, medicine, arms, and pay. Many troops had deserted and some departed after fulfilling their term of enlistments without new recruits replacing them in the ranks. Washington wrote:

> "We have been half our time without provisions and are like to continue so. We have no Magazines, nor money to form them and in a little time we shall have no men [even] if we had money to pay them. We have lived on expedients till we can live no longer."[494]

Americans' Prayers Are Answered

Just as God, through his miracles, provided food and water to the Hebrew people during their misery in the wilderness, he too provided relief to the American people during their war misery of 1779-1780. First, the French landed five thousand much-needed troops at Newport, Rhode Island. Second, Washington sent Nathanael Greene to take over for Gates as commander of the American Southern Department. Third, elements of Greene's army defeated elements of Cornwallis' at Cowpens, South Carolina and King's Mountain, North Carolina.

---

492   Willard M. Wallace, *Appeal to Army: A Military History of the American Revolution* (Chicago, Quadrangle Books, 1951), 210.
493   Spivey, 195.
494   Ward, 866.

Clinton and Cornwallis Disagree

Clinton believed America could be pacified by establishing a chain of fortified posts at strategic coastal bases throughout the colonies, from which campaigns could be launched against American military positions. He assumed the British navy would maintain supremacy of the seas despite France's entry into the war.

Cornwallis, now operating independently in the South, did not agree with Clinton's strategy. Cornwallis believed the British should hold as few posts as possible, but that wherever they had a force, it should be substantial. He considered the pacification of North Carolina as essential to defeating Greene, commanding the last major American force in the South. In so doing, he hoped to convince the elusive masses of southern Loyalists that it was safe to show themselves.[495]

Cornwallis Pursues Greene

After Greene's subordinate, Dan Morgan, defeated elements of Cornwallis's army under the command of Colonel Banastre Tarleton at Cowpens, Cornwallis immediately advanced into North Carolina in pursuit of Morgan and Greene. The British general abandoned large amounts of equipment and stores to speed his advance so he could catch Greene and force a decisive engagement.

Cornwallis also obtained permission from London to correspond directly with Germain, the secretary of state for America, on the basis that Clinton in New York was too far away to control affairs in the South. Clinton was unaware that Cornwallis's plan was gaining support in England. Clinton had not received any correspondence from Cornwallis since a January 18, 1781, letter relating the Cowpens defeat. His next communication came on April 10, 1781, from Wilmington, North Carolina. By that point Cornwallis had already entered North Carolina, despite his original orders from Clinton to pacify South Carolina and Georgia. Clinton had effectively lost control of events in the South. He was intentionally cut out of the loop when Cornwallis corresponded directly with Germain, bypassing the established chain of command. Jumping the chain of command was one of the lessons the British should have learned from their loss at Saratoga. Failure to coordinate the efforts of two British armies in the field was another critical mistake from Saratoga that had not been learned.

Greene Does Not Take the Bait

Instead of confronting the pursuing Cornwallis, Greene retreated over two hundred miles across North Carolina, not allowing himself to be pinned down. At the same time he forced Cornwallis to extend his supply lines, thus reducing the British general's effective combat power.

495   Morrissey, 17.

Battle of Guilford Court House

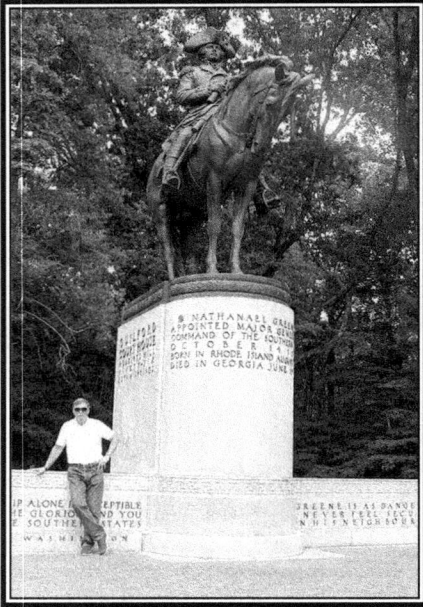

General Nathanael Greene—Guilford Court House Battlefield

Greene, reinforced by troops from Virginia and Maryland, saw an opportunity to give battle to Cornwallis on favorable terms at Guilford Court House, the current Greensboro, North Carolina. On March 15, he amassed forty-five hundred troops, mostly militia, to oppose Cornwallis and his force of twenty-one hundred.

Although Cornwallis drove the Americans from the field and was awarded a tactical victory, he suffered considerable losses in men and material, similar to the British experience at Bunker Hill. So much so that he retreated southeast to the port of Wilmington to resupply. His plan had failed. He had expended most of his supplies. The predicted masses of Loyalist support in North Carolina never materialized. He had not destroyed Greene's army, and he had not held South Carolina. The results of this battle would have a critical impact for the future of America.

Confused British Command and Control

Throughout the Revolutionary War, the British command and control network was one of the weakest aspects of its military establishment. On paper, the British chain of command was simple. Cornwallis as subordinate reported to Clinton. Clinton, as British military leader in America, reported to Germain in London. The problem was execution, or lack thereof, which was driven by the personalities of those involved.

Germain was the main problem, as witnessed in his lack of coordination between Howe and Burgoyne during the Hudson River Grand Strategy campaign. Germain's poor coordination resulted in the disaster at Saratoga. Germain did not learn his lessons from Saratoga. He ensured continued confusion in America by dealing directly with Cornwallis when it suited him, thus undercutting Clinton.

Clinton was against Cornwallis' decision to abandon South Carolina, but Germain overruled him. In early 1781, Germain directed Clinton to make Cornwallis's proposed advance through North Carolina and Virginia the "principle object for the employment of all forces under your command."[496] As commander of British forces in North America, Clinton's view was that his "principle object" was to hold the key ports, New York and Charleston. He was now ordered to react to the initiatives of his subordinate, Cornwallis, despite facing America's primary army, led by Washington, which was camped just miles from Clinton's position in New York City.[497]

Cornwallis Departs for Virginia

Without coordination with anyone, Cornwallis departed Wilmington for Virginia on April 25, 1781, after being resupplied and refitted. Cornwallis had concluded that the war was to be won in America's largest state, Virginia. His plan was to join the British army of twenty-five hundred currently raiding Virginia, led by Major Generals William Phillips and the turncoat Benedict Arnold. Phillips and Arnold were operating on the James River between Williamsburg and Richmond.

Lafayette to Virginia

As early as the winter and spring of 1781, Clinton had pursued weakening Virginia's support of the war effort by sending these raids up the James. Phillips' and Arnold's forces sacked Williamsburg, Richmond, and Petersburg. They burned and captured war materiel at Warwick Plantation and Chesterfield Court House. Virginia had only local militia to respond to the British raids; there was no regular Continental Army in the state at this time.

Thomas Jefferson, Virginia's governor, pleaded his case for protection to Washington and the Continental Congress. As a result, Washington released the French

Marquis de Lafayette by Charles Willson Peale

general, the Marquis de Lafayette and a force of three thousand from his army in New Jersey. Their mission was to protect Virginia against the British raids, and also to capture the traitor Arnold. Lafayette arrived in Richmond in time to stop Phillips from capturing the city for a second time.

---

496   Don Cook, *The Long Fuse: How England Lost the American Colonies, 1760-1785* (New York: Atlantic Monthly Press, 1995), 335.
497   Spivey, 199.

A Confused Clinton by Design or Divine Providence?

Phillips would die of typhoid before his friend Cornwallis could rendezvous with him at Petersburg. After his long march from Wilmington, Cornwallis reached Petersburg on May 20. His army was once again exhausted, weakened by malnutrition and heat exhaustion. Cornwallis was unable to attack the American army in Virginia. He found Lafayette was not willing to confront the combined British forces commanded by Cornwallis, the deceased Phillips and Arnold. Instead, Lafayette retreated north and west toward the Virginia mountains, with Cornwallis in pursuit. Unsuccessful in catching the elusive Lafayette, Cornwallis returned to Richmond.

Thomas Jefferson by Rembrandt Peale
Courtesy of Monticello.org

The British high command was now completely confused as to American intentions. The British had captured correspondence from Washington, intended for Lafayette. On May 31, Washington wrote to Lafayette detailing plans for a combined French and American attack on New York. This plan never materialized; the French Lieutenant General Jean-Baptiste Rochambeau persuaded Washington that the better strategy was a campaign to defeat Cornwallis in Virginia.

Clinton's confusion over Washington's intentions and doubts about Cornwallis' campaign produced one of the most bewildering sequences of orders ever issued by a commander. Clinton thought New York was to be attacked by a combined American and French force that would include a French fleet that had been entering American waters from the Caribbean each summer since 1778. On June 11, Clinton ordered Cornwallis to return six battalions of his infantry and all possible artillery and cavalry to New York. Two weeks later, Cornwallis got a new letter from Clinton that downplayed the threat to New York and, instead, introduced a new plan. Now he wanted Cornwallis to send the troops to Philadelphia instead of New York and establish a base on the Chesapeake Bay. Then a month later, yet another letter arrived from Clinton. This one insisted that Cornwallis immediately disembark troops he was loading on ships to send north, and with his entire force establish a naval base at Old Point Comfort. This is where Fort Monroe sits today, at the southern tip of Hampton, Virginia. Clinton thought this site, where the James and York Rivers join, was a perfect place to control Hampton Roads.

Clearly, Clinton's confusion as to Washington's intentions clouded his vision. It caused him to miss a great opportunity to attack and completely defeat Washington's army when it evacuated its positions in New Jersey and New York and marched south to confront Cornwallis.

Clinton also confused his southern commander as Cornwallis considered opportunities to defeat Lafayette. The intercepted Washington letter finding its way into Clinton's hands and the British general's response to it was an act of Divine Providence.

Cornwallis on the Defense

Cornwallis proceeded to carry out Clinton's order to establish a naval base at Old Point Comfort to control the entrance to Hampton Roads and the Chesapeake Bay. But on further investigation, Cornwallis' chief engineer, Lieutenant Alexander Sutherland, and the naval officers present found Old Point Comfort unsuitable as an anchorage.

Cornwallis surmised that the best location from a naval point of view would be Yorktown on the York River. With the labor of his men and hundreds of runaway slaves, Cornwallis immediately began to build fortifications at Yorktown and at Gloucester Point across the York River.

By August, Cornwallis began to consolidate his scattered units into his new position at Yorktown where he would await the arrival of British naval support and further orders.

Washington's Problems

Washington was still looking for opportunities to recapture New York. While operating in northern New Jersey, he was not without his own problems. He had Greene fighting in the Carolinas and Lafayette defending Virginia against Cornwallis and the raids by Phillips and Arnold. Rochambeau's French army was in Newport, Rhode Island and the French fleet was reported to be somewhere in the Caribbean. Pressure from Virginia was building to help Lafayette suppress the British raids. Washington also wanted to see to it personally that Arnold was captured and tried for treason.

With his own and allied forces so dispersed, it took weeks to get information from and to those units. Planning for their coordination was nearly impossible. Uncertain lines of authority between the Americans and their French allies was an even greater concern.[498] Washington became frustrated with the inaction of

---

498   Ibid, 200.

Rochambeau's army at Newport and the uncertain whereabouts of the main French naval force.

Washington's Decision Made for Him

On May 22 Washington and Rochambeau met to discuss two possibilities. Either they would wait for the French fleet and attack Clinton in New York, or support Lafayette in Virginia to defeat Cornwallis. The conference concluded without reaching a decision, as neither general had detailed information about French naval movements. Washington was pressing hard for an attack on New York, but Rochambeau considered it too risky. While he did not publicly disapprove of Washington's plan, Rochambeau knew that to carry out the plan the French fleet would be needed to defeat or contain the British fleet. He wrote directly to the French naval commander in the Caribbean and requested that he designate Virginia's Chesapeake Bay as his fleet's destination instead of New York.[499]

French General Rochambeau
Courtesy of Mount Vernon Ladies' Association

By August, Rochambeau had his response. He proceeded to inform Washington that Admiral Francois de Grasse would come up only as far as Chesapeake Bay because he would have to return his ships to the Caribbean for the winter.

After surveying Clinton's defenses in detail, Washington was already having second thoughts about his plans to attack New York. About this same time, Lafayette reported to Washington that Cornwallis was moving down the York peninsula towards the entrance to Chesapeake Bay. After learning the French fleet's intentions to make Chesapeake Bay its American destination, Washington abandoned all further discussion of an attack on Clinton. He formed a new plan to move a combined American and French force of seven thousand to the head of the Elk River, now Elkton, Maryland, then to be transported by ship down Chesapeake Bay to Virginia. He and Rochambeau agreed: the objective was to trap Cornwallis.

499   E. B. Potter and Chester Nimitz, *Seapower: A Naval History* (Englewood Cliffs, NJ: Prentice-Hall Inc., 1960). 89.

Washington's Ruse and March South

Washington put half of his army and all of Rochambeau's on the road south toward Virginia. His remaining Americans were left under the command of General William Heath to hold the Hudson Highlands and deceive the British in New York.

Washington's route of march south was chosen to influence Clinton's thinking that the allies would attack either Staten Island or Sandy Hook, New Jersey, which commanded the entrance to New York Harbor. For eleven days the ruse worked. It wasn't until Washington's columns veered towards Princeton that the trick was exposed. By that time Clinton had lost his opportunity to either attack Washington while on the march or beat him in a foot race to Virginia.

Washington's Combined Forces Arrive at Head of Elk

By the first week of September, Washington's force was at Head of Elk waiting to be transported down the Chesapeake Bay to Yorktown. Messages were sent directing Lafayette to expect Admiral de Grasse and to deploy all available troops to prevent Cornwallis' escape. Orders were given to the French naval squadron in Newport, under Admiral Jacques-Melchior de Barras, also to proceed to the Chesapeake with all dispatch. But neither Washington and Rochambeau, nor Clinton and Cornwallis, were aware of the events that were unfolding in the Atlantic off the mouth of Chesapeake Bay.

The Naval Components

To understand the significant role the British and French navies played in the outcome at Yorktown, one must first have a sense of the composition of each fleet and the advantages each had over its opponent.

Actually, four naval squadrons participated in the Yorktown campaign. The British and French had two each. The British had one squadron at New York City and another in the West Indies. The French had a squadron at Newport and another sailing in the Caribbean. The British ships were faster than the French. British ships had copper bottoms, which resisted the buildup of marine life on their submerged surfaces. That "fouling" increases friction, resulting in reduced speeds. The French ships, not "coppered," thus were slower than the British. Also, by and large, the British ships carried heavier armament than the French. The French ships, on the other hand, were newer and for the most part more seaworthy.

Another phenomenon during the days of sailing ships was the advantage the "weather gauge"

The British Fleet

Admiral Marriot
Arbuthnot, commanding

Robust (64 guns)
Europe (64 guns)
Prudent (64 guns)
Royal Oak (74 guns)
London (90 guns)
Adamant (50 guns)
Bedford (64 guns)
America (64 guns)

The French Fleet

Admiral Charles Chevalier
Destouches, commanding

Conquerant (74 guns)
Provence (64 guns)
Ardent (64 guns)
Neptune (74 guns)
Bourgogne (74 guns)
Romulus (44 guns)
Janson (64 guns)
Eveille (64 guns)

could provide. As sailing ships-of-war had a row of guns on their main deck and other rows of guns below decks, sailing with the "weather gauge" was extremely important. This could negate a ship's superior firepower over one with fewer guns. As an example, if a ship that had ninety guns sailed on a tack to windward, it would heel over toward its opponent. Its below-deck gun ports would have to be closed in order not to flood the ship. The sixty-four gun ship that was downwind would heel in the opposite direction, allowing for the use of all its guns. The sixty-four gun ship-of-war, by sailing with the "weather gauge," now has an armament advantage over a vessel laden with much heavier armament.

First Naval Action off the Virginia Capes

Looking back to the spring of 1781, Washington and his army opposed Clinton and his army in New York City. As Washington pondered his next move—attack New York or go south after Cornwallis—Phillips and Arnold were raiding Virginia up the James River. Cornwallis, fighting his way north through North Carolina, was confronted by Greene. Washington saw an opportunity to catch the traitor Arnold by trapping him between Lafayette's forces in Virginia and a French naval force in the Chesapeake Bay. This plan came to fruition when the French squadron in Newport, commanded by Admiral Charles Chevalier Destouches at the time, set sail for Virginia on March 8, 1781. He took the entire squadron, which included eight ships and carried 1,220 French soldiers.[500]

To avoid getting bottled up in New York Harbor, the British squadron was anchored off Long Island. Its commander, Vice Admiral Marriott Arbuthnot, got a tip that the French had departed from Newport.

Within thirty-six hours, he sailed in pursuit. At dawn on March 16, the two opposing squadrons sighted each other off the Virginia Capes. Heavy seas and a westerly wind prevented either force from entering the Chesapeake Bay, so Arbuthnot turned to engage the French. His poor tactical maneuvering decisions, and a changing wind during the battle allowed the French to obtain "the weather gauge" and the use of all their guns; the British could use only their upper deck guns, thus conceding the gunnery advantage to the French. Sailing in a line, the three forward-most British ships took most of the French assault while the remaining British ships were not in a position to participate. The three ships in Arbuthnot's van were so badly damaged that he elected not to pursue the French further. Instead,

---

500   Morrissey, 50-51.

he headed west and entered the bay. Destouches had won a tactical victory, clearly outfighting and outmaneuvering Arbuthnot despite having slower ships and fewer guns. But Destouches handed Arbuthnot a strategic victory by deciding to break off contact and return to Newport. That left the French admiral unable to complete his mission of helping to capture Benedict Arnold. Arbuthnot's strategic victory by default probably saved Arnold's neck.

Arbuthnot and his crippled squadron returned to New York on April 6. There, he struggled to repair his damaged vessels, as New York lacked shipyards that could handle such large ships. In ill health, Arbuthnot returned to England. He was replaced by Rear Admiral Thomas Graves, who arrived on July 4, 1781. This change of command within the British Admiralty, along with a similar change in the British fleet in the Caribbean, would have disastrous consequences for the empire.

Another British Navy Change of Command

Arguably the best naval commander operating in the Western Hemisphere on either side was British Admiral George Brydges Rodney. He commanded a squadron in the Caribbean consisting of twenty-four ships. Rear Admiral Samuel Hood was his principal deputy commander. When de Grasse entered the Caribbean in the spring of 1781, both the French and British were anxious for combat. Hood and de Grasse had a brief skirmish off Martinique in late April. Then in early May, de Grasse captured Tobago. He then sailed to Cap Haitien, where he found a frigate awaiting him with dispatches from Washington and Rochambeau. That summer, neither Rodney nor de Grasse could find the other's opposing force. On July 7, Admiral Rodney wrote to Admiral Graves in New York, warning him that a French naval force, might be heading north. He also suggested that both the Graves' squadron in New York and his own Caribbean squadron rendezvous off the Virginia Capes, consolidating their forces to oppose the large French fleet.

This message never made it to Graves. The captain of the sloop of war that carried it, not finding Graves at New York, sailed in search of him. Almost immediately, he encountered three American privateers. To escape the Americans he ran his ship aground on Long Island and sank all his cargo, including his dispatches, to keep the letter from falling into American hands.[501]

Graves did not learn of its contents until mid-August. By that time, Rodney had become sick, and with three of his ships, returned to England. That left the Caribbean squadron under Hood's command. Hood, while tactically skilled, was subordinate in rank to Graves. When the two British squadrons eventually joined, Graves would command the combined fleet. The working relationship between the two British admirals was no better than that between the generals, Clinton and

---

501   Benson Bobrick, *Angel in the Whirlwind – The Triumph of the American Revolution* (New York: Simon & Schuster, 1997), 451.

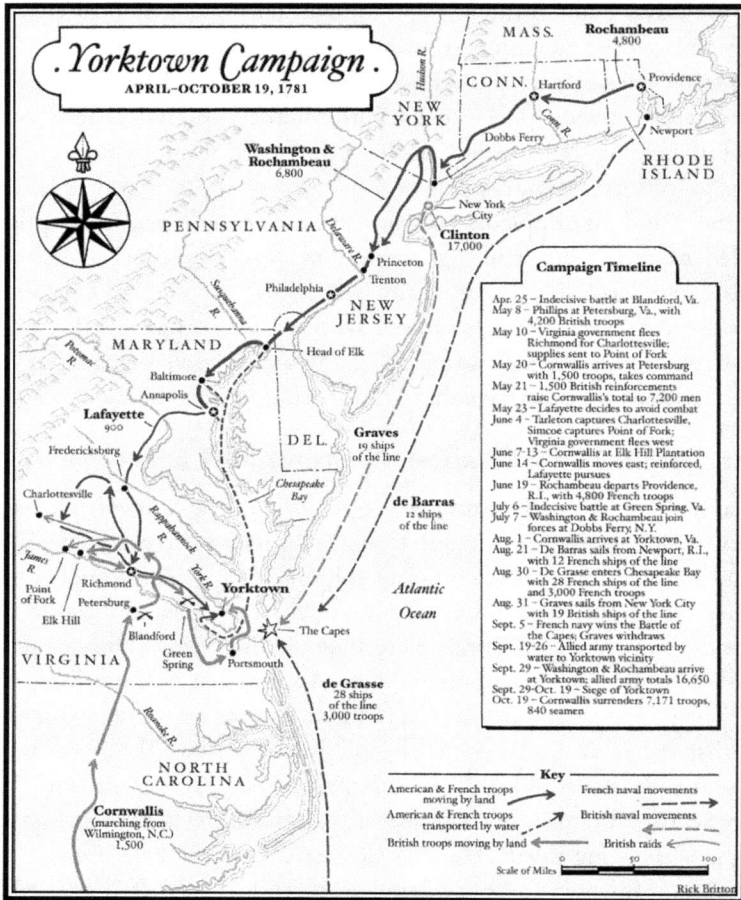

Yorktown Campaign
Courtesy of Mount Vernon Ladies' Association

Cornwallis, or before them, Howe and Burgoyne. The Graves-Hood relationship would have dire consequences for the British at Yorktown. Also, of the twenty-one British ships Rodney had left behind, only fourteen were fit for service.[502]

The Sea Race to Virginia

On August 5, de Grasse departed Haiti with twenty-six ships and five frigates, carrying thirty-two hundred French troops under the command of Major General Marquis de Saint Simon. De Grasse, knowing his ships were much slower than those of the British, sailed an indirect course between Florida and the Bahamas to confuse the enemy. Along the way, he captured three British ships.[503]

502   Morrissey , 53.
503   Ibid.

Hood, with fourteen ships, sailed north five days later but he took a more direct route to Virginia, arriving on August 21, a full five days before the French squadron. Finding neither the French fleet nor Graves's Squadron from New York at the Chesapeake Bay, Hood immediately set sail for New York, where he assumed de Grasse must be. Hood recognized that the only way to confront the larger French force was to concentrate the two British squadrons.

Hood Arrives in New York

Hood arrived in New York on August 28 to learn that his superior, Rear Admiral Graves, was out to sea. Hood also learned that on August 25, the French squadron in Newport under de Barras had set sail. Graves returned to New York on August 31 and at this point had no knowledge of de Grasse's approach from the Caribbean or of de Barras' departure from Newport.

Correctly, Graves surmised that the French squadrons under de Barras and de Grasse planned to meet at the Chesapeake. Both Graves and Hood set sail immediately, hoping to overtake de Barras and his slower French Squadron of eight ships, four frigates and eighteen transports, which carried Rochambeau's siege artillery. Like de Grasse, de Barras sailed a roundabout way, farther off shore, to avoid interception by the faster British ships pursuing him.

De Grasse Arrives in the Chesapeake Bay

When de Grasse arrived off the Virginia coast on August 30, he found the Chesapeake Bay unprotected. He anchored his ships in Lynnhaven Bay. De Grasse sent four ships to block a British escape from Yorktown. He unloaded Saint Simon's corps on the James River to link up with Lafayette. The French admiral sent smaller ships up the Chesapeake Bay to ferry both Washington's American and Rochambeau's French forces, which had marched from New Jersey and were waiting at the head of the Elk River in Maryland.[504]

Second Battle of the Virginia Capes

On September 5th the French frigate *Aigrette* signaled de Grasse's flagship *Ville de Paris* that ten sail were approaching from the northeast. Initial assumptions were that de Barras was arriving from Rhode Island, but these thoughts quickly dissolved as more sails came over the horizon. This force was larger than de Barras and could only be British. De Grasse, anxious to protect the arrival of the squadron from Rhode Island, weighed anchor and put out to sea to engage the British with twenty-four of his ships, despite having left a large contingent of his men ashore looking for forage and firewood. De Grasse did leave four ships behind to continue blockading Cornwallis at Yorktown.

504   Ibid.

<table>
<tr><td colspan="2">The French Fleet</td></tr>
</table>

The French Fleet

**Second Battle of the
Virginia Capes
5-13 September 1781**
Admiral Francois
Joseph Paul de Grasse,
commanding

Pluton (74 guns)
Marseilles (74 guns)
Bourgogne (74 guns)
Diademe (74 guns)
Reflcche (64 guns)
Auguste (80 guns)
Saint-Esprit (80 guns)
Canton (64 guns)
Cesar (74 guns)
Destin (74 guns)
Victoire (74 guns)
Ville de Paris (110 guns—De
  Grasse's flagship)
Sceptre (74 guns)
Northumberland (74 guns)
Palmier (74 guns)
Solitaire (64 guns)
Citoyen (74 guns)
Scipione (74 guns)
Hercule (74 guns)
Magnanime (74 guns)
Languedoc (80 guns)
Zele (74 guns)
Hector (74 guns)
Souverain (74 guns)

The two fleets were less evenly matched than the sheer numbers indicate: twenty-four French ships to nineteen British. The French had the weather gauge, so they could use all their guns. The British, to windward, had to keep their lower gun ports closed. The French ships were in a much better state of repair.

As Graves saw the French emerging from the Chesapeake Bay, he followed the Admiralty's Fighting Instructions and gave the signal to turn and parallel the French course. This however, reversed the normal British line of battle and placed the weaker of the British ships against stronger French opponents. Also, the best of the British commanders, Hood, was placed farthest from the French ships, which negated his superior seamanship. Hood's rear division hardly fired a shot.

The battle lasted two hours, in which more than three hundred men were killed and wounded on each side, virtually all the fighting falling to the vans and centers. French gunnery disabled five of the leading British ships. The French ships were damaged too, but de Grasse kept his numerical superiority. Most important, with both fleets now heading away from the Virginia Capes, de Grasse held the strategic advantage. The British did not lift the blockade, and the Chesapeake remained open for de Barras' arrival.

Graves shadowed de Grasse for four days, looking for another opportunity to engage him. Not knowing what to do—resume the battle, return to New York or head for the Chesapeake—he asked Hood for advice. Hood was still upset by Graves' tactics from the earlier engagement. In a fit of rage, he refused to provide Graves with any advice.

De Grasse had achieved his goals: maintaining the blockade, drawing Graves away from the Chesapeake, and allowing de Barras to enter the bay. He turned his fleet around and headed back to the Chesapeake Bay where, on September 11, he found de Barras at anchor in Lynnhaven Bay.[505]

---

505   Ibid, 57.

If the British had prevailed in this sea battle, Washington's march to Virginia would have been in vain. Additionally, his army could have been caught on the Chesapeake being transported to Yorktown without a naval escort. His army might have been sunk in their transports or captured by the British fleet. Those results would have made possible a British victory in the war.

Instead, Graves elected to return his battered fleet to New York for repairs, having concluded that the French fleet looked less badly damaged. Graves arrived in New York on September 20.

Allied Troops Arrive

While the two fleets did battle off the Virginia Capes, the main bodies of the American and French forces were ferried from Head of Elk to Williamsburg. Washington and Rochambeau rode ahead of their forces to Baltimore and completed their journey overland. They spent three days at Mount Vernon. Washington had not seen his home in six years. Washington and Rochambeau arrived in Williamsburg on September 14, ahead of their arriving armies. By September 26, the entire allied force—sixteen thousand strong—was encamped near Williamsburg. [506] Washington's force consisted of nine thousand Americans and seven thousand French.

Cornwallis Fortifies

On his arrival in Yorktown, Cornwallis commenced building a defensive perimeter. The town would not have been his choice for a defensive stand. It was chosen because Clinton had ordered Cornwallis to construct a naval

> ### The British Fleet
> **Second Battle of the Virginia Capes**
> **5-13 September 1781**
> Rear-Admiral Thomas Graves, commanding
> Alfred (74 guns)
> Belligeux (64 guns)
> Invincible (74 guns)
> Barfleur (98 guns—Hood's flagship)
> Monarch (74 guns)
> Centaur (74 guns)
> America (64 guns)
> Resolution (74 guns)
> Bedford (74 guns)
> London (90 guns—Graves's flagship)
> Royal Oak (74 guns)
> Montagu (74 guns)
> Europe (64 guns)
> Terrible (74 guns)
> Ajax (74 guns)
> Princessa (70 guns)
> Alcide (74 guns)
> Intrepid (64 guns)
> Shrewsbury (74 guns)

British Inner Defenses—Yorktown

---

506   Bobrick, 453.

The British Army
Yorktown, Virginia
General Charles Cornwallis, commanding
Fusiliers Redoubt (23rd Foot)
17th Foot
23rd Foot
33rd Foot
43rd Foot
71st Foot
76th Foot
80th Foot
Foot Guards
Queen's Rangers/British Legion Infantry
Queen's Rangers/British Legion Cavalry
1st Light Battalion
2nd Light Battalion
Light Company, 82nd Foot
1st Anspach-Bayreuth Regiment
2nd Anspach-Bayreuth Regiment
Regiment Von Bose
Regiment Prince Hereditaire
Loyalists

station with stout defensive works. Cornwallis now had to defend his chosen naval station with little to no navy to support his army.

Benjamin Franklin marveled afterwards at how not only had the French and American forces been able to coalesce with such perfect timing "from different places by land and sea, to form their junction punctually without the least regard for cross accidents or wind or weather or interruption from the enemy" and "that the [enemy] army which was their object should in the meantime have had the goodness to quit a situation from whence it might have escaped, and place itself in another from whence an escape was impossible."[507]

Under the circumstances, Cornwallis had done rather well. His defenses consisted of two entrenched lines, an exterior line and a main line closer to the town. These defensive lines included ten redoubts. Redoubts 1 and 2 lay outside the town overlooking the steep banks of Yorktown Creek; Redoubts 3, 4, and 5 faced inland overlooking a ravine behind the town; beside them was the Hornwork, a more substantial defense designed to cover the Hampton Road into Yorktown; Redoubts 6, 7, and 8 faced southeast toward Wormley Creek; while Redoubts 9 and 10 stood two hundred to three hundred yards outside the main line, commanding a small mound and the beach below riverside cliffs. Minor works were constructed in the town, to cover roads and gullies, along with fourteen batteries mounting sixty-five guns, some of them taken from British ships in the harbor.[508] A large star-shaped redoubt, named the Fusilier Redoubt, was northeast of Yorktown to cover the river road. Across the York River, Cornwallis also fortified Gloucester Point with four redoubts and twenty guns in three batteries.

Clinton's Rescue Mission

In early September, Clinton became intuitively aware of Cornwallis' predicament but thought that Cornwallis could hold out throughout October. Even letters from Cornwallis to Clinton dated mid-September reveal that Cornwallis thought he could last six weeks.

---

507   Ibid, 455-456.
508   Morrissey, 60.

Clinton conducted a council of war on September 24 where it was proposed that as soon as Graves' fleet could be repaired the British would set sail with five thousand troops to relieve Cornwallis. Graves's estimate for a sailing date, based on the time needed to repair his ships, was around October 5.

Those repairs progressed slowly due to the lack of dockyards and shortages of naval stores in New York. When Graves relayed to Clinton that repairs would not be completed until October 12, Clinton considered attacking Philadelphia, instead of launching the rescue mission, to relieve the pressure on Cornwallis. Further delays deferred the actual expedition from New York to Yorktown until October 19.

The British departed Sandy Hook, sailing with twenty-eight ships of the line and eight frigates, escorting 7,149 troops embarked in the transports. Clinton was commanding the expedition with Graves as the naval commander. Even as this large force sailed, it was unclear whether it would arrive in time to save Cornwallis, or if Graves could force his way into Chesapeake Bay past de Grasse's large French fleet that stood in the way.[509]

The Allied Army

Yorktown, Virginia
General George Washington, commanding
Maryland Continentals
New Jersey Continentals
New York Continentals
Pennsylvania Continentals
Rhode Island Continentals
Virginia Continentals
Virginia Militia (Weeden)
Virginia Militia (Stevens)
Virginia Militia (Lawson)
Hazen's Light Infantry Brigade
Muhlenberg's Light Infantry Brigade
Advance Guard
American artillery park
Sappers and miners
French Marines from De Grasse's fleet
Lauzun's Legion
Regiment Touraine
Regiment Gatenois
Regiment Agenois
Regiment Saintonge
Regiment Soissonnois
Regiment Dieux-Ponts
Regiment Bourbonnois
Voluntaires de Saint Simon
French artillery park

The Siege Begins

On September 28, Washington and his allied forces marched from Williamsburg to Yorktown. They met little British resistance along the route. When they were within six miles of Yorktown the American and French forces diverged, the Americans heading right and the French left. About noon, they pitched their respective camps about two miles from the British. Washington's allied army spread out into a semicircular line around the British position. The ends of the allied lines rested on the York River. Cornwallis was surrounded with his back to the York, which was controlled by the French navy.

Almost as soon as Washington had assumed his siege position, Cornwallis abandoned his outer line and moved all his forces to his main line of defense, much closer to the town. Washington was amazed that Cornwallis had abandoned his outer

---

509   Morrissey, 58.

Siege of Yorktown
Courtesy of Mount Vernon Ladies' Association

defenses without a fight. The allies had regarded this British position as completely defensible and from the British perspective, worth the struggle to hold. Defending the outer line would have helped deplete the allied forces. More important, it would buy time for the Clinton rescue expedition to arrive from New York. Cornwallis would argue afterwards that he had just received a dispatch from Clinton that a mighty fleet of twenty-three ships of the line bearing five thousand men would soon sail from New York to lift the siege. With this information Cornwallis thought it better to hold out by consolidating his inner line. In a response to Clinton, Cornwallis reveals his confidence of success, hinging on the timely arrival of the relief expedition.

> "I have ventured these last two days to look General Washington's whole force in the face . . . and have the pleasure to assure your Excellency that there is but one wish throughout the army, which is that the enemy would advance . . . I shall retire this night within the works, and have no doubt, if relief arrives in any reasonable time, York and Gloucester will be both in the possession of His Majesty's troops."[510]

Little did he know that Clinton would not be able to sail on October 5 as originally planned due to the delays in repairing Graves's ships.

Washington's allied army promptly occupied the evacuated British outer defensive line and turned it against its builder, as well as adding new redoubts.

---

510   Bobrick, 456.

The British evacuation of their outer position saved the allies considerable time and labor, plus of course the many lives it would have cost to take it by force. Additionally, from this position the allies were able to view the town's defenses and the small but commanding knolls and ravines that previously protected the British. By occupying the abandoned outer line, the allies gained much-needed cover from the British artillery.

With Tarleton's Legion and Simcoe's Queen's Rangers across the river in Gloucester, Washington needed to prevent them from launching foraging expeditions and to stop them from providing an escape route. To counter Tarleton and Simcoe, Washington deployed eighteen hundred infantry, three hundred cavalry and eight hundred French marines. [511]

Siege Warfare

The siege of Yorktown progressed along the classic rules for investiture that had been established more than a century before by the French Marshal Sébastien de Vauban. The first of a series of parallel encircling trenches was opened by the allies about six hundred yards from the besieged British fortifications. These trenches were dug out of range of small-arms fire and grape and canister shot. The earth removed from the parallels was thrown over bundles of sticks called fascines in front of the parallel trench to form parapets, and earthen artillery batteries were constructed and connected to the parallels by additional trenches.

Smaller trenches called saps, protected by earth-filled basket-like gabions, were dug

First Allied Siege Line—Yorktown

in a manner that zigzagged toward the enemy's walls. Meanwhile siege guns had been landed from the French ships and heavy guns brought up from the James River.

Effects of the Siege

The surrounding of the British forces by sea and land had an almost immediate effect. Supplies started running short. One British soldier complained:

"We get terrible provisions now . . . putrid meat and wormy biscuits that have spoiled on the ships. Many of the men have taken sick here with

---

511   Ibid, 457.

dysentery or the bloody flux and diarrhea . . . Foul fever is spreading . . . we have had little rest day or night."[512]

For meat, the British began to kill their horses in great numbers and for days afterward the skinned and butchered carcasses were seen floating down the York River.[513]

Several hundred blacks who had been deliberately infected with smallpox were expelled from Yorktown in an attempt to cause an epidemic in the allied camp. It was clear that Cornwallis was willing to do anything to keep his hopes alive.[514]

Tightening the Noose

On October 6, the allies commenced to dig their first parallel entrenchment,

Second Allied Siege Line—Yorktown

eight hundred yards from the British lines. Over forty-three hundred allied troops entered the initial trenches to protect the fifteen hundred others who were tasked to dig them deep enough to protect those who manned the positions. By October 9, the first parallel was complete and artillery was brought forward. After two days of continuous firing, all the British guns were knocked out of action. It was rumored that Washington personally fired the first salvo. By this point, Cornwallis had received word that the Clinton rescue mission had been delayed.[515]

Capture of Redoubts 9 and 10

On the night of October 11, the allies started digging second parallel trench only three hundred fifty to four hundred yards from the British. Two days were spent bringing up the artillery and strengthening the line. The second parallel could not be completed without capturing British Redoubts 9 and 10, which were forward and outside the main defensive line.

---

512   Ibid.
513   Ibid.
514   Ibid.
515   U.S. Department of Interior, National Park Service, "Yorktown - *The Siege*", https://www. nps.gov/york/learn/historyculture/the-siege.htm, February 27, 2015. (July 20, 2018).

During the night of October 14, four hundred French soldiers from the Deux Ponts and Gatenois Regiments stormed Redoubt 9. Defended by 120 British and Hessians, it put up a spirited thirty-minute defense but quickly surrendered as they were over matched.

Redoubt 9—Yorktown

Barely one hundred yards from Redoubt 9 was Redoubt 10. Defended by seventy British troops, it too was attacked this night by four hundred men of Gimat's, Hamilton's and Laurens's Light Infantry Battalions. Alexander Hamilton led the way, his men advancing with unloaded muskets. The redoubt fell within ten minutes. All the British were either killed or captured.[516]

Redoubt 10—Yorktown

Redoubts 9 and 10 were immediately incorporated into the second parallel. With the loss of Redoubts 9 and 10, Cornwallis reported to Clinton:

> "The safety of the place is, therefore, so precarious that I cannot recommend that the fleet and army should run any great risk in endeavoring to save us."[517]

Last Stand

Cornwallis decided that it would be dishonorable to surrender without attempting to test the allied siege line. Before sunrise on October 16, Cornwallis attacked the allied center. He desired to silence a couple of French artillery batteries. Attacking with three hundred fifty Light Infantry and Foot Guards, the British were initially successful in spiking several French and American cannons but were eventually driven off. The allied artillery was firing again within six hours.[518]

---

516   Morrissey, 71.
517   Ibid.
518   National Park Service, Yorktown

British Attempt to Escape

That evening Cornwallis attempted to evacuate Yorktown with his entire force by crossing the York River to his other defenses at Gloucester Point. Once his forces were consolidated there, he planned to break out and march north.

Using sixteen boats that could hold one hundred men each, Cornwallis

Patriot Militia Reenactment—Gloucester County, Virginia

was successful in ferrying a thousand men of the Guards and Light Infantry over to Gloucester Point. But another act of Divine Providence derailed his plan when a violent storm arose at midnight that scattered his boats. All ferrying stopped during the storm and Cornwallis concluded not enough time remained during the darkness to complete ferrying his entire force. He recalled the thousand troops that had already made their escape to Gloucester.

Surrender

As the sun rose on October 17, a British drummer climbed on top of a parapet and began beating the signal for parley. It's most likely that the drummer was

Moore House—Yorktown

unheard over the noise of the allied bombardment. Soon an officer emerged from the British line with a white handkerchief and approached the American lines, clearly indicating a request to cease fire. A number of notes were passed between Washington and Cornwallis during the day that set the framework for a British surrender. Cornwallis wrote Washington:

"Sir I propose a cessation of hostilities for twenty-four hours, and that two officers may be appointed by each side, to meet at Mr. Moore's house, to settle terms for the surrender of the post of York and Gloucester."[519]

---

519   Ibid.

The next day a party of four officers, one American, one French, and two British, met at the home of Augustine Moore, one mile outside of Yorktown, to settle the conditions of surrender.

Fourteen Articles of Capitulation were drawn up and would be signed by both Cornwallis and Washington. One article stated that the surrender ceremony contained a provision that deprived the British of the honors of war.

It was the custom in this period to allow the surrendering troops to march out of their works with their regimental flags flying and playing an enemy's tune in honor of the victor. Washington demanded that "the same honors will be granted to the surrendering army as granted the garrison of Charleston." In May 1780, when the American army surrendered Charleston, it was humiliated by not being given the honors of war, therefore, in retribution, the British would not be granted honors at Yorktown. The British were to march out with shouldered arms, battle flags cased, and drums beating a British or German march. They were then to lay down their arms and return to their encampment, where they were to remain until they were marched to the places of their captivity.

At 2 p.m. on October 19, 1781, Cornwallis's army marched, sullen and dispirited, out of Yorktown on the Hampton Road, past the French on the left and Americans on the right. Cornwallis was not at the head of his surrendering army, pleading that he was sick. He instead sent his deputy, Brigadier-General Charles O'Hara, to present Cornwallis's sword. O'Hara offered the sword to Rochambeau, who properly declined and pointed towards Washington, who also refused

Surrender Field—Yorktown

to accept it. Instead, he directed O'Hara to Washington's own second-in-command, Benjamin Lincoln—who had been the American commander who surrendered at Charleston.

As the sword ceremony played out, the British garrison from Yorktown and the cavalry laid down their arms in a nearby field. The remainder of the Gloucester garrison surrendered the next day. Thus ended the last major battle of the American Revolution.

As these surrender ceremonies were taking place, Clinton was setting sail from New York to rescue Cornwallis. He arrived in Hampton Roads five days later to

Washington before Yorktown by Rembrandt Peale

discover the disaster. In all, the allies captured 7,247 British officers and men, 840 British sailors, and 244 pieces of artillery. [520]

Making Peace

In February 1782 a Whig government was elected in England with the intent of making peace. In March, Parliament agreed to a cessation of hostilities. Both

520   Morrissey, 76.

England and America, as well as France, appointed commissioners to conduct peace negotiations in Paris. On January 20, 1783, a peace treaty was signed in Paris. America had won its freedom. The news of the Treaty of Paris did not reach America until March, and hostilities did not officially cease until April 19, exactly eight years to the day after the first Patriots had fallen at Lexington, Massachusetts.

Washington Says His Goodbyes to the Army

The last British forces left New York City by November 25, 1783. On December 4, Washington met with his ranking officers in the Fraunces Tavern on the corner of Broad and Pearl Streets to say farewell. He was preparing to depart for Annapolis, Maryland and a meeting with Congress. In Annapolis he was prepared to surrender his commission as commander-in-chief.

This was a most difficult period in American history. The Department of Finance was empty, government salaries were in arrears, and fundamental prior commitments to those who had served in the army could not be met.[521] Inflation made paper money worthless. Some argued that Washington could have appointed himself king of America and America would have accepted it. Washington had in fact received correspondence to that effect from Colonel Lewis Nicola, the former commander of Fort Mifflin, one of the defenses of Philadelphia. Nicola urged Washington to seize power and with the army's help, enthrone himself king or dictator to establish a strong stable government. Washington responded:

"With a mixture of great surprise and astonishment I have read [your proposal] which to me seems big with the greatest mischiefs that can befall my Country. If I am not deceived in myself, you could not have found a person to whom your schemes were more disagreeable . . . Let me conjure you then, if you have any regard for your Country, for yourself or posterity, or respect for me, to banish these thoughts from your Mind, and never communicate, as from yourself, or anyone else, a sentiment of like nature."[522]

Washington poured himself a glass of wine in the Fraunces Tavern and addressed his men:

"With a heart full of love and gratitude, I now take leave of you. I most devoutly wish that your latter days may be as prosperous and happy as your former ones have been glorious and honorable. I cannot come to each of you to take my leave, but shall be obliged if each of you will come and take me by hand."[523]

521   Bobrick, 473.
522   Ibid.
523   Ibid, 478.

Each man came forward and shook Washington's hand and embraced him, starting with Henry Knox. Lieutenant Colonel Benjamin Tallmadge describes the event:

> "Such a scene of sorrow and weeping, I have never before witnessed, and hope I may never be called upon to witness again . . . The simple thought that we were then about to part from the man who had conducted us through a long and bloody war, and under whose conduct the glory and independence of our country had been achieved, and that we should see his face no more in this world, seemed to me utterly insupportable."[524]

Washington Resigns His Commission

On December 23, at the Old Maryland State House in Annapolis, before the Congress of the United States, George Washington submitted his resignation as commander in chief of the Continental Army. He wanted to do everything in his power to display his humility before the civilian government. Washington's resignation was a carefully prepared affair, to show a doubting world that this new republic would not degenerate into disorder.

Washington arrived wearing his familiar uniform for the last time. He was greeted by Charles Thomson, the secretary of Congress, who led him to his seat on the dais. About twenty representatives sat in the audience. The doors were opened, and the town gentry poured into the hall. Everyone pressed into the hall to sneak a peek at the historic transaction.[525]

Following a precise script, Washington rose and bowed to the congressmen. As he spoke, he held the speech in his right hand, which began to shake so violently that he had to steady it with his left. In a voice hoarse with emotion, he recalled his feelings of inadequacy when first appointed and stated that he had been sustained only "by confidence in the rectitude of our cause, the support of the supreme power of the union, and the patronage of heaven."[526] He paid honor to the men who had served with him and mildly urged Congress to take care of them, reminding them of the troops who had been sent home unpaid. It was at this stage that he had to grasp the speech with two trembling hands. When he commended "our dearest country to the protection of Almighty God," said James McHenry, "his voice faltered and sank and the whole house felt his agitations."[527] After a pause, he recovered his composure and closed on a poetic note, implying his permanent withdrawal:

> "Having now finished the work assigned me, I retire from the great theater of action; and bidding an affectionate farewell to this august body

---

524 Ibid.
525 Chernow, 454-455.
526 Ibid, 456.
527 Ibid.

under whose orders I have so long acted, I here offer my commission and take my leave of all the employments of public life."[528]

The emotional impact was overpowering. "The General was so much affected himself that everybody felt for him," commented a woman named Mary Ridout, who said that "many tears were shed.'"[529]

As Thomas Jefferson wrote:

"The moderation and virtue of a single character . . . probably prevented this revolution from being closed, as most others had been, by subversion of that liberty it was intended to establish."[530]

The resigning of his commission was a momentous act, establishing a precedent for the subordination of military to civilian authority, no matter how great that military power was. This precedent remains today. Alexis de Tocqueville, a French diplomat who wrote about America in the nineteenth century, once observed that the fight for American independence had "contracted no alliance with the turbulent passion of anarchy." "Not a single political murder was committed before the war began, and at the end of the war, no military coup or dictatorship subverted its ideals." Recalling the excesses of his own country's revolution, Tocqueville wrote, "Nor were there bloodthirsty revolutionary tribunals, to mete out Justice to dissenters or unseated administrators in years to follow. All the men who signed the Declaration of Independence died in bed."[531] We can thank George Washington for this.

After a closing speech by the president of the Congress, Thomas Mifflin, Washington shook hands and said his farewells with each member of Congress. He had already checked out

Washington Resigns—Old State House, Annapolis

of the George Mann Tavern and his bags were packed, horse and attendants waiting outside the State House door. He mounted his horse, and rode off in a rush. "It was a solemn and affecting spectacle, such a one as history does not present," McHenry

---

528   "From George Washington to the United States Congress, 23 December 1783." *Founders Online,* National Archives, https://founders.archives.gov/documents/washington/99-01-02-12223. (April 11, 2019).
529   Chernow, 456.
530   Ibid.
531   Bobrick, 492.

said.[532] "The spectators all wept and there was hardly a member of Congress who did not drop tears."[533] A small group escorted Washington to the South River ferry. Then he was finally alone on horseback with his two aides and servants, heading for Mount Vernon.[534] Washington arrived at Mount Vernon just as the sun was setting on Christmas Eve 1783.

The Road to Yorktown – Luck or Divine Providence

Could all the events and incredible timing that lead to the allied victory at Yorktown have been just luck or was Divine Providence in play? How could it be that the British could never coordinate the actions of two armies without one ending in defeat? Yet, in this case, Washington's coordination with three armies and two navies was not only brilliant but precise. The timing of the allied armies and French fleet was perfect despite all the trappings of coordinating over vast distances. I argue that this victory was God's hand at work. I'm not alone. Admiral Chester Nimitz writes in *Seapower*:

> "Miracles do not often occur in military and naval operations, but
> Yorktown was a miracle. At a time the American cause was disintegrating,
> it brought victory. At a time when the British could not effectively
> coordinate two armies in the colonies . . . it was an example of perfect
> coordination of a fleet with the armies of two different nations. At a time
> when communications were slow and unreliable, it demonstrated precise
> timing on the part of forces fifteen hundred miles apart."[535]

The combination of the most amazing and bizarre events of the war brought about the outcome.

- **The Letters:** When General Washington's uncoded letter of May 31, 1781, fell into Clinton's hands, the British commander thought he had evidence that Washington intended to attack New York. Clinton completely missed his opportunity to attack and defeat Washington as his enemy marched out of his positions around New York en route to Virginia. Also, after acquiring Washington's correspondence, Clinton proceeded to confuse not only himself but Cornwallis with contradictory orders. While Washington's letter caused great confusion within the British leadership, Admiral Rodney's correspondence to Graves warning him of de Grasse's departure from the Caribbean and the need to consolidate British naval forces at the Chesapeake was clear and "spot on." However, it did not find its intended recipient.

---

532   Chernow, 456.
533   Ibid.
534   Ibid, 457.
535   Potter and Nimitz, 90.

The ship that transported the British message was intercepted by American privateers, ran itself aground, and sank with the letter still aboard. Had this letter found its destination—Graves—the British fleet would have joined off the Virginia Capes setting the trap for the arrival of de Grasse's French fleet. Instead, when Hood arrived off Virginia, he did not find either the French fleet or Graves waiting as had been ordered in the Rodney correspondence. Hood in turn assumed, incorrectly, that the French had sailed to New York. And so did he. The French, sailing more slowly and in a more round-about route than the much faster British, would later sail into Chesapeake Bay unopposed and commence the blockade of Cornwallis.

- **British Chain of Command:** Even though Cornwallis was subordinate to Clinton, he was allowed to correspond directly with Germain, the British secretary of state in England, bypassing the chain of command. The lack of coordination between Cornwallis and Clinton can be directly attributed to Germain allowing Cornwallis to correspond directly with him without first going to Clinton. This kept Clinton in the dark as to Cornwallis's activities in the Carolinas during the winter and spring of 1781. It is inexplicable that this was still an issue within the British communication network, especially since the same issue contributed to the surrender of Burgoyne's army at Saratoga in 1777.

- **Admiral Rodney's Illness:** Rodney was England's most experienced naval commander. His untimely illness caused him to return to England prior to the Second Battle of the Virginia Capes. He turned his command over to Hood, who was up to the task. But when Hood's squadron combined with the Graves's New York squadron, it was Graves who was senior and who commanded at the Second Battle of the Virginia Capes. Graves did not have the same expertise as Rodney or Hood, and made poor decisions, despite having the advantage of faster and more maneuverable ships. Throwing away his advantages, Graves was defeated by the French. Had Rodney—or even Hood,—commanded at the Second Battle of the Virginia Capes, the outcome may well have been different.

- **Cornwallis's Decision:** Cornwallis's decision to evacuate his outer defensive line at Yorktown cost him the time needed for Clinton to transport his rescue force to the Chesapeake. Clinton's letter informing Cornwallis when to expect his rescue force was the basis of that decision. However, the letter was obviously written when the plan was drafted and did not address the delays that Graves would experience in repairing his ships. Those delays caused the British to depart New York two weeks later than projected and arrive five days after Cornwallis surrendered. If Cornwallis had forced Washington to fight to obtain those outer defensive positions, the time required to accomplish that task would have been enough for Clinton's rescue mission to arrive.

- **Storm at Gloucester Point:** Cornwallis attempted to evacuate his entire force at night across the York River to Gloucester Point. After successfully ferrying over a thousand troops across the river, gales completely scattered his boats and forced him to give up the escape attempt.

- **The Timing Miracle:** Washington and the French allies made many sound decisions that led to the victories at the Virginia Capes and Yorktown. Historians have rightly recognized them for the brilliance of the campaign. Only when one considers the complexity of these events and the precise timing of the arriving forces over vast distances with little to no communications, do we lay witness to the miraculous nature of this victory and the hand of God at work.[536]

As Benson Bobrick articulates in *Angels in the Whirlwind*, "If some angel did not ride in this whirlwind, what can we say?" I agree. What can we say?

Gloucester County Militia

Chapter 10

Mount Sinai and the New Republic

You will think me transported with enthusiasm, but I am not. I am well aware of the toil, and blood, and treasure that it will cost us to maintain this Declaration, and support and defend these states. Yet through all the gloom, I can see the rays of ravishing light and glory. I can see that the end is more than worth all the means, and that posterity will triumph in that day's transaction, even though we should rue it, which I trust in God we shall not.

John Adams to Abigail Adams
July 3, 1776

B ack at Mount Vernon after the war, Washington was content to live the quiet life on the Potomac River. After leaving public service he would find the crowing of the morning rooster and mooing of the cow replacements for the rattle of the restless army camp, and the beating of the drum that awakened him from his sleep for the previous eight years. Washington devoted himself to animal husbandry, the cultivation of his land, and the running of the many diverse businesses associated with his plantation.

But all was not well in America. Governed by the Articles of Confederation, the government still struggled financially, and disorder was growing commercially as each state pursued its own economic interests. The economy was wrecked by inflation. Congress was slow to grant pensions for the soldiers who fought in the war. Congress had been unable to impose taxes or regulate currency, credit or commerce; to exercise full control over the military; or to enforce any civil law.[537] The Articles of Confederation, which loosely held the thirteen states together, had managed to win a long and complex war, but with the increase in dissatisfaction came social unrest. America had a staggering national debt and the Congress, as organized, had no answers to the nation's problems.

Even Washington felt the effects of the war and the country's new found freedom. Mount Vernon had been in neglect for eight years; he found conditions worse than he had assumed. Eighteen slaves had run away and nine had to be sold

---

537   Chernow, 488.

during the war's most difficult years to pay the taxes.[538] Plantation industries like his fishery and ferry had done well on paper, but inflation made payment in paper almost worthless. Lund Washington, who had maintained the plantation during the war, was delinquent in his bookkeeping and in collecting rent from western lands. Washington had to settle most of his debts by selling land, as he was land rich but cash poor.

In America there were those with separatist tendencies, some desiring to divide into thirteen separate countries. At this time an American when referring to his or her "country" meant his or her own state. Imperial union had departed but national unity had yet to take its place.[539] Americans complained about their new-found freedom.

Similar to the Israelites in the Desert

The post-war Americans were similar to the Israelites in the desert on their Exodus journey. After receiving their freedom, for the first months in the desert the "stiff-necked" Israelites complain to Moses about the lack of food and water. If only we had died "in the land of Egypt," they cried, "when we sat by the fleshpots." These incidents in the wilderness have a clear theme: the Israelites were not yet truly free. They were still trapped in the slavishness of the past and unable to cope with being a liberated people. The Moses narrative contains at least a dozen different rebellion stories in which the people gripe about everything from water and food, to their leadership, to God. The Israelites had this misplaced notion that freedom means lack of responsibility.[540]

Freedom then Law

After two months, the Israelites arrived at Mount Sinai and God summoned Moses to the top of the mountain, saying; "I bore you on eagles' wings" so you could become a "holy nation." God provided Moses ten commandments and 613 additional laws, then gave Moses two stone tablets containing their pact. The solution for Israel was to voluntarily commit itself to a new form of bondage. To "reenslave" oneself. For them this meant accepting the law God handed down to Moses on Mount Sinai. [541]

America's Mount Sinai—Philadelphia 1787

State delegates met in Annapolis in September 1786 to discuss what was to be done to solve America's problems. The delegates unanimously agreed that the states

---

538   Douglas Southall Freeman, *George Washington* Volume Six *Patriot and President* (Charles Scribner's Sons: New York), 1954, 4.
539   Chernow, 488.
540   Fielder, 91.
541   Ibid, 17.

should send delegates to a convention in Philadelphia on the second Monday in May 1787. The purpose of the assembly was to:

> ". . . take into consideration the situation of the United States, to devise such further provisions as shall appear to them necessary to render the constitution of the federal government adequate to the exigencies of the Union; and to report such an act for that purpose to the United States in Congress assembled, as, when agreed to by them, and afterwards confirmed by the legislatures of every State will effectually provide for the same."[542]

Most thought this meant making adjustments to the ineffective Articles of Confederation.

Even though Virginia selected Washington as one of its delegates to the convention, he initially refused. He had his doubts that the country could be saved. Particularly troubling was an uprising that had broken out in Massachusetts, what became known as Shay's Rebellion. Washington was reluctant to accept his nomination. He wavered back and forth between passionate concern for saving the union and an insistence that he couldn't go to Philadelphia. He saw America as a "house on fire," saying that unless emergency measures were taken, the building would be "reduced to ashes," and somebody else would have to extinguish the blaze.[543]

Washington realized that some citizens would suspect that the Convention was nothing more than a ploy to create a quasi-royal central government seeking to seize power from the states. Washington also knew he would most likely be elected the Convention's leader, and as such, proposed as the nation's first executive. He did not want to be perceived as grasping for power. Being an active participant in the Convention with its implied presidential caveat, he would certainly be perceived as such by the public.[544] But he knew from his experience as commander in chief during the war that a more effective government with central powers was needed to keep the colonies unified. He wrote to his friend William Gordon:

> "Certain I am that unless adequate powers are given to Congress for the general purposes of the Federal Union that we shall soon moulder into dust and become contemptible in the eyes of Europe, if we are not made the sport of her politics . . . To suppose that the general concerns of this country can be directed by thirteen heads, or one head without competent powers, is a solecism, the bad effects of which every man who has had the

---

542   Ibid.
543   Chernow, 523.
544   William P. Kladky, Ph.D. "Constitutional Convention," *George Washington's Mount Vernon*, https://www.mountvernon.org/library/digitalhistory/digital-encyclopedia/article/constitutional-convention/. (February 24, 2019).

practical knowledge to judge from that I have, is fully convinced of; though none perhaps has felt them in so forcible a degree. The People at large and at a distance from the theatre of action, who only know that the machine was kept in motion and that they are at last arrived at the first object of their wishes, are satisfied with the event without investigating the slow progress to it or the expenses which have been incurred."[545]

To many Americans, insufficient power at the national level meant that one thing was lacking: a king. This sentiment was outrageous to Washington, even though he undoubtedly would have been chosen for the position. He wrote John Jay:

"I am told that even respectable characters speak of a monarchical form of government without horror. What a triumph for the advocates of despotism to find that we are incapable of governing ourselves, and that systems founded on the basis of equal liberty are merely ideal and fallacious!"[546]

James Madison and Henry Knox convinced Washington to accept his nomination. As one of Virginia's delegates, Washington arrived in Philadelphia on May 13, 1787, lodging in the home of Mr. and Mrs. Robert Morris. He renewed his acquaintance with Benjamin Franklin, also a delegate to the Constitutional Convention. Like Washington, Franklin's, name would add legitimacy to the proceedings.

The convention, held in Philadelphia's Independence Hall during a hot and steamy summer season, was slow to assemble. On May 14, the date set for the convention's start, only Virginia and Pennsylvania were represented.

The Virginia delegation took advantage of the time spent waiting for enough delegates to form a quorum. The group from Virginia included James Madison and George Mason. Working two to three hours per day, led by Madison, the Virginians developed a new plan of government. By May 25, enough delegates had arrived and the convention officially met. Immediately adding to the discomfort and tension, the

Philadelphia's Independence Hall

545   Chernow, 489.
546   W.W. Abbot, ed., *The Papers of George Washington*, Confederation Series, vol 4, *2 April 1786-31 January 1787* (Charlottesville: University Press of Virginia, 1995), 212-213.

Benjamin Franklin, by Charles Willson Peale

delegates demanded that the hall's windows be kept shut so they could meet in secret.

As he expected, Washington was selected as president of the Convention. His colleagues certainly knew that at crucial times during this process, Washington's prestige might be the only thing holding the Convention together, while impatience, heated arguments, mistrust, and the delegates' unfamiliarity with each other threatened to tear it apart.

Sun Carving on Washington's Chair

Assembly Room—Washington's Chair

The role of president of the Convention was perfect for Washington. By accepting the position, he was lifted above the partisan debate. His was a nonspeaking role that was perfect for his discreet nature. It spared him the need to voice opinions or to make speeches, and enabled him to lend both ears to all, thereby learning much that he had not acquired from his wartime experiences or from running his plantation. The Constitutional Convention was much like his years as a surveyor and French and Indian War soldier under General Braddock. It provided him an education and preparation for something bigger yet to come.

As the Convention's president, Washington assumed his position in the front of the Assembly Room. A desk and tall wooden chair were placed on an elevated platform. The chair had a rising sun carved on its back slat. As heated deliberations progressed, Benjamin Franklin remarked that all through the hot summer he wondered if the gilded sun on Washington's chair was rising or setting.

So our comparison of Moses and Washington continues. The Constitutional Convention would play the part of Mount Sinai. Like Moses, who delivered God's laws to the Hebrew nation, Washington as president of the Convention would deliver the new laws to the Congress and the American people.

Washington's position would be difficult if not impossible. Holding these diverse delegates together and on point proved to be like herding cats. Jealous states would find it impossible to consent to create a government greater than their own. Douglas Southall Freeman observed, "Every self-esteemed little Caesar had rather be first in an Atlantic village than second at a western Rome."[547]

On May 29, Edmund Randolph of Virginia "laid before the House, for their consideration, sundry propositions, in writing, concerning the American

---

547   Freeman, Vol Six, 91.

confederation and the establishment of a national government."[548] What Randolph was proposing was the body of work developed by the delegates from Virginia, which became known as the Virginia Plan.

The Virginia Plan

Under the proposed Virginia Plan, the government would consist of three branches: legislative, executive, and judicial. The legislature was to consist of two chambers, one elected by the people of the various states and the other chosen by the elected branch from a list of nominees submitted by the individual state legislatures. This central two-house lawmaking body was to have the relevant powers vested in Congress by the Articles of Confederation and, in addition, the power to pass laws where states were unable to act or were not in harmony. All state laws that contravened the terms of union could be "negated" by the "National Legislature," which likewise could "call forth the force of the Union against any member of the Union failing to fulfill its duty under the articles thereof." A "National Executive" would have the powers suggested by the title, insofar as the Articles of Confederation conferred authority of this type of Congress. "A general authority to execute the national laws" was added. The "National Judiciary" was to have particular regard to "questions which may involve the national peace and harmony."[549]

Debate

After hearing the Virginia Plan and another plan of government proposed by Charles Pinckney of South Carolina, the assembly quickly resolved to replace instead of merely rewriting the Articles of Confederation. Debate and compromise centered on the Virginia Plan. Division of power between branches of government and between the federal and state governments, slavery, trade, taxes, foreign affairs, representation and the procedure to elect the president were a few of the contentious issues. Diverging ideas, egos, regional demands and states' rights made solutions difficult.

On June 28, a heated, passionate debate almost shut down the Convention. Franklin rose to the occasion by appealing to a higher perspective and suggested that each day's proceedings open with a prayer. He addressed his statement to Washington as president.

> "I have lived, Sir, a long time, and the longer I live, the move convincing proofs I see of this truth—that God governs in the affairs of men. And if a sparrow cannot fall to the ground without his notice, is it possible that an empire can rise without his aid? We have been assured, Sir, in the sacred writings, that 'except the Lord built the House they labour in vain that built

---

548   Ibid, 92.
549   Ibid, 92-93.

it.' I firmly believe this; and I also believe that without his concurring aid we shall succeed in this political building no better than the Builders of Babel. I therefore beg leave to move—that henceforth prayers imploring the assistance of Heaven, and its blessings on our deliberations be held in this Assembly every morning before we proceed to business."[550]

Clearly, at eighty-one years of age, and all that he had witnessed, Franklin believed that God's hand had guided the forming of this American republic.

After four months of exhausting debate, compromise, and creative ideas, a new Constitution was produced that created a federal republic with a strong central government. It also left most of the power with the state governments. Washington's most significant contribution to the new Constitution was the fact that he allowed for the connection of his name with the Convention, as its president, and its final product.

The Miracle of the Constitution

Washington was a strong supporter of the newly written Constitution. As he stated, it was "the result of a spirit of amity and mutual concession" and more coherent than anyone had a right to expect from so many discordant delegates with passionate opinions.[551] The miracle of the writing of the American Constitution was the fact that such a document could be produced from such a diverse body of Americans. George Washington thought so too, writing to Lafayette that it struck him as "little short of a miracle" and that "delegates from so many different states . . . should unite in forming a system of national government so little liable to well-founded objections."[552] Like Franklin, Washington too thought God had his hand in the writing of the United States Constitution. He said, "We may, with a kind of pious and grateful exultation, trace the finger of Providence through those dark and

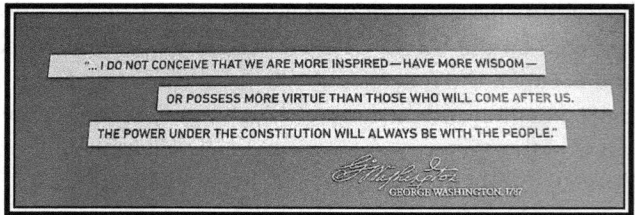

"... I DO NOT CONCEIVE THAT WE ARE MORE INSPIRED— HAVE MORE WISDOM—
OR POSSESS MORE VIRTUE THAN THOSE WHO WILL COME AFTER US.
THE POWER UNDER THE CONSTITUTION WILL ALWAYS BE WITH THE PEOPLE."
GEORGE WASHINGTON 1787

Washington's Words from the National Constitution Center—Philadelphia

mysterious events." He also warned generations to come that he had confidence that the new government would prevent oppression "so long as there shall remain any virtue in the body of the people."[553]

550   Carl Van Doren, *Benjamin Franklin* (New York: Bramhall House 1938), 747-748.
551   Chernow, 538.
552   W.W. Abbot, ed., *The Papers of George Washington,* Confederation Series, vol 6, *1 January 1788-23 September 1788* (Charlottesville: University Press of Virginia, 1997), 95-98.
553   Spivey, 80.

Like Moses, who delivered God's laws to the Hebrew nation, on September 17, 1787, Washington delivered the proposed new laws—the United States Constitution—to the Congress and the American people.

Franklin determined that the sun carved into the back of Washington's chair was in fact rising, a symbol a young nation ascending at the dawn of its new government.

Ratification

The second miracle of the United States Constitution was its ratification. The Constitution was ferociously controversial at first and produced impassioned arguments from all quarters. The country was as divided in 1787 as it is today in 2019. Consider the difficulty, if not impossibility, of adding an amendment to the Constitution in 2019. The ratification of the Constitution in 1787-1788 was just as difficult. Of the fifty-five delegates who started the convention, only forty-two remained at the end. Only thirty-nine put their signature on the document.

To ensure that the Constitution would derive its lawfulness from the people, not state governments, the framers required that the ratification process would require approval by a special convention in each state. The Constitution would become the law of the land only after ratification from nine states.

Washington returned to Mount Vernon and moved silently into the background of the ratification process. He worried that those with an unfavorable opinion of the Constitution would be more vocal and successful in influencing the ratification process than those who were supporters.

Of immediate concern was the fact that both Edmund Randolph, the governor of Virginia, and George Mason, both of whom were Virginia delegates to the Constitutional Convention, were among the three who refused to sign the document. Washington feared that another influential Virginian, Patrick Henry, would also join with the dissenters. Washington engaged in low-key lobbying.[554] Additionally, of concern to Washington, if Virginia failed to ratify the Constitution, he would not be eligible for the presidency.

To help advocate in favor of the Constitution and explain the framers' intent, Alexander Hamilton, James Madison, and John Jay published a series of essays under the anonymous name "Publius." The essays were called *The Federalist*. *The Federalist* must have appeared to the Constitution's advocates as an answered prayer; they transcended journalism and would take on a classic status. Washington told Hamilton that "when the transient circumstances and fugitive performances which attended this crisis shall have disappeared, that work will merit the notice of posterity." Washington was right, for *The Federalist Papers* are still referenced today on critical legal and constitutional issues. Washington routinely spread issues of *The Federalist* to influential Virginians for advocacy and publication.

554   Chernow, 545.

By mid-January 1788, the five states of Pennsylvania, New Jersey, Delaware, Georgia, and Connecticut had ratified the Constitution. Washington was still concerned about New York and Virginia, particularly his own state. As the United States' biggest, richest, and most populous state, its ratification would be key.

By May three more states had ratified the Constitution—Massachusetts, Maryland, and South Carolina—bringing the total to eight. This put additional pressure on states that had yet to hold their conventions.

In June, Virginia held its Ratifying Convention. At this point, Governor Randolph had changed his opinion and joined the Federalists—those in favor of the Constitution. On June 21, when New Hampshire became the ninth state to ratify, all the uncertainty associated with the Constitution's future was over. America's new form of government was born. Four days later Virginia ratified, followed by New York in July.

Washington celebrated at Wise's Tavern in Alexandria, Virginia, where he ate dinner and drank thirteen toasts, punctuated by cannon salutes. Upon returning home to Mount Vernon, Washington wrote:

> ". . . we may rationally indulge the pleasing hope that the Union will now be established upon a durable basis and that Providence seems still disposed to favor the members of it, with unequalled opportunities for political happiness."[555]

Presidential Election

Once the Constitution was the law of the land, the question became: who would become the first president of the United States? Washington could not ignore the question; he stood in a "league of his own" among America's Founding Fathers. But like many of the founders, he regarded any open interest in power as unbecoming to a gentleman. He preferred to be recruited for the position. Washington also worried that the public would think he had yielded to the allure of worldly pomp and had cynically broken his pledge not to return to public life.[556]

Washington's name recognition alone would be to his advantage in the presidential election. Not to mention the many thousands of voters who had served under his charge during the Revolution; they would surely vote for his continued public service.

Many attempted to influence Washington to seek the Presidency. Hamilton, Madison, Robert and Gouverneur Morris, and Lafayette were the most persuasive. Gouverneur Morris told Washington that among the "thirteen horses now about to be coupled together, there are some of every race and character. They will listen to

---

555   W.W. Abbot, ed., *The Papers of George Washington,* Confederation Series, Vol 6. *1 January 1788—23 September 1788* (Charlottesville: University Press of Virginia, 1997). 360-362.

556   Chernow, 547.

Alexander Hamilton by John Trumbull

your voice and submit to your control. You therefore must, I say, must mount this seat."[557]

---

557   Ibid, 548.

James Madison
Courtesy of Britannica.com

Still, Washington underwent a protracted period of indecision about the presidency. Portions of him felt burdened by public life, and he was torn by unacknowledged ambition, mingled with self-doubt.[558] He wrote down all the considerations that carried weight to him on the decision. The five primary arguments in his mind against accepting the office were:

- His age, his interest in agricultural pursuits and his love of retirement—in short, his personal circumstances and inclination.

558   Ibid, 547.

- Fear that a return to public life after his deliberate retirement in 1783 might be regarded as inconsistent, if not, indeed, as evidence of rashness and ambition.

- Disinclination to assume new and unfamiliar duties, though he was resolved that this "terror of encountering new fatigues and troubles" should not be decisive with him.

- Doubt whether his election would be acceptable to the Anti-Federalists—those who had opposed the Constitution.

- The absence of any proof that the duties of the office could not be discharged as readily by someone else as by him.

His arguments for acceptance were primarily these unanswered questions:

- Much as he prized the good opinion of his fellow Americans, would he not be violating principles to which he had adhered since young manhood if he sought to retain his popularity at "the expense of one social duty or moral virtue?"

- If clamor were raised against him and censure were imposed, could he not endure these plagues of public life, so long as he gave no just occasion for public disapproval?

- Was the good of the country involved? If it was, did he not have a duty to discharge, even though he might risk the reputation he had earned and cherished?

- Might it not be possible to answer the call, to hold the office briefly and, when the government was in operation, to resign and to return to Mount Vernon, there "to pass an unclouded evening after the stormy day of life?"[559]

Washington could not come to grips with his decision about the presidency, and unless convinced that this would have "very disagreeable consequences" to America and to himself, he would remain in retirement. Those who wished it otherwise would have to demonstrate the absolute necessity that Washington, and not someone else, should assume the burden of the presidency.[560]

Hamilton made his last arguments that Washington had no choice but to assume the Presidency if elected. The success of the new government was hardly undisputable, and only Washington, Hamilton argued, could put the new Constitution to a fair test. If the first government failed, "the framers of it will have to encounter the disrepute of having brought about a revolution in government, without substituting anything that was worthy of the effort." Hamilton also argued that Washington's

559   Freeman, Vol Six, 149.
560   Ibid, 150.

refusal to become president would "throw everything into confusion". This was what Washington desired to hear: that overwhelming necessity demanded that he make the supreme sacrifice and serve as president.[561]

Another act of Divine Providence ended Washington's indecisiveness. The act was the timeline that Congress established for the election. Presidential electors would be chosen in January 1789 and the vote would be conducted in February. With this short timetable, no presidential candidate would be required to engage in electioneering. Washington lacked the requisite skills for making speeches or debating on the stump. In a drawn-out election with debates and stump speeches, he would have not fared very well. This first presidential election was tailor-made for this transitional moment between the patrician style of the colonial past and the rowdy populism of the Jacksonian era. Washington could remain incommunicado as the electors voted.[562] His national reputation, name recognition and residence in America's largest state should assure a landslide victory.

Washington believed the new government needed a fair trial and a positive start. He always believed in the power of first impressions and now imagined that "the first transactions of a nation, like those of an individual upon his first entrance into life, make the deepest impression" To Madison, he said: "To be shipwrecked in sight of the port would be the severest of all possible aggravations to our misery."[563] Washington decided that if elected he would serve as the first president of the United States.

The presidential election of 1789 was not even close. George Washington received sixty-nine votes to thirty-four for John Adams and nine for John Jay. The process had been just as Washington had envisioned. Instead of clutching for power, he had let it descend slowly upon his shoulders, as if deposited there by the gentle hand of fate.[564]

Luck or Divine Providence

Was it God sitting behind the steering wheel of history that drove Washington's great-grandfather to America and shipwrecked his vessel in the Potomac, causing him to take up residence in America? Was it just good luck that caused a distant Washington cousin to sue to return the child, Augustine Washington, from England to be raised in America? The early death of Augustine Washington precluded his son George being educated in England and allowed for the introductions and mentoring

561   Dorothy Twohig, ed., *The Papers of George Washington,* Presidential Series, vol 1, *24 September 1788 – 31 March 1789* (Charlottesville: University Press of Virginia, 1987), 23-25.
562   Chernow, 550.
563   W.W. Abbot, ed., *The George Washington Papers,* Confederation Series, vol 6, *1 January 1788 – 23 September 1788* (Charlottesville: University Press of Virginia, 1997), 533-534.
564   Chernow, 551.

by his older brother, Lawrence: that was his destiny? Was it just good timing when

Crypt of George and Martha Washington—Mount Vernon

Lawrence Washington introduced his brother to the Fairfaxes and they spread their influence on George's life? Was it good fortune that saved Washington's life during battles in the French and Indian War when all other officers were killed or wounded? No, I would argue that these were acts of the gentle hand of Divine Providence. God had chosen Washington as his instrument, just as he had chosen Moses. Becoming America's Founding Father was his destiny as ordained by God.

Washington's first inaugural address was focused on God. He expressed the thanks of a grateful nation and asked for God's continued blessing. Washington implored all to keep God at the center of the nation's business. Remembering all that God had already done, for himself personally, he also thanked God for sustaining the nation, delivering freedom, and instituting law. Washington said:

> "No people can be bound to acknowledge and adore the invisible hand, which conducts the Affairs of men more than the People of the United States. Every step, by which they have advanced to the character of an independent nation, seems to have been distinguished by some token of providential agency. "[565]

---

[565] "First Inaugural Address: Final Version, 30 April 1789", *The Papers of George Washington: Presidential Series*, vol. 2, ed. Dorothy Twohig, Charlottesville: University Press of Virginia, 1987, 173-177.

Epilogue

There is no such thing as coincidence. God wills his world according to his design.

George Washington
1773

O
ne of the last orders of business of the Continental Congress on July 4, 1776, was to design a new seal for the United States. After adopting the Declaration of Independence, a committee was chartered consisting of Benjamin Franklin, John Adams, and Thomas Jefferson to design and propose a Great Seal of the United States. It is interesting that both Franklin and Jefferson created seal designs that transmit the story of Moses and the Bible's Exodus story. Franklin's proposal reads as follows:

"Moses in the Dress of High Priest standing on the Shore, and extending his Hand over the Sea, thereby causing the same to overwhelm Pharaoh who is sitting in an open Chariot, a Crown on his Head and Sword in his Hand. Rays from a Pillar of Fire in the Clouds reaching to Moses, to express that he acts by the Command of the Deity."[566]

Franklin's Proposed Seal by Benson J. Lossing

Neither Franklin's nor Jefferson's proposed designs was accepted, but this clearly reveals their thinking at the time of our nation's founding.

Time and time again over the centuries, Americans have drawn similarities to their Israelite forebears. They have found both purpose and meaning to their cause by drawing parallels between their ongoing struggles and those of the central figures

---

[566]   Jonathan Mulinix, "Rejected Designs for the Great Seal of the United States," *Mentalfloss. com,* June 13, 2012, www://mentalfloss.com/article/30912/rejected-designs-great-seal-united-states, (March 6, 2019).

of the Hebrew Bible. As with every crisis in American life—from the Pilgrims to the starvation at Valley Forge; from the bloody battlefields of the Civil War to the chaos in the streets of the civil rights movement—Americans turned to the Exodus for direction, inspiration and hope.[567]

In the Bible's Exodus story, God executed his plan to bring freedom to the enslaved Hebrew people and to form them into a nation. To achieve his purpose he used great and small men with all their inherent strengths and weaknesses, and he also performed miracles. Through the writing of this book, I have attempted to make a compelling argument that the same can be said of America and its Revolution for independence. America's independence story is filled with miracles and both great and small men. Like Moses, George Washington was the major instrument used by God to execute his designs for America.

America's own Exodus involved a long war and years of sacrifice and hardship. Freedom did not come easily to America. Many saw God's miracles working to sustain a cause frequently on the verge of defeat. The path to becoming a nation was difficult. Unity came slowly and painfully over a period of years as the war touched one region after another. Through all of this time of shared hardship, sacrifice and danger, a new nation was formed.[568]

Washington was indispensable to the Revolution and to the first years of the young American republic. I have shown that incident after incident of what was reported as Divine Intervention interceded to protect Washington for a purpose. The evidence of God's hand being on the steering wheel of America's Exodus story is plainly visible in the historical record presented in this book. Even Washington himself believed that he was protected by Providence. He wrote to his wife, Martha, after the Continental Congress elected him as commander in chief of the Continental Army:

"I shall rely, therefore, confidently on that Providence which has heretofore, preserved and been bountiful to me, not doubting but that I shall return safe to you . . . ."[569]

He also stated to the Virginia Legislature on April 27, 1790:

"If I have been enabled to make use of whatever abilities Heaven has been pleased to confer upon me, with any advantage to our common Country, I consider it not less owing to the fostering encouragement I received in early life from the Citizens of the Commonwealth in which I was born, than to the persevering support I have since experienced from my fellow-

567   Fielder, 6.
568   Spivey,229.
569   John White, "George Washington and the Hand of God," *Atlantis Rising Magazine*, March/April 2013, 46.

citizens collectively, in the course of their exertions which, under Divine Providence, saved their Liberties and established their Independence."[570]

Throughout his extensive military career, which included fifteen years of combat, he was never wounded in battle.

As stated in the Introduction, I'm sure the cynic may be unconvinced by my explanation of the events in Washington's life and the battles of the American Revolution. Some could argue that most of the miracles I have presented can be attributed to natural phenomena. Taken individually, each event does have a logical explanation. But looking at the entire Washington ancestral record and the entire war, there is a convincing case that something other than human skill or luck orchestrated this extraordinary sequence of events.[571]

Washington's story should be better known in America today. He was once revered by all. Even his enemy King George III called him "the greatest man in the world," after hearing that Washington had given up his power after the war. Without a constitution at the time, he easily could have been crowned king of America. Washington would have none of that. General Henry Lee eulogized him as "first in war, first in peace, and first in the hearts of his countrymen." John Adams praised him: "Washington's example is complete; and it will teach wisdom and virtue to Magistrates, Citizens and Men, not only in the present age, but in future generations." Decades later, Abraham Lincoln—who some would argue was another American Moses—added his praise:

"Washington is the mightiest name on earth . . . . To add brightness to the sun or glory to the name of Washington is alike impossible. Let none attempt it. In solemn awe pronounce the name, and in its naked deathless splendor leave it shining on."[572]

Our nation is as divided today as it was in 1776. We should reflect on the purpose of the freedoms that have been provided. The benefits of freedom are all around us. America has been lavishly blessed for over two hundred years and never more so than today. But why?[573]

I believe we can find the answer to the question in our own spiritual roots. These roots predate the Revolution. They go back as far as the reasons why the first settlers came to America. Many came to seek religious freedom and to serve God according to one's own conscience.

570   Dorothy Twohig, Mark A. Mastromarino, and Jack D. Warren, *The Papers of George Washington*, Presidential Series, Vol 5, *16 January 1790-30 June 1790*, (Charlottesville: University Press of Virginia, 1996),349-352.
571   Spivey, 233.
572   White.
573   Spivey, 241.

I argue that our ability to find a national sense of purpose and reclaim our national unity might depend on our ability to recall the Biblical story of the Exodus and our own American Exodus. Both Moses and George Washington, who each led their own Exodus, inspired leaders across all sociological, political, and religious divides. Is it possible that the perseverance of their stories could serve as a reminder of our shared national values? If God could split the Red Sea, could he unsplit America?[574]

It is important to remember that God will accomplish his purposes in his own way and on his schedule. Only God knows who will be the next Moses or Washington. God's actions are never easy to determine and few mortals understand them. But clearly, if this work has done nothing else, it has demonstrated that God is on America's side.

America will experience difficult times again. Perhaps as we look for answers to the issues that drive our anxieties; we should be less concerned with peace and prosperity and more concerned with spiritual revitalization. Perhaps as Benjamin Franklin recommended to save the Constitutional Convention from disintegration, we too should open our daily business by "imploring the assistance of Heaven, and its blessings on our deliberations."

May the same wonder-working deity, who long since delivered the Hebrews from their Egyptian oppressors, planted them in the promised land, whose providential agency has lately been conspicuous in establishing these United States as an independent nation, still continue to water them with the dews of Heaven.[575]

George Washington
To the Hebrew Congregation of Savannah, Georgia
June 14, 1790

---

574   Fielder, 5.
575   Dorothy Twohig, Mark A. Mastromarino, and Jack D. Warren, ed., *The Papers of George Washington,* Presidential Series, vol 5, *16 January 1790 – 30 June 1790* (Charlottesville: University Press of Virginia, 1996), 448-450.

Washington at Princeton by Charles Willson Peale

223

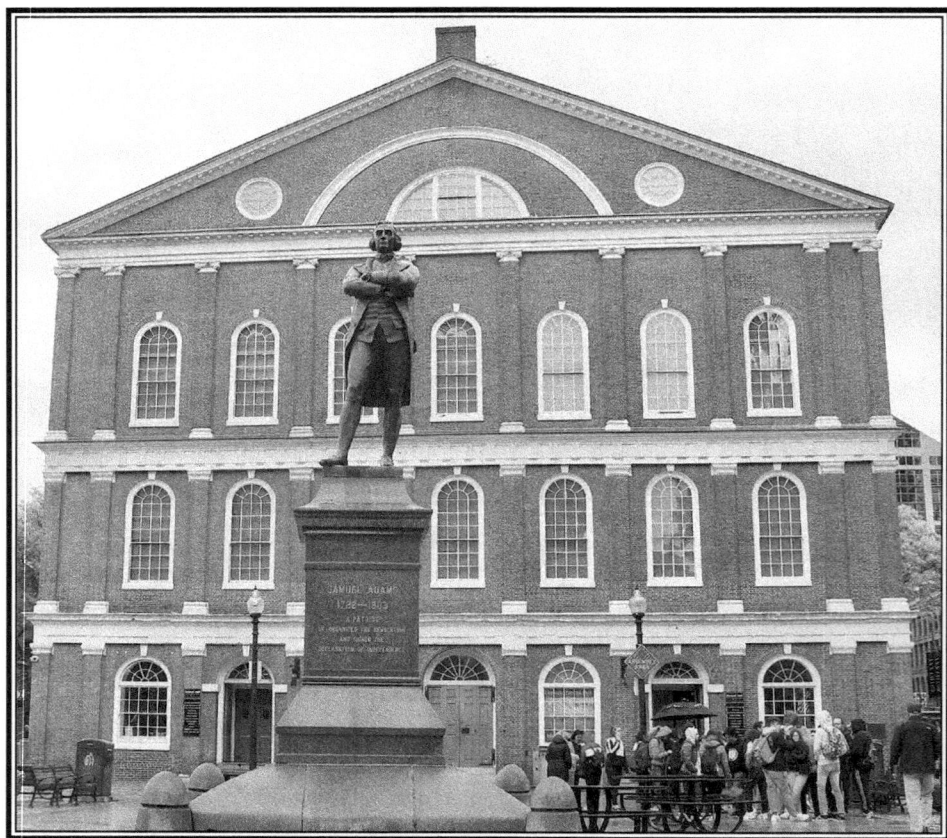

Samuel Adams statue at Faneuil Hall–Boston

Works/References Cited

Abbot, W.W., ed. *The Papers of George Washington,* Colonial Series, vol 1, *7 July 1748 – 14 August 1755,* Charlottesville: University Press of Virginia. 1983.

Abbot, W.W., ed., *The Papers of George Washington,* Colonial Series, vol 6, *4 September 1758 – 26 December 1760*. Charlottesville: University Press of Virginia, 1988.

Abbot, W.W. eds. *The Papers of George Washington,* Confederation Series*, vol 4, *2 April 1786-31 January 1787*. Charlottesville: University Press of Virginia, 1995.

Abbot, W.W. *The Papers of George Washington,* Confederation Series, vol 6, *1 January 1788-23 September 1788*. Charlottesville: University Press of Virginia, 1997.

Adams, Samuel. "Letter to Charles Dick, Charles Washington and George Thornton of Spotsylvania County, Virginia" March 1775. Library of Virginia Archives.

Allen, W.B. *George Washington: A Collection*. Indianapolis: Liberty Classics, 1988.

Aratani, Lori. "Historic Alexandria Church Decides to Remove Plaques Honoring Washington, Lee." *Washington Post*, October 28, 2017.

Barton, David. *The Bulletproof George Washington*. Aledo, Texas: WallBuilders, 2016.

"Battle of Bennington." *BritishBattles.com*, https://www.britishbattles.com/war-of-the-revolution-1775-to-1783/battle-of-bennington/(accessed July, 7, 2018).

"Battle of Freeman's Farm" "Battle of Saratoga." *BritishBattles.com*. https://www.britishbattles.com/war-of-the-revolution-1775-1783/battle-of-saratoga/ (accessed June 5, 2018).

"Battles of Lexington and Concord." *History.Com.* https://www.history.com/topics/american-revolution/battles-of-lexington-and-concord. A+E Networks (accessed July 1, 2018)

Bible. Life Application Study, King James Version. Wheaton, Illinois: Tyndale House Publishing, 1996.

Bliven, Jr, Bruce. *Battle for Manhattan*. Papamoa Press, 1956.

Bobrick, Benson. *Angel in the Whirlwind – The Triumph of the American Revolution,* New York: Simon & Schuster 1997.

"Boston Tea Party Ships and Museum December 16, 1773 A Revolutionary Experience." *Boston Tea Party Ships.com*. https://www.bostonteapartyship.com/ (accessed March 20, 2017).

Works/References Cited

"Bunker Hill Plan Photo." United States Military Academy West Point, Department of History. https://www.westpoint.edu/history/SiteAssets/SitePages/American%20Revolution/05aBunkerHillPlan.pdf. February 3, 2012. (accessed April 1, 2018).

Chase, Philander D. ed., *The Papers of George Washington*, Revolutionary War Series, vol 1, *16 June 1775 – 15 September 1775*. Charlottesville: University Press of Virginia, 1985.

Chase, Philander D. ed. *The Papers of George Washington*, Revolutionary War Series, vol 3, *1 January 1776 – 31 March 1776*. Charlottesville: University Press of Virginia, 1988.

Chase, Philander D. ed. *The Papers of George Washington*, Revolutionary War Series, vol 7, *21 October 1776 – 5 January 1777*. Charlottesville: University Press of Virginia, 1997.

Chidsey, Donald Barr. *The Tide Turns: An Informal History of the Campaign of 1776 in the American Revolution*. New York: Crown Publishers, Inc, 1966.

"Colonial America." *Land of the Brave*. https://www.landofthebrave.info (accessed March 19, 2018).

Cook, Don. *The Long Fuse: How England Lost the American Colonies, 1760-1785*. New York: Atlantic Monthly Press, 1995.

Darnell, Nathaniel. "1776: Providence & Perseverance — How George Washington Won the War." *The American Vision*. https://americanvision.org/6039/1776-providence-perseverance/ (accessed December 30, 2017).

Ellis, Joseph J. *His Excellency George Washington*. New York: Vintage Books 2005.

Elstner, Carolyn Jones and Katherine Porter Clark. *Dear Old Ellwood*. Washington: Virginia Rappahannock Historical Society, 2016.

Evans, Tony. *Detours The Unpredictable Path to Your Destiny*. Nashville, Tennessee: B&H Publishing Group, 2017.

Fairfax, Hugh. *Fairfax of Virginia: The Forgotten Story of America's Only Peerage 1690-1960*. London: The Fairfax Family, 2017.

Farley, William P. "Old Ironsides: Oliver Cromwell and the Puritan Revolution." *Assemblies of God Enrichment Journal*. www.enrichmentjournal.ag.org/200402/200402_115_ironsides.cfm (accessed January 18, 2018).

Works/References Cited

Federer, Susie. *Miracles in American History 32 Amazing Stories of Answered Prayer.* Virginia Beach, Virginia: Amerisearch, Inc, 2017.

Feiler, Bruce. *American's Prophet.* New York: Harper Collins Publishers, 2009.

Felder, Paula S. *George Washington's Fredericksburg.* Fredericksburg: Donning Company Publishers, 2011.

Founders Online National Archives. "The Adams Papers." https://founders. archives.gov/documents/Adams.99-02-02-4098 (accessed March 22, 2019).

Founders Online National Archives. "The Washington Papers." https://founders. archives.gov/documents/washington/99-01-02-12223 (accessed 11 April 2019).

Founders Online National Archives. "To Thomas Jefferson from John Page, 20 July 1776," version of January 18, 2019, https://founders.archieves.gov.documents/ Jefferson.01-01-02-0189 (accessed June 15, 2018).

Freeman, Douglas Southall. *George Washington Volume One Young Washington.* New York: Scribner's and Sons, 1948.

Freeman, Douglas Southall. *George Washington Volume Two, Young Washington.* New York: Charles Scribner's Sons, 1948.

Freeman, Douglas Southall. *George Washington Vol Four, Leader of the Revolution.* New York: Charles Scribner's Sons, 1951.

Freeman, Southall Freeman. *George Washington Volume Six, Patriot and President.* New York: Charles Scribner's Sons, 1954.

"French and Indian Wars." *History Central.* www.historycentral.com/Revolt/ French.html (accessed March 15, 2018).

Freund, Michael. "How the Exodus Story Created America." *Pundicity*.org www. michaelfreund.org/13124/exodus-america (accessed January 18, 2017).

Gangi, Carol Kelly. *The Essential Wisdom of the Founding Fathers.* New York: Fall River Press, 2018.

"George Washington Quotes." *NotableQuotes.* http://www.notable-quotes. com/w/washington_george.html (accessed December 25, 2017).

Hart, Benjamin. *Faith and Freedom Recovering America's Christian Heritage.* Ottawa, Illinois: Jameson Books, 2004.

Hatch, Charles Jr. *Chapters in the History of Popes Creek* Washington DC: US Department of Interior, December 1, 1968.

Works/References Cited

Hay, Robert P. "George Washington: American Moses." *American Quarterly Vol. 2, No 4,* 1969.

History.com Staff. "Battles of Trenton and Princeton." *History.com.* http://www.history.com/topics/american-revolution/battles-of-trenton-and-princeton. A+E Networks (accessed May 25, 2018).

Horwitz, Tony. "The True Story of the Battle of Bunker Hill." *Smithsonian.com.* https://www.smithsonianmag.com/history/the-battle-of-bunker-hill-36721984 (accessed April 1, 2018).

Hudson, Winthrop S. and John Corrigan. *Religion in America: An Historical Account of the Development of American Religious Life.* Upper Saddle River, NJ: Prentice Hall, 1999.

Johnson, Henry P. *The Campaign of 1776 Around New York and Brooklyn.* Brooklyn: Long Island Historical Society, 1878.

Kladky, William P. Ph.D. "Constitutional Convention," *George Washington's Mount Vernon.* https://www.mountvernon.org/library/digitalhistory/digital-encyclopedia/article/constitutional-convention/ (accessed February 24, 2019).

Kostyal, K.M. *Founding Fathers The Fight for Freedom and the Birth of American Liberty.* Washington D.C: National Geographic Society, 2014.

Lass, Cody. "Battle of Trenton." *George Washington's Mount Vernon.* www.mountvernon.org/library.digitalhistory/digital-encyclopedia/article.battle-of-trenton (accessed May 28, 2018)

Luzader, John. *Decision on the Hudson, The Battles of Saratoga.* Fort Washington, Pa: Eastern National, 2002.

Marshall, Logan. "The Story of Moses, the Child who was Found in the River." *Bible Hub.* www.biblehub.com/library/marshall/the_wonder_book_of_bible_stories/the_story_of_moses_the.htm (accessed January 19, 2017).

Morrissey, Brendan. *Yorktown 1781.* Botley, Oxford: England, Osprey Publishing, 1997.

Mulinix, Jonathan, "Rejected Designs for the Great Seal of the United States." *Mentalfloss.com.* www.mentalfloss.com/article/30912/rejected-designs-great-seal-united-states (accessed March 6, 2019).

Myers, J. Jay. "George Washington: Defeated at the Battle of Long Island," *American History Magazine,* History Net, June 2001.

TECTION OF A KIND PROVIDENCE: WASHINGTON AND AMERICA'S EXODUS

Works/References Cited

National Historical Park Service. *Saratoga.* U.S. Department of Interior. Government Printing Office-2018, 403-332/82045, 2018.

Ohotto, Robert. *Transforming Fate into Destiny A New Dialogue with Your Soul.* Carlsbad, California: Hay House, Inc, 2008.

"On This Day May 28, 1754." *Revolutionary War and Beyond.* www.revolutionary-war-and-beyond.com/george-washington-starts-french-and-indian-war.htm (accessed February 17, 2018).

O'Reilly, Bill and Martin Dugard. *Killing England The Brutal Struggle for American Independence.* New York, New York: Henry Holt and Company. 2017.

Plan of Princeton Map. *Library of Congress.* http://lccn.loc.gov/gm71000925 (accessed May 30, 2018).

Potter, E.B. and Chester Nimitz. *Seapower: A Naval History.* Englewood Cliffs, NJ: Prentice-Hall, Inc., 1960.

Rose, Alexander. *Washington's Spies, The Story of America's First Spy Ring,* New York: Bantam Dell, 2006.

Smith, Gary. "The Faith of George Washington." *The Center of Vison and Values/Grove City College.* http://www.visionandvalues.org/2008/02/the-faith-of-george-washington/ (accessed December 26, 2017).

Spivey, Larkin. *Miracles of the American Revolution Divine Intervention and the Birth of the Republic.* Chattanooga, Tennessee: God and County Press, 2010.

"Stamp Act." *History.com.* www.history.com/topics/American-revolution/stamp-act (accessed March 18, 2017).

Stoltz, Joseph F. "The Battle of Princeton." *George Washington's Mount Vernon.* www.mountvernon.org/library/digitalhistory/digital-encyclopedia/article/battle-of-Princeton/. (accessed June 3, 2018).

"The Story of Moses and the Exodus from Egypt." *Bible History Online.* www.bible-history.com/old-testament/moses.html. 2016. (accessed January 20, 2018).

Torrence, Clayton. "A Virginia Lady of Quality and Her Possessions: Mrs. Mildred Willis of Fredericksburg." *The Virginia Magazine of History and Biography* Volume 56, No. 1. Richmond: Virginia Historical Society, 1948).

Twohig, Dorothy, ed. *The Papers of George Washington,* Presidential Series, vol 1, *24 September 1788 – 31 March 1789.* Charlottesville: University Press of Virginia, 1987.

Works/References Cited

Twohig, Dorothy, ed. *The Papers of George Washington,* Presidential Series, vol 1, *24 September 1788 – 31 March 1789.* Charlottesville: University Press of Virginia, 1987.

Twohig, Dorothy, ed. *The Papers of George Washington:* Presidential Series, vol. 2. Charlottesville: University Press of Virginia, 1987.

Twohig, Dorothy, Mark A. Mastromarino, and Jack D. Warren ed. *The Papers of George Washington,* Presidential Series, Vol 5, *16 January 1790-30 June 1790.* Charlottesville: University Press of Virginia, 1996.

Twohig, Dorothy, Mark A. Mastromarino, and Jack D. Warren. ed. *The Papers of George Washington,* Presidential Series, vol 5, *16 January 1790 – 30 June 1790.* Charlottesville: University Press of Virginia, 1996.

U.S. Department of Interior. "George Washington Birthplace National Monument." Washington, D.C.: National Park Service 1941.

U.S. Department of Interior. "Fort Necessity." Washington, D.C.: National Park Service.

U.S. Department of Interior. "Yorktown: The Siege." National Park Service. https://www.nps.gov/york/learn/historyculture/the-siege.htm (accessed February 26, 2019).

Wallace, Willard M. *Appeal to Army: A Military History of the American Revolution.* Chicago: Quadrangle Books, 1951.

Ward, Christopher. *The War of the Revolution.* Vol 2. New York: The Macmillan Company, 1952.

White, John. "George Washington and the Hand of God." *Atlantis Rising Magazine.* March/April 2013.

Van Doren, Carl. *Benjamin Franklin.* New York: Bramhall House ,1938.

White, R.J. *The Age of George III.* New York: Walker and Company, 1968.

Index

Index

Index

Index

Index

Index

Index

Index

Index

Index

Index

Paul Revere House—Boston

Independence Hall - Downtown Philadelphia

About the Author

Captain Tom A. Russell, United States Navy, Retired, was born and raised in Thomasville, North Carolina. He graduated from the United States Naval Academy with the class of 1977. A career pilot, Tom served in the Navy for twenty-six years. He made deployments to the Atlantic Ocean, Mediterranean Sea, Western Pacific Ocean, and Indian Ocean and was decorated for meritorious service while flying missions in the Persian Gulf during Operation Desert Storm. He retired with the rank of captain. Captain Russell received a Master's of Arts in Management from Webster University, Saint Louis, Missouri and a Master's of Arts in National Security and Strategic Studies from the United States Naval War College, Newport, Rhode Island. He is married to Mary Shawn Webb of Pensacola, Florida, who is an author and a descendant of the Washington family. She serves as the historian general for The National Society of Washington Family Descendants. They reside on the southeast coast of North Carolina.

Notes

Notes

Printed in the United States of America

www.ingramcontent.com/pod-product-compliance
Lightning Source LLC
Chambersburg PA
CBHW060303100426
42742CB00011B/1849